Lecture Notes in Computer Science 16086

Founding Editors

Gerhard Goos
Juris Hartmanis

Editorial Board Members

Elisa Bertino, *Purdue University, West Lafayette, IN, USA*
Wen Gao, *Peking University, Beijing, China*
Bernhard Steffen, *TU Dortmund University, Dortmund, Germany*
Moti Yung, *Columbia University, New York, NY, USA*

The series Lecture Notes in Computer Science (LNCS), including its subseries Lecture Notes in Artificial Intelligence (LNAI) and Lecture Notes in Bioinformatics (LNBI), has established itself as a medium for the publication of new developments in computer science and information technology research, teaching, and education.

LNCS enjoys close cooperation with the computer science R & D community, the series counts many renowned academics among its volume editors and paper authors, and collaborates with prestigious societies. Its mission is to serve this international community by providing an invaluable service, mainly focused on the publication of conference and workshop proceedings and postproceedings. LNCS commenced publication in 1973.

Zihan Wang · Jinyuan Fang · Giacomo Frisoni ·
Zhuyun Dai · Zaiqiao Meng · Gianluca Moro ·
Emine Yilmaz
Editors

Knowledge-Enhanced Information Retrieval

Second International Workshop, KEIR 2025
Lucca, Italy, April 10, 2025
Revised Selected Papers

Editors
Zihan Wang
University of Amsterdam
Amsterdam, The Netherlands

Giacomo Frisoni
University of Bologna
Cesena, Italy

Zaiqiao Meng
University of Glasgow
Glasgow, UK

Emine Yilmaz
University College London
London, UK

Jinyuan Fang
University of Glasgow
Glasgow, UK

Zhuyun Dai
Google DeepMind
Mountain View, CA, USA

Gianluca Moro
University of Bologna
Cesena, Italy

ISSN 0302-9743 ISSN 1611-3349 (electronic)
Lecture Notes in Computer Science
ISBN 978-3-032-02898-3 ISBN 978-3-032-02899-0 (eBook)
https://doi.org/10.1007/978-3-032-02899-0

© The Editor(s) (if applicable) and The Author(s), under exclusive license
to Springer Nature Switzerland AG 2026

This work is subject to copyright. All rights are solely and exclusively licensed by the Publisher, whether the whole or part of the material is concerned, specifically the rights of translation, reprinting, reuse of illustrations, recitation, broadcasting, reproduction on microfilms or in any other physical way, and transmission or information storage and retrieval, electronic adaptation, computer software, or by similar or dissimilar methodology now known or hereafter developed.
The use of general descriptive names, registered names, trademarks, service marks, etc. in this publication does not imply, even in the absence of a specific statement, that such names are exempt from the relevant protective laws and regulations and therefore free for general use.
The publisher, the authors and the editors are safe to assume that the advice and information in this book are believed to be true and accurate at the date of publication. Neither the publisher nor the authors or the editors give a warranty, expressed or implied, with respect to the material contained herein or for any errors or omissions that may have been made. The publisher remains neutral with regard to jurisdictional claims in published maps and institutional affiliations.

This Springer imprint is published by the registered company Springer Nature Switzerland AG
The registered company address is: Gewerbestrasse 11, 6330 Cham, Switzerland

If disposing of this product, please recycle the paper.

Preface

Over the past few years, pretrained language models (PLMs) have become the backbone of modern information retrieval (IR). Their latent knowledge—encoded within millions or billions of parameters—has enabled a leap in semantic understanding. However, PLMs remain fundamentally static: their knowledge is frozen in time at the training point, and they typically lack mechanisms for dynamically incorporating new, domain-specific, or user-specific contexts. In addition, they operate as black boxes, making it difficult to audit their reasoning processes or update specific associations without retraining the entire model. These inherent limitations pose significant challenges in real-world scenarios, where users frequently seek up-to-date and specialized data that may extend beyond the training corpora, demanding grounded and trustworthy predictions. The mismatch between the static knowledge of PLMs and the dynamic nature of information needs often leads to severe problems, such as imprecise, non-factual, or non-personalized results and shallow representation of long-tail concepts. To overcome these challenges, a growing body of research has focused on *knowledge-enhanced IR*, which aims to augment PLMs with access to external knowledge sources. These sources can be either unstructured (e.g., textbooks, guidelines, user descriptions) or structured (e.g., knowledge graphs, relational databases), possibly generated by large language models (LLMs) and covering multiple modalities. Such augmentation approaches have shown promising results in various natural language processing tasks—including open-domain question answering and dialogue systems—but their potential in IR remains underexplored.

The 2nd Workshop on Knowledge-Enhanced Information Retrieval (KEIR 2025) aimed to provide a venue to present and discuss modern, efficient, and effective methods for incorporating external knowledge into PLM-based IR systems. KEIR 2025 was held as a half-day, in-person event co-located with the 47th European Conference on Information Retrieval (ECIR 2025) in Lucca, Italy, on 10 April 2025.[1] We previously organized the 1st edition of KEIR at ECIR 2024 in Glasgow, UK, which was among the most popular workshops at the conference and was broadly welcomed by attendees. Compared to the inaugural edition, and in response to evolving trends in the literature and community, the 2025 workshop placed greater emphasis on LLMs, retrieval-augmented generation (RAG), and all related subtopics—ranging from query rephrasing and chunking techniques to LLM-generated context and agentic retrieval. A notable change from the previous year was the option for authors of accepted papers to publish their work in a non-archival format.

In total, 10 papers from authors across four countries were submitted. The final program included 4 papers, which corresponds to an acceptance rate of 40%. All submissions were double-blind peer-reviewed by 3 international program committee members to ensure the highest relevance and quality. For contributions co-authored by any committee members, reviewer assignment was carefully handled to ensure impartiality: such submissions were assigned exclusively to reviewers from other institutions, with

---

[1] https://keir-ecir2025.github.io/.

no conflicts of interest. The accepted papers target orthogonal themes of equal importance: ontology-based RAG, late chunking and contextual retrieval, learnable sparse representations, decoder-based models for embedding, and personalized query reformulation. Addressed applications are automatic coding and document retrieval in medicine, general-domain web search, and conversational information seeking. The KEIR 2025 workshop featured poster presentations of accepted papers and two keynotes, delivered by Alessandro Lenci (University of Pisa, Italy) and Andrew Yates (Johns Hopkins University, USA). Thanks to the association with a major international AI conference, the workshop offered a stimulating forum for interaction among researchers from both academia and industry. Approximately 25 participants attended the event, contributing to a lively and valuable exchange of ideas. This volume includes extended and revised versions of 3 accepted papers from KEIR 2025, for which the authors opted for archival publication, along with 4 invited contributions that complement the workshop themes. Each invited paper was evaluated by at least two independent reviewers with expertise in the relevant subject area. Reviewers assessed the submissions according to established scholarly standards. Final decisions were made by the organizers, based on the reviewers' recommendations and the alignment of each contribution with the workshop's objectives.

We thank the ECIR 2025 organizers and chairs for accepting our workshop proposal. We extend our gratitude to the keynote speakers for their insightful talks. We wish to thank all the student volunteers who helped to create a great experience for attendees. Special thanks are also due to the program committee for reviewing the paper submissions and providing valuable guidance to the contributors. But, of course, KEIR 2025 would not have been possible without the dedicated involvement of the contributing authors and participants.

June 2025

Zihan Wang
Jinyuan Fang
Giacomo Frisoni
Zhuyun Dai
Zaiqiao Meng
Gianluca Moro
Emine Yilmaz

Acknowledgments

We would like to thank the entire workshop organization team for their dedication and contributions, without which this event would not have been possible. In particular, we are grateful to Zihan Wang and Jinyuan Fang for taking the lead in organizing the workshop and coordinating its many logistical and scientific aspects. We sincerely appreciate Giacomo Frisoni for his efforts in managing the preparation of the proceedings, presenting the in-person event, and maintaining communication with Springer throughout the publication process. We also thank Zaiqiao Meng and Gianluca Moro for their valuable advice and feedback during the planning and review phases. Finally, we extend our warmest thanks to the members of the Program Committee for their time, expertise, and thoughtful reviews, which helped ensure the quality and rigor of the accepted papers.

Organization

Workshop Chairs

Zihan Wang	University of Amsterdam, The Netherlands
Jinyuan Fang	University of Glasgow, UK
Giacomo Frisoni	University of Bologna, Italy
Zhuyun Dai	Google DeepMind, USA
Zaiqiao Meng	University of Glasgow, UK
Gianluca Moro	University of Bologna, Italy
Emine Yilmaz	University College London, UK

Program Committee

Jingwei Kang	University of Amsterdam, The Netherlands
Jingfen Qiao	University of Amsterdam, The Netherlands
Yongkang Li	University of Amsterdam, The Netherlands
Xinhao Yi	University of Glasgow, UK
Lubingzhi Guo	University of Glasgow, UK
Jack McKechnie	University of Glasgow, UK
Zhaohan Meng	University of Glasgow, UK
Zixuan Yi	University of Glasgow, UK
Siwei Liu	University of Aberdeen, UK
Ruihong Zeng	Sun Yat-sen University, China
Zhengliang Shi	Shandong University, China

Contents

Advances in Knowledge-Enhanced Retrieval Models

Reconstructing Context: Evaluating Advanced Chunking Strategies
for Retrieval-Augmented Generation 3
   Carlo Merola and Jaspinder Singh

Leveraging Decoder Architectures for Learned Sparse Retrieval 19
   Jingfen Qiao, Thong Nguyen, Evangelos Kanoulas, and Andrew Yates

Enhancing Representation Learning for Content-Based Information
Retrieval: A Knowledge-Enhanced Geometric Approach 36
   Manuel Alejandro Goyo, Giacomo Frisoni, Gianluca Moro,
   and Claudio Sartori

Applications of Knowledge-Enhanced IR

OntologyRAG: Better and Faster Biomedical Code Mapping
with Retrieval-Augmented Generation (RAG) Leveraging Ontology
Knowledge Graphs and Large Language Models 71
   Hui Feng, Yuntzu Yin, Emiliano Reynares, and Jay Nanavati

I Know About "Up"! Enhancing Spatial Reasoning in Visual Language
Models Through 3D Knowledge Reconstruction 87
   Hao Zhou, Zaiqiao Meng, and Yifang Chen

BladeLoRA: An Enhanced LoRA Method with Adaptive Rank Selection
and Pruning for Efficient Fine-Tuning 105
   Anqi Liu, Baoyuan Qi, and Xuedan Hu

Evaluating Knowledge Graph Sources for Non-personalized Financial
Asset Recommendation: 10K Reports vs. Wikidata 120
   Lubingzhi Guo, Javier Sanz-Cruzado, and Richard McCreadie

Author Index 151

Advances in Knowledge-Enhanced Retrieval Models

Reconstructing Context
Evaluating Advanced Chunking Strategies for Retrieval-Augmented Generation

Carlo Merola[✉][iD] and Jaspinder Singh[✉][iD]

Department of Computer Science and Engineering, University of Bologna, Bologna, Italy
merolacarlo99@gmail.com, singhjaspinder10@gmail.com

Abstract. Retrieval-augmented generation (RAG) has become a transformative approach for enhancing large language models (LLMs) by grounding their outputs in external knowledge sources. Yet, a critical question persists: how can vast volumes of external knowledge be managed effectively within the input constraints of LLMs? Traditional methods address this by chunking external documents into smaller, fixed-size segments. While this approach alleviates input limitations, it often fragments context, resulting in incomplete retrieval and diminished coherence in generation. To overcome these shortcomings, two advanced techniques—late chunking and contextual retrieval—have been introduced, both aiming to preserve global context. Despite their potential, their comparative strengths and limitations remain unclear. This study presents a rigorous analysis of late chunking and contextual retrieval, evaluating their effectiveness and efficiency in optimizing RAG systems. Our results indicate that contextual retrieval preserves semantic coherence more effectively but requires greater computational resources. In contrast, late chunking offers higher efficiency but tends to sacrifice relevance and completeness.

Keywords: Contextual Retrieval · Late Chunking · Dynamic Chunking · Rank Fusion

1 Introduction

Retrieval Augmented Generation (RAG) is a transformative approach that enhances the capabilities of large language models (LLMs) by integrating external information retrieval directly into the text generation process. This method allows LLMs to dynamically access and utilize relevant external knowledge, significantly improving their ability to generate accurate, contextually grounded, and informative responses. Unlike static LLMs that rely solely on pre-trained data, RAG-enabled models can access up-to-date and domain-specific information. This dynamic integration ensures that the generated content remains both relevant and accurate, even in rapidly evolving or specialized fields.

J. Singh—Equal contribution.

© The Author(s), under exclusive license to Springer Nature Switzerland AG 2026
Z. Wang et al. (Eds.): KEIR 2025, LNCS 16086, pp. 3–18, 2026.
https://doi.org/10.1007/978-3-032-02899-0_1

RAG models combine two key components: a retrieval mechanism and a generative model. The retrieval mechanism fetches relevant documents or data from a large corpus, while the generative model synthesizes this information into coherent, contextually enriched answers. This synergy enhances performance in knowledge-intensive natural language processing (NLP) tasks, enabling models to produce well-informed responses grounded in the retrieved data.

The Context Dilemma in Classic RAG: Managing extensive external documents poses significant issues in RAG systems. Despite advancements, many LLMs are limited to processing a few thousand tokens. Although some models have achieved context windows up to millions of tokens [4], these are exceptions rather than the norm. Moreover, research indicates that LLMs may exhibit positional bias, performing better with information at the beginning of a document and struggling with content located in the middle or toward the end [6,11]. This issue is exacerbated when retrieval fails to prioritize relevant information properly. Thus, documents are often divided into smaller segments or "chunks" before embedding and retrieval. However, this chunking process can disrupt semantic coherence, leading to:

- *Loss of Context:* dividing documents without considering semantic boundaries can result in chunks that lack sufficient context, impairing the model's ability to generate accurate and coherent responses.
- *Incomplete Information Retrieval:* important information split across chunks may not be effectively retrieved or integrated.

To address these issues, we analyse and compare two recent techniques—contextual retrieval[1] and late chunking [8]—within a unified setup, evaluating their strengths and limitations in tackling challenges like context loss and incomplete information retrieval. Contextual retrieval preserves coherence by prepending LLM-generated context to chunks, while late chunking embeds entire documents to retain global context before segmenting.

Our study rigorously assesses their impact on generation performance in question-answering tasks, finding that neither technique offers a definitive solution. This work highlights the trade-offs between these methods and provides practical guidance for optimizing RAG systems.

To further support the community, we release all code, prompts, and data under the permissive MIT license, enabling full reproducibility and empowering practitioners to adapt and extend our work.[2]

2 Related Work

Classic RAG. A standard RAG workflow involves four main stages: document segmentation, chunk embedding, indexing, and retrieval. During segmentation,

---

[1] https://www.anthropic.com/news/contextual-retrieval.
[2] https://github.com/disi-unibo-nlp/rag-when-how-chunk.

documents are divided into manageable chunks. These chunks are then transformed into vector representations using encoder models, often normalized to ensure unit magnitudes. The resulting embeddings are stored in indexed vector databases, enabling efficient approximate similarity searches. Retrieval involves comparing query embeddings with the stored embeddings using metrics such as cosine similarity or Euclidean distance, which identify the most relevant chunks. Seminal works like [15] and [13] have demonstrated the effectiveness of RAG in tasks such as open-domain question answering. More recent studies, including [7], have introduced advancements in scalability and embedding techniques, further establishing RAG as a foundational framework for knowledge-intensive applications.

Document Segmentation. Document segmentation is essential for processing long texts in RAG workflows, with methods ranging from *fixed-size segmentation* [7] to more adaptive techniques like *semantic segmentation*,[3] which detects semantic breakpoints based on shifts in meaning. Recent advancements include *supervised segmentation models* [12,14] and *segment-then-predict models*, trained end-to-end without explicit labels to optimize chunking for downstream task performance [16]. In 2024, *late chunking* and *contextual retrieval* introduced novel paradigms. Both techniques have proven effective in retrieval benchmarks but remain largely untested in integrated RAG workflows. Despite several RAG surveys [5,7,10], no prior work has compared these methods within a comprehensive evaluation framework. This study addresses this gap by holistically analyzing late chunking and contextual retrieval, offering actionable insights into their relative strengths and trade-offs.

3 Methodology

To guide our study, we define the following research questions (RQs), aimed at evaluating different strategies for chunking and retrieval in RAG systems:

- **RQ#1:** Compares the effectiveness of **early versus late chunking** strategies, utilizing **different text segmenters** and embedding models to evaluate their impact on retrieval accuracy and downstream performance in RAG systems.
- **RQ#2:** Compares the effectiveness of **contextual retrieval versus traditional early chunking** strategies, utilizing **different text segmenters** and embedding models to evaluate their impact on retrieval accuracy and downstream performance in RAG systems.

---

[3] https://docs.llamaindex.ai/en/stable/examples/node_parsers/semantic_chunking/.

3.1 RQ#1: Early or Late Chunking?

In this workflow, the main architectural modification compared to the standard RAG lies in the document embedding process Fig. 1. Specifically, we experiment with various embedding models to encode document chunks, tailoring them to align with the early and late chunking strategies under evaluation. This adjustment allows us to explore how different embedding techniques influence the retrieval quality and, subsequently, the overall performance of the RAG system. Additionally, we test dynamic segmenting models to refine the chunking process further, providing an adaptive mechanism that adjusts chunk sizes based on content characteristics. By evaluating the impact of these dynamic segmenting models, we aim to improve the overall retrieval efficiency and response generation within the RAG framework.

Early Chunking. Documents are segmented into text chunks, and each chunk is processed by the embedding model. The model generates token-level embeddings for each chunk, which are subsequently aggregated using mean pooling to produce a single embedding per chunk.

Late Chunking. Late chunking [8] defers the chunking process. As shown in Fig. 1, instead of segmenting the document initially, the entire document is first embedded at the token level. The resulting token embeddings are then segmented into chunks, and mean pooling is applied to each chunk to generate the final embeddings. This approach preserves the complete contextual information within the document, potentially leading to superior results across various retrieval tasks. It is adaptable to a wide range of long-context embedding models and can be implemented without additional training. The two approaches are tested with different embedding models.

3.2 RQ#2: Early or Contextual Chunking?

In this workflow, traditional retrieval is compared to Contextual Retrieval with Rank Fusion technique. This has been introduced by Anthropic in September 2024.[4] Three steps are added to the Traditional RAG process: Contextualization, Rank Fusion, Reranking.

Contextualization. After document segmentation, each chunk is enriched with additional context from the entire document, ensuring that even when segmented, each piece retains a broader understanding of the content (Fig. 2). In fact, when documents are split into smaller chunks, it might arise the problem where individual chunks lack sufficient context. For example, a chunk might contain the text: "The company's revenue grew by 3% over the previous quarter". However, this chunk on its own does not specify which company it is referring to or the relevant time period, making it difficult to retrieve the right information or use the information effectively. For this reason, after segmenting the

---

[4] https://www.anthropic.com/news/contextual-retrieval.

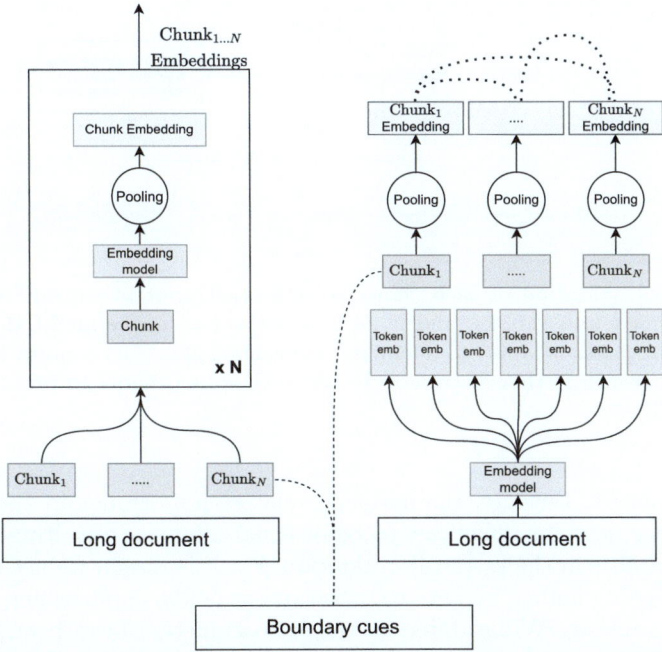

Fig. 1. Comparison of early chunking (left) and late chunking (right) approaches for processing long documents. In early chunking, the document is divided into chunks before embedding, with each chunk processed independently by the embedding model and then pooled. In contrast, late chunking processes the entire document to generate token embeddings first, using boundary cues to create chunk embeddings, which are subsequently pooled.

document into chunks, each chunk is paired with its corresponding document and formatted into a prompt template for querying an LLM (Sect. A). The LLM generates contextual information from the document specific to each chunk. This generated context is then prepended to the chunk before being processed by the embedding model to create the final chunk embedding. By preserving contextual integrity, this approach enhances the relevance and accuracy of retrieved information.

Rank Fusion. In our methodology, we employ a rank fusion strategy that integrates dense embeddings with sparse embeddings of BM25 [19] to improve retrieval performance. Although embedding models adeptly capture semantic relationships, they may overlook exact matches, which is particularly useful for unique identifiers or technical terms. BM25 uses a ranking function that builds upon Term Frequency-Inverse Document Frequency (TF-IDF), addressing this limitation by emphasizing precise lexical matches. To combine the strengths of both approaches, we conduct searches across both dense embedding vectors and BM25 sparse embedding vectors generated from both the chunk and its

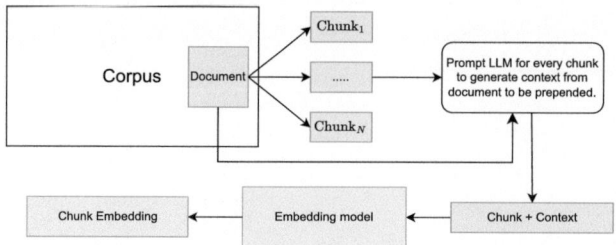

Fig. 2. Contextualization of each chunk is performed prior to embedding. The document is divided into chunks, and a prompt is used to query an LLM to generate contextual information from the document for each chunk. The context is prepended to the chunk, which is then processed by the embedding model to produce the final chunk embedding.

generated context. Initially, the assigned relative importance in the search for the two vector fields has been set to be of equal intensity, resulting in lowering the scoring results in the retrieval evaluation. For this reason we use a weighting strategy assigning higher weights to dense vector fields, emphasizing them more in the final ranking. While different weight parameters have been tested, the final decision has been to define a ratio of importance 4:1 assigning weight 1 for the dense embedding vectors and 0.25 for the BM25 sparse embedding vectors. This ratio reflects Anthropic weight assignment.[5] By applying these weights, dense embeddings are emphasized more heavily, while still incorporating the contributions of the BM25 sparse embeddings. This weighted rank fusion approach leverages the complementary strengths of semantic embeddings and lexical matching, aiming to improve the accuracy and relevance of the retrieved results.

Reranking Step. To boost and obtain consistent improved performance, the retrieval and ranking stages have been separated. This two-stage approach improves efficiency and effectiveness by leveraging the strengths of different models at each stage. After retrieving the initial set of document chunks, we implement an additional reranking step to enhance the relevance of the results to the user's query. This process involves reassessing and reordering the retrieved chunks based on their pertinence, prioritising the most relevant information. The reranker operates by evaluating the semantic similarity and contextual relevance between the query and each retrieved chunk. It assigns a relevance score to each chunk, and the chunks are then reordered based on these scores, with higher-scoring chunks placed at the top of the list presented to the user. This method ensures that the most pertinent information is readily accessible, improving the overall effectiveness of the retrieval system. Implementing this reranking step addresses potential limitations of the initial retrieval process, such as the inclusion of less relevant chunks or the misordering of pertinent information.

---

[5] https://github.com/anthropics/anthropic-cookbook/blob/main/skills/contextual-embeddings/guide.ipynb.

4 Experimental Setup

This study has focused on testing these techniques with open-source models. A particular focus was also given to resource usage, for real-world scenarios that lead towards the choice of the LLM for the question answering task to Microsoft's `Phi-3.5-mini-instruct`.[6] [1] This language model is designed to operate efficiently in memory- and compute-constrained environments which is a crucial aspect of our work. The same language model has been used also to generate additional context to prepend to each chunk in the Contextual Retrieval Setup.

For what regards the embedding models these ones have been tested: `Jina V3` [20], `Jina Colbert V2` [9], `Stella V5` and `BGE-M3` [3], all present in the `MTEB` [17] leaderboard (see Table 1 for more details).

Dataset and Hardware. There are severe limitations in current datasets available for RAG systems evaluation. Many do not include together the labels for retrieval quality evaluation and answers labels for the quality of the generation in a question answering system. In our system initial Retrieval performance has been tested on the `NFCorpus` [2] dataset, while the subsequent Generation performance in question answering has been conducted over `MSMarco` [18].

Another important note for Contextual Retrieval (`RQ#2`). The `NFCorpus` dataset is characterised by a long average document length. Here appear the first limitations of the Contextual Retrieval approach to RAG. For the intrinsic nature of this approach, the segmented chunks are enhanced with a generated context taken from the document, prompting an LLM for the task, leveraging the new advents of Instruction Learning. Chunks and documents are passed together in a formatted prompt to the model. When a document reaches long lengths, the VRAM of the GPU gets filled up quickly. For chunk contextualization, around 24GB of VRAM use can be reached, limiting batch dimensions for generation and slowing down the times needed for effective chunk contextualization. To avoid exceeding the GPU's memory capacity, the LLM has been quantized to 4-bit, ensuring a more efficient and sustainable process.

In our experimental setup, we utilized an Nvidia RTX 4090 with 24GB of VRAM. Due to GPU memory constraints, we employed a subset of the dataset, corresponding to 20% of the entire `NFCorpus` for `RQ#2`, while the full dataset was used for `RQ#1` workflow.

For datasets such as `MsMarco`, which include only passage texts rather than full documents, the system operates within a more constrained context for generating responses. This limitation arises because passages are typically shorter segments of text, providing less information for contextual understanding. As a result in `RQ#2`, the system's ability to generate contextually relevant and comprehensive responses can be affected by the brevity of the input text, potentially impacting the quality and depth of the generated content.

---

[6] https://huggingface.co/microsoft/Phi-3.5-mini-instruct

Table 1. Embedding models.

Model	MTEB Rank	Model Size (M)	Memory (GB)	Embedding Dim	Max Tokens
Stella-V5	5	1,543	5.75	1,024	131,072
Jina-V3 [20]	53	572	2.13	1,024	8,194
Jina-V2 [9]	123	137	0.51	1,024	8,194
BGE-M3 [3]	211	567	2.11	1,024	8,192

In `RQ#1`, the evaluation was conducted on the first 1,000 queries and approximately 5,000 documents/passages. For `RQ#2`, due to the significant computational requirements and hardware limitations, the experiments were restricted to 50 queries and around 300 documents.

4.1 Embedding Generation

Common to both RQs. To generate embeddings for our experiments, we utilized different embedding models, as detailed previously (see Sect. 4). Each segmentation model approach outlined was paired with an appropriate embedding model to evaluate its influence on downstream tasks.

For fixed-size segmentation, we divided the text into equal-sized chunks with a predefined length of 512 tokens. This approach ensures uniform chunk sizes, simplifying processing and offering a baseline for comparison with more adaptive methods.

For semantic segmentation, we used the `Jina-Segmenter API`,[7] which dynamically adjusts chunk boundaries based on the semantic structure of the text. This ensures that the segments capture meaningful content, improving the quality of embeddings generated.

All the generated embeddings were normalized to unit vectors, facilitating cosine similarity computations during the retrieval phase and ensuring uniformity across experiments.

RQ#1: In addition to the mentioned segmentation approaches, for this workflow, dynamic segmentation was tested, testing two models to assess their performance. The first model, `simple-qwen-0.5`,[8] is a straightforward solution designed to identify boundaries based on the structural elements of the document. Its simplicity makes it efficient for basic segmentation needs, offering a computationally lightweight approach.

The second model, `topic-qwen-0.5`, inspired by Chain-of-Thought reasoning, enhances segmentation by identifying topics within the text. By segmenting text based on topic boundaries, this approach captures richer semantic relationships, making it suitable for tasks requiring a deeper understanding of document content.

---

[7] https://jina.ai/embeddings/.
[8] https://huggingface.co/Qwen/Qwen2-0.5B.

RQ#2: In this workflow, for the Contextual Retrieval evaluation, contextualization of the chunks before the embedding is necessary. To contextualize each chunk, we prompt Microsoft's LLM model `Phi3.5-mini-instruct` to generate a brief summary that situates the chunk within the overall document, formatting the prompt with the chunk and its relative original document.

4.2 Retrieval Evaluation

RQ#2: In this workflow, specifically for the Contextual Retrieval retrieval, the document retrieval has been enhanced with two additional steps (see Sect. 3.2). In the reranking step, Rank Fusion was allowed through `Milvus` Vector Database, which integrates with `BM25` through the `BM25EmbeddingFunction` class, enabling hybrid search across dense and sparse vector fields.

After retrieving the top documents, these are reordered through the reranker model `Jina Reranker V2 Base` model,[9] that employs a cross-encoder architecture that processes each query-document pair individually, outputting a relevance score. This design enables the model to capture intricate semantic relationships between the query and the document before being given to the LLM.

Scorings. For both approaches in `RQ#1` and `RQ#2`, when querying the embedding database (generated in Sect. 4.1), the output will be a ranked list of chunks, ordered from the most similar to the query to the least similar. We employ a straightforward aggregation strategy to transition from chunk-level rankings to document-level rankings. Specifically, for each document, we consider the score of its most significant chunk as the representative value for the entire document. This approach ensures that a document's relevance is determined by its most relevant chunk.

Once the document scores are determined, we generate a ranked list of documents based on these scores. From this ranking, we extract the top-k documents, focusing on the Top 5 or Top 10 documents, depending on the specific evaluation scenario. This final document ranking is then used to assess the effectiveness of the retrieval process.

This methodology highlights the importance of individual chunks in influencing the overall document ranking and ensures that highly relevant chunks directly impact the document's position in the final ranking.

Metrics. To evaluate the performance of our model, we utilize three key metrics: NDCG, MAP, and F1-score. Each metric serves a specific purpose in assessing different aspects of the results. *Normalized Discounted Cumulative Gain (NDCG):* It measures the usefulness of an item based on its position in the ranking, assigning higher weights to items appearing at the top of the list. By using NDCG, we aim to assess the relevance of predictions in a way that prioritizes higher-ranked items. *Mean Average Precision (MAP)*: It calculates the

---

[9] https://huggingface.co/jinaai/jina-reranker-v2-base-multilingual.

Table 2. Comparative results on a subset of the `NFCorpus` dataset. 20% of the whole shuffled dataset was taken, deleting labels of documents not present in the subset dataset for retrieval evaluation. Scorings will be higher on the whole dataset.

Model	CM	RM	NDCG@5	MAP@5	F1@5	NDCG@10	MAP@10	F1@10
Jina-V3	FUC	TR	0.303	0.137	0.193	0.291	0.154	0.191
		RFR	0.289	0.130	0.185	0.288	0.150	0.193
	SUC	TR	0.307	0.143	0.197	0.292	0.159	0.187
		RFR	0.295	0.135	0.194	0.287	0.152	0.189
	FCC	TR	0.312	0.144	0.204	0.295	0.159	0.190
		RFR	**0.317**	**0.146**	0.206	0.308	0.166	0.202
	SCC	TR	0.305	0.136	0.197	0.296	0.155	0.198
		RFR	0.317	0.146	**0.209**	**0.309**	**0.166**	**0.204**
Jina-V2	FUC	TR	0.206	0.084	0.138	0.202	0.096	0.137
		RFR	0.256	0.119	0.166	0.251	0.133	0.161
	SUC	TR	0.231	0.100	0.152	0.223	0.112	0.149
		RFR	0.274	0.127	0.179	0.262	0.140	0.168
	FCC	TR	0.232	0.098	0.155	0.219	0.109	0.143
		RFR	0.288	0.130	0.182	0.274	0.144	0.173
	SCC	TR	0.231	0.099	0.156	0.220	0.110	0.148
		RFR	0.297	0.134	0.191	0.283	0.148	0.180
BGE-M3	FUC	TR	0.017	0.006	0.015	0.018	0.007	0.014
		RFR	0.032	0.012	0.018	0.033	0.012	0.020
	SUC	TR	0.012	0.003	0.001	0.012	0.003	0.011
		RFR	0.029	0.008	0.017	0.026	0.009	0.018
	FCC	TR	0.007	0.001	0.003	0.012	0.003	0.012
		RFR	0.040	0.015	0.026	0.040	0.016	0.027
	SCC	TR	0.002	0.001	0.001	0.006	0.002	0.007
		RFR	0.034	0.014	0.021	0.030	0.015	0.019

CM: Chunking Methods (FUC: Fixed-Window Uncontextualized Chunks, SUC: Semantic Uncontextualized Chunks, FCC: Fixed-Window Contextualized Chunks, SCC: Semantic Contextualized Chunks).
RM: Retrieval Methods (TR: Traditional Retrieval, RFR: Rank Fusion with weighted strategy (1, 0.25) respectively for dense embedder models and BM25 embeddings – additional Reranking step for RFR).

mean of the Average Precision (AP) scores for all queries, where AP considers the precision at each relevant item in the ranked list. With MAP, we aim to quantify how effectively the model retrieves relevant results across different scenarios. *F1-score:* The F1-score, a harmonic mean of precision and recall, is employed to balance the trade-off between false positives and false negatives.

4.3 Generation Evaluation

Generation evaluation was assessed through the MSMarco dataset using a question answering task. While for the Late Chunking technique, the scoring on the generation respects the retrieval performance, for the Contextual Retrieval Setup, chunks are enriched with additional generated context from the document that influences the output generation of an LLM. Although some differences were measured in the scorings, they were not notable enough to assess a significant difference in generation performance.

5 Results and Analysis

5.1 Traditional Retrieval Versus Contextual Retrieval

From the results in Table 2, and especially focusing the attention on the best performing embedding model Jina-V3, we show that Fixed-Window Chunking versus Semantic Chunking techniques do not differ much in terms of performance or not at all, while the first one being far easier implementable and faster than the second one. A more important finding underlines in the Rank Fusion technique. This technique shows improved results especially when chunks are enriched with additional context from the document. In this way, BM25 matches search terms in both segments and contexts, leading to very good results. It is important to note that adding the final reranking step in the workflow is crucial to leverage this potential and see consistent improvements in the results.

5.2 Traditional Retrieval Versus Late Chunking Retrieval

Upon analyzing the results in Table 3, we observe that the novel Late Chunking approach performs well in most cases when compared to the Early version. This indicates its potential as an effective retrieval strategy for many scenarios. However, it is important to note that Late Chunking does not consistently outperform the Early approach across all models and datasets.

For instance, with the BGE-M3 model applied to the NFCorpus, the Early version demonstrates superior performance, highlighting a case where the Late Chunking approach falls short. This observation is further confirmed through testing on the MsMarco dataset using the Stella-V5 model (Table 4), where once again the Early version outperforms the Late Chunking approach.

These findings suggest that while Late Chunking introduces promising improvements in certain contexts, its efficacy may vary depending on the dataset and model used, emphasizing the need for careful selection of retrieval strategies based on specific use cases.

5.3 Late Chunking Versus Contextual Retrieval

In Table 5 we compare the best results obtained for Contextual Retrieval with Late Chunking on the same subset of NFCorpus in order to compare the two techniques. The embedding model used is Jina-V3, for Fixed-Window Chunks. Contextual Retrieval obtains better results overall.

Table 3. Early Chunking Vs Late Chunking Retriever comparison on `NFCorpus`. Bold values indicate the best performance for each metric.

Model	Chunk	Segm	Length	NDCG@5	MAP@5	F1@5	NDCG@10	MAP@10	F1@10
Stella-V5	Early	Fix-size	512	0.443	**0.137**	**0.226**	**0.414**	**0.161**	**0.247**
	Late	Fix-size	512	**0.445**	0.133	0.225	0.410	0.158	0.242
Jina-V3	Early	Fix-size	512	0.374	0.107	0.186	0.346	0.127	0.204
	Late	Fix-size	512	0.380	0.103	0.185	0.354	0.125	0.210
	Early	Jina-Sem	–	0.377	0.111	0.192	0.353	0.130	0.210
	Late	sim-Qwen	–	0.384	0.105	0.185	0.356	0.126	0.206
	Late	top-Qwen	–	0.383	0.102	0.179	0.351	0.122	0.203
Jina-V2	Early	Fix-size	512	0.261	0.064	0.124	0.237	0.075	0.137
	Late	Fix-size	512	0.280	0.069	0.125	0.255	0.081	0.146
	Early	Jina-Sem	–	0.294	0.079	0.144	0.269	0.092	0.158
	Late	sim-Qwen	–	0.278	0.071	0.130	0.253	0.083	0.146
	Late	top-Qwen	–	0.279	0.070	0.135	0.254	0.081	0.147
BGE-M3	Early	Fix-size	512	0.246	0.059	0.120	0.225	0.069	0.130
	Late	Fix-size	512	0.070	0.010	0.029	0.067	0.013	0.038
	Early	Jina-Sem	-	0.260	0.066	0.122	0.240	0.079	0.144
	Late	sim-Qwen	-	0.091	0.015	0.038	0.081	0.018	0.045
	Late	top-Qwen	-	0.110	0.019	0.044	0.097	0.022	0.048

Table 4. Early Chunking Vs Late Chunking Retriever comparison `MsMarco`. Bold values indicate the best performance for each metric.

Model	Chunk	Segm	Length	NDCG@5	MAP@5	F1@5	NDCG@10	MAP@10	F1@10
Stella-V5	Early	Fix-size	512	**0.630**	**0.501**	**0.019**	**0.632**	**0.502**	**0.011**
	Late	Fix-size	512	0.503	0.340	0.018	0.505	0.341	0.010

5.4 Dynamic Segmenting Models

As shown in Table 3, the performance of pipelines utilizing dynamic segmentation, such as with `Jina-V3`, is superior to other approaches. However, this improvement comes at the cost of increased computational requirements and longer processing times. Specifically, embedding the `NFCorpus` dataset entirely with our experimental setup with fixed-size or semantic segmenter takes approximately 30 min. In comparison, the `Simple-Qwen` model requires twice the time, while the `Topic-Qwen` model requires four times as long.

Another drawback of these models is their generative nature, which can lead to inconsistencies. They do not always produce the exact same wording for chunks, rendering them less reliable in certain scenarios.

Table 5. Late Chunking (Late) comparison versus Contextual Retrieval (Contextual) best performances, on same `NFCorpus` dataset subset (20% of the whole). Embedding Model: `Jina-V3`. Chunking Method: Fixed-Window Chunking.

Method	NDCG@5	MAP@5	F1@5	NDCG@10	MAP@10	F1@10
Late	0.309	0.143	0.202	0.294	0.160	0.192
Contextual	**0.317**	**0.146**	**0.206**	**0.308**	**0.166**	**0.202**

6 Conclusion

Both late chunking and contextual retrieval aim to preserve context in document retrieval, each with its own advantages and trade-offs. Late Chunking involves embedding the entire document before dividing it into chunks. This method maintains contextual relationships across the document, leading to improved retrieval performance. It is computationally efficient, as it requires embedding only once per document, making it suitable for large-scale applications. However, its effectiveness is limited by the embedding model's context window size, which may not capture dependencies in very long documents.

Contextual Retrieval embeds each chunk along with additional context from surrounding sections or the entire document. This approach enhances semantic accuracy, especially for queries needing a comprehensive understanding of the document. However, it incurs higher computational costs due to repeated context generation and embedding processes. Additionally, the quality of the added context significantly influences performance, and smaller, more efficient models may underperform in this setup. In practical scenarios where computational resources are limited, late chunking offers a balanced solution by maintaining context with lower computational demands. Contextual Retrieval may be more suitable when sufficient computational resources are available.

Furthermore, the lack of datasets supporting both retrieval benchmarking and generation performance evaluation highlights the need for dedicated dataset construction. This would enable more comprehensive benchmarking and further advancements in this research area.

Acknowledgments. We would like to express our sincere thanks to Professor Gianluca Moro, Giacomo Frisoni, and Lorenzo Molfetta for their continuous support, guidance, and valuable insights throughout the development of this work.

A Prompt for Contextualization

(See Fig. 3).

Prompt Templates

Task: Chunk Contextualization
User:

```
    DOCUMENT:
    {doc_content}


    Here is the chunk we want to situate within the whole document
    CHUNK:
    {chunk_content}


    Provide a concise context for the following chunk, focusing on
    ↪ its relevance within the overall document for the purposes
    ↪ of improving search retrieval of the chunk.
    Answer only with the generated context and nothing else.
    Output your answer after the phrase "The document provides an
    ↪ overview".
    Think step by step.


    Here there is an example you can look at.
    EXAMPLE:
    {examples}
```

Fig. 3. Prompt template to instruct the LLM to generate contextual information from the document specific to each chunk.

References

1. Abdin, M.I., et al.: Phi-3 technical report: a highly capable language model locally on your phone. CoRR abs/2404.14219 (2024). https://doi.org/10.48550/ARXIV.2404.14219
2. Boteva, V., Gholipour, D., Sokolov, A., Riezler, S.: A full-text learning to rank dataset for medical information retrieval. In: Ferro, N., et al. (eds.) ECIR 2016. LNCS, vol. 9626, pp. 716–722. Springer, Cham (2016). https://doi.org/10.1007/978-3-319-30671-1_58
3. Chen, J., Xiao, S., Zhang, P., Luo, K., Lian, D., Liu, Z.: BGE m3-embedding: multi-lingual, multi-functionality, multi-granularity text embeddings through self-knowledge distillation. CoRR abs/2402.03216 (2024). https://doi.org/10.48550/ARXIV.2402.03216

4. Ding, Y., et al.: Longrope: extending LLM context window beyond 2 million tokens. In: Forty-first International Conference on Machine Learning, ICML 2024, Vienna, Austria, 21–27 July 2024. OpenReview.net (2024). https://openreview.net/forum?id=ONOtpXLqqw
5. Fan, W., et al.: A survey on RAG meeting LLMs: towards retrieval-augmented large language models. In: Baeza-Yates, R., Bonchi, F. (eds.) Proceedings of the 30th ACM SIGKDD Conference on Knowledge Discovery and Data Mining, KDD 2024, Barcelona, Spain, 25–29 August 2024, pp. 6491–6501. ACM (2024). https://doi.org/10.1145/3637528.3671470
6. Gao, M., Lu, T., Yu, K., Byerly, A., Khashabi, D.: Insights into LLM long-context failures: when transformers know but don't tell. In: Al-Onaizan, Y., Bansal, M., Chen, Y. (eds.) Findings of the Association for Computational Linguistics: EMNLP 2024, Miami, Florida, USA, 12–16 November 2024, pp. 7611–7625. Association for Computational Linguistics (2024), https://aclanthology.org/2024.findings-emnlp.447
7. Gao, Y., et al.: Retrieval-augmented generation for large language models: a survey. CoRR abs/2312.10997 (2023). https://doi.org/10.48550/ARXIV.2312.10997
8. Günther, M., Mohr, I., Wang, B., Xiao, H.: Late chunking: contextual chunk embeddings using long-context embedding models. CoRR abs/2409.04701 (2024). https://doi.org/10.48550/ARXIV.2409.04701
9. Günther, M., et al.: Jina embeddings 2: 8192-token general-purpose text embeddings for long documents. CoRR abs/2310.19923 (2023). https://doi.org/10.48550/ARXIV.2310.19923
10. Gupta, S., Ranjan, R., Singh, S.N.: A comprehensive survey of retrieval-augmented generation (RAG): evolution, current landscape and future directions. CoRR abs/2410.12837 (2024). https://doi.org/10.48550/ARXIV.2410.12837
11. Hsieh, C., et al.: Found in the middle: calibrating positional attention bias improves long context utilization. In: Ku, L., Martins, A., Srikumar, V. (eds.) Findings of the Association for Computational Linguistics, ACL 2024, Bangkok, Thailand and virtual meeting, 11–16 August 2024, pp. 14982–14995. Association for Computational Linguistics (2024). https://doi.org/10.18653/V1/2024.FINDINGS-ACL.890
12. Jina.ai: Finding optimal breakpoints in long documents using small language models (2024). https://jina.ai/news/finding-optimal-breakpoints-in-long-documents-using-small-language-models/
13. Karpukhin, V., et al.: Dense passage retrieval for open-domain question answering. In: Webber, B., Cohn, T., He, Y., Liu, Y. (eds.) Proceedings of the 2020 Conference on Empirical Methods in Natural Language Processing, EMNLP 2020, Online, 16–20 November 2020, pp. 6769–6781. Association for Computational Linguistics (2020). https://doi.org/10.18653/V1/2020.EMNLP-MAIN.550, https://doi.org/10.18653/v1/2020.emnlp-main.550
14. Koshorek, O., Cohen, A., Mor, N., Rotman, M., Berant, J.: Text segmentation as a supervised learning task. In: Walker, M.A., Ji, H., Stent, A. (eds.) Proceedings of the 2018 Conference of the North American Chapter of the Association for Computational Linguistics: Human Language Technologies, NAACL-HLT, New Orleans, Louisiana, USA, 1–6 June 2018, Volume 2 (Short Papers), pp. 469–473. Association for Computational Linguistics (2018). https://doi.org/10.18653/V1/N18-2075

15. Lewis, P.S.H., et al.: Retrieval-augmented generation for knowledge-intensive NLP tasks. In: Larochelle, H., Ranzato, M., Hadsell, R., Balcan, M., Lin, H. (eds.) Advances in Neural Information Processing Systems 33: Annual Conference on Neural Information Processing Systems 2020, NeurIPS 2020, 6–12 December 2020, virtual (2020). https://proceedings.neurips.cc/paper/2020/hash/6b493230205f780e1bc26945df7481e5-Abstract.html
16. Moro, G., Ragazzi, L.: Align-then-abstract representation learning for low-resource summarization. Neurocomputing **548**, 126356 (2023). https://doi.org/10.1016/J.NEUCOM.2023.126356
17. Muennighoff, N., Tazi, N., Magne, L., Reimers, N.: MTEB: massive text embedding benchmark. In: Vlachos, A., Augenstein, I. (eds.) Proceedings of the 17th Conference of the European Chapter of the Association for Computational Linguistics, EACL 2023, Dubrovnik, Croatia, 2–6 May 2023, pp. 2006–2029. Association for Computational Linguistics (2023). https://doi.org/10.18653/V1/2023.EACL-MAIN.148
18. Nguyen, T., et al.: MS MARCO: a human generated machine reading comprehension dataset. In: Besold, T.R., Bordes, A., d'Avila Garcez, A.S., Wayne, G. (eds.) Proceedings of the Workshop on Cognitive Computation: Integrating neural and symbolic approaches 2016 Co-located with the 30th Annual Conference on Neural Information Processing Systems (NIPS 2016), Barcelona, Spain, 9 December 2016. CEUR Workshop Proceedings, vol. 1773. CEUR-WS.org (2016). https://ceur-ws.org/Vol-1773/CoCoNIPS_2016_paper9.pdf
19. Robertson, S.E., Zaragoza, H.: The probabilistic relevance framework: BM25 and beyond. Found. Trends Inf. Retr. **3**(4), 333–389 (2009). https://doi.org/10.1561/1500000019
20. Sturua, S., et al.: jina-embeddings-v3: multilingual embeddings with task LoRA. CoRR abs/2409.10173 (2024). https://doi.org/10.48550/ARXIV.2409.10173

Leveraging Decoder Architectures for Learned Sparse Retrieval

Jingfen Qiao[1]($\boxtimes$), Thong Nguyen[1], Evangelos Kanoulas[1], and Andrew Yates[1,2]

[1] University of Amsterdam, Amsterdam, The Netherlands
{j.qiao,t.nguyen2,e.kanoulas}@uva.nl, andrew.yates@jhu.edu
[2] Johns Hopkins University, Baltimore, USA

Abstract. Learned Sparse Retrieval (LSR) has traditionally focused on small-scale encoder-only transformer architectures. With the advent of large-scale pre-trained language models, their capability to generate sparse representations for retrieval tasks across different transformer-based architectures, including encoder-only, decoder-only, and encoder-decoder models, remains largely unexplored. This study investigates the effectiveness of LSR across these architectures, exploring various sparse representation heads and model scales. Our results highlight the limitations of using large language models to create effective sparse representations in zero-shot settings, identifying challenges such as inappropriate term expansions and reduced performance due to the lack of expansion. We find that the encoder-decoder architecture with multi-tokens decoding approach achieves the best performance among the three backbones. While the decoder-only model performs worse than the encoder-only model, it demonstrates the potential to outperform when scaled to a high number of parameters.

Keywords: Learned Sparse Retrieval · LLMs · Information Retrieval

1 Introduction

Modern LLMs are knowledgeable about a wide range of topics and have achieved remarkable performance in their application to information retrieval [17,28,30]. However, much of the research has focused on using LLMs to generate dense vectors rather than sparse ones [17,18]. Learned sparse retrieval (LSR) utilizes LLMs to encode queries and documents into lexical sparse vectors, i.e. vectors where most of the elements are zero. Compared to dense retrieval, LSR's lexical representations are more interpretable as each output dimension is aligned with a term in a vocabulary. In addition, LSR relies on an inverted index for retrieval, which is smaller in size than a vector index (e.g., HNSW [21]) employed by dense retrieval. Recent studies have demonstrated that LSRs could efficiently achieve strong first-stage retrieval performance [4,15]. Its effectiveness, efficiency and transparency make LSR a compelling alternative to dense retrieval in many information retrieval applications [12,23].

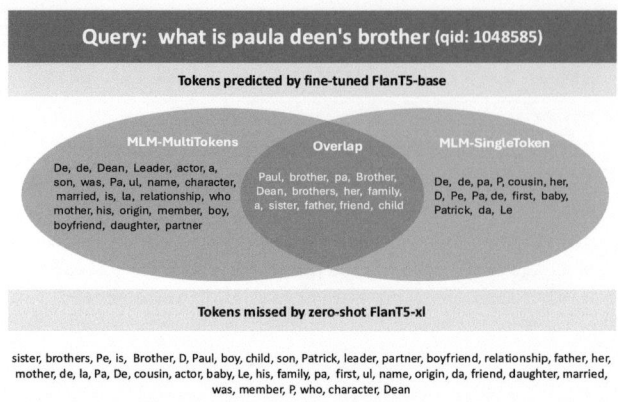

Fig. 1. Output Bags of Tokens Produced by Different Sparse Representation Heads; Zero-shot encoder (FlanT5-xl) misses many important expansion terms. The MLM-MultiTokens head captures more relevant tokens than the MLM-SingleToken head by gathering contextual information from all input token rather than a single token.

When evaluating the capabilities of LLMs for sparse retrieval, a key question is whether they can generate effective sparse representations in zero-shot settings. Our analysis shows that while LLMs excel in many generative tasks, they struggle with zero-shot sparse retrieval. As illustrated in Fig. 1, which shows the tokens predicted by different sparse representation heads with a zero shot or fine-tuned model, LLMs not only fail to expand the input text to include semantically relevant terms, but they often introduce noise, leading to semantic drift and poor retrieval performance. This limitation highlights the need for supervised training to enhance LLMs' effectiveness and raises the question of whether fine-tuning could enable LLMs to outperform smaller-scale learned sparse retrieval (LSR) methods.

Previous research on LSR has predominantly focused on small-scale encoder-only transformer architectures [2,12,19,27,34]. For instance, Splade [12], a state-of-the-art LSR model, is built upon Cocondenser [13], which utilizes a BERT-base architecture with 110M parameters, specifically pre-trained for Information Retrieval (IR) tasks. The generalizability of LSR to other transformer architectures, such as decoder-only and encoder-decoder, remains unclear, as does its scalability concerning model size. Decoders are trained to sequentially generate a subsequent token based on the given input text and previously generated tokens. This is different from sparse representation learning which requires weighting existing tokens within the input and expanding them with contextually relevant terms. To learn a sparse representation from the decoder output, we investigate using a multi-tokens decoding approach. This adaptation allows the decoder to work more like an encoder, making better use of the parameters within the decoder module. Our results indicate that the multi-tokens decoding approach

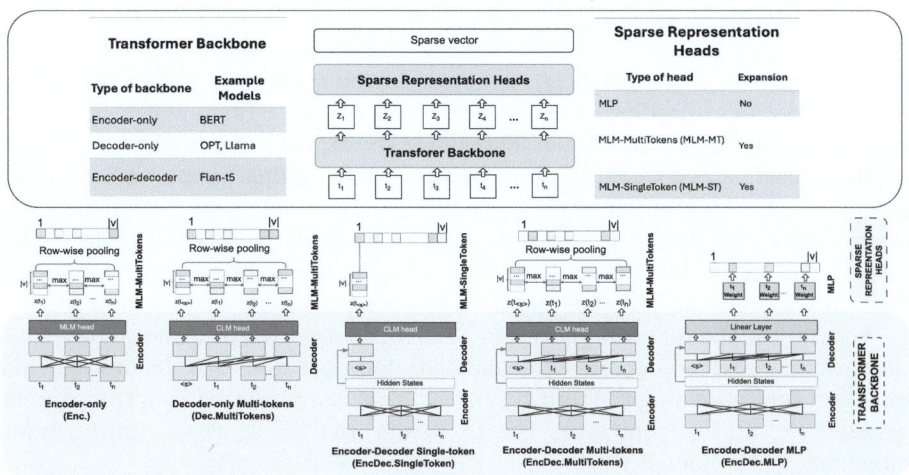

Fig. 2. Learned sparse retrieval architectures consist of (1) a transformer backbone that takes query or document text as input and outputs hidden state(s) and (2) a sparse representation head that takes the hidden state(s) as input and outputs sparse lexical representations.

for encoder-decoder models helps to effectively utilize the parameters in both encoder and decoder modules.

This paper aims to address these gaps by investigating LSR across different transformer architectures (encoder-only, decoder-only, and encoder-decoder) at several scales and exploring the capabilities of LLMs under zero-shot and fined-tuning settings. Our findings are as follows: **(1)** Without fine-tuning, LLMs struggle to generate meaningful sparse representations due to inappropriate term expansions; **(2)** the ability of decoder-only architectures to produce sparse representations is limited and comparable results to encoder-only models are only achieved when the model is scaled to a large size, such as 3 billion parameters; **(3)** by copying the encoder's input to the decoder we enable the encoder-decoder to perform multi-tokens decoding effectively aggregating lexical information across the input sequence and creating a significantly more effective sparse representation compared to the single-token approach; and **(4)** encoder-decoder architectures with multi-tokens decoding can outperform encoder-only and decoder-only.[1]

2 LSR Architectures

In LSR, queries and passages are encoded into sparse representations over terms (Fig. 2). In this section, we describe how to generate sparse representations from various transformer-based architectures, including encoder-only, decoder-only, and encoder-decoder.

---

[1] Code: https://github.com/JingfenQiao/Decoder4LSR.

2.1 Transformer Backbones

Given a sequence of n tokens $(t_1, t_2, \ldots, t_n)$ in the query or passage, the task of a LSR model is to predict term weights based on the hidden states output by the transformer-based backbone. Therefore, the transformer backbone aims to transform each input token t_i into a hidden state (latent vector) h_i. A sparse representation of the input is then produced by passing these hidden states to a sparse representation head. In this section, we first describe how the hidden states h_i are produced by encoder-only backbone in the previous research, and then illustrate how to leverage decoders to construct sparse representations.

We will use the following notation to describe each transformer-based backbone in this paper: $\oplus$ denotes the concatenation operator, $h_{1:n}$ denotes the hidden states corresponding to input tokens $t_{1:n}$ that are produced by a transformer-backbone, v_i and e_i represents the i_{th} token and transformer's initial input embedding in the model vocabulary $|V|$, where $i \in \{0, \ldots, |V|-1\}$.

Encoder-Only (Enc.): When using a transformer encoder stack as the backbone, we feed text directly into the encoder, which produces a contextualized embedding of each input term. We refer to these as hidden states h_i for consistency with the decoder-based backbone that we introduce in this paper.

$$h_{1:n} = \text{Encoder}(t_1, t_2, \ldots, t_n) \qquad (1)$$

When using an encoder backbone, the hidden states are produced using bi-directional attention that considers terms both before and after a given term t_i when producing hidden states to represent the input sequence. This is an intuitive property for the transformer backbone to have. With the exception of the zero-shot PromptRep model [37] and orthogonal document expansion approaches like doc2query [26], all existing learned sparse retrieval models use backbones based on a transformer encoder [23].

Decoder-Only with Multi-tokens (Dec. MultiTokens): In contrast to encoder models, decoders are designed with causal attention, where the generation of a hidden state h_i depends only on the previously generated tokens, and the decoder starts with the start symbol of a model <s>. We concatenate the start symbol of the model <s> in front of the token t_1.

$$h_{1:n} = \text{Decoder}(<\text{s}>, t_1, t_2, \ldots, t_n) \qquad (2)$$

When using decoder-based backbones, rather than invoking the decoder repeatedly for each token, we feed the entire input text to the decoder in a single pass to generate sparse representations. This contrasts with the typical token-by-token decoding approach, where a new hidden state is produced at each decoding step. As illustrated in Fig. 2, the row-wise pooling of MLM outputs demonstrates how the hidden state of every token contributes to the final multi-token representation.

Encoder-Decoder with Single-Token (EncDec. SingleToken): In encoder-decoder with single-token, similar to the Sentence-T5 embedding model [24], input text is fed into the encoder and only the start token <s> is fed into the decoder. Therefore, it only yields a single latent vector h_1 that is derived from the hidden state of the input token <s>, which is in turn derived from the hidden states of the entire input text produced by the encoder stack.

$$h^{enc}_{1:n} = \text{Encoder}(t_1, t_2, \ldots, t_n) \quad (3)$$

$$h_1 = \text{Decoder}(h^{enc}_{1:n} \oplus e_{<s>})_{n+1} \quad (4)$$

Encoder-Decoder with Multi-tokens (EncDec. MultiTokens): We hypothesize that the output representation of the encoder-decoder architecture is bottlenecked by the single decoder input, the start token <s>, which limits the model's ability to aggregate lexical information from the entire input sequence. To overcome this bottleneck, we propose a multi-tokens decoding approach that allows the model to gather information from any input token. As shown in Fig. 2, the Encoder-Decoder with multi-tokens model receives full input text both in the encoder and decoder, and the decoder's input is prepended with the start token.

$$h^{enc}_{1:n} = \text{Encoder}(t_1, t_2, \ldots, t_n) \quad (5)$$
$$h_{1:n} = \text{Decoder}(h^{enc}_{1:n} \oplus e_{<s>} \oplus t_1, t_2, \ldots, t_n) \quad (6)$$

2.2 Sparse Representation Heads

A sparse representation head takes a hidden state produced by the transformer backbone as input and produces one or more term weights.[2] These term weights are then aggregated to produce a sparse representation of the entire input text, which can then be used for retrieval by taking the dot product of a query representation and a document representation. More formally, a sparse representation head takes a sequence of n hidden states output by a transformer backbone $h_{1:n} = (h_1, h_2, \ldots, h_n)$ as input. The head outputs a sparse vector with $|V|$ dimensions where v_i corresponds to a term t_i in the vocabulary.

MLP Head: The MLP head, used in models like DeepCT [14], uniCOIL [16] and DeepImpact [22], uses a multi-layer perceptron to process contextualized embeddings for each input term in the query or passage. It assigns non-zero weights to terms that occur only in the input text. The importance $MLP(h)_i$ of each term v_i within a model vocabulary V for a given input t_n is defined by Eq. 7, where W and b are the weight and bias of the linear head, respectively. $1(v_i = t_n)$ ensures to that only tokens in the input receive weights, the other terms are zero.

$$MLP(h_{1:n})_i = \sum_{j=1}^{n} \log\left(1(v_i = t_j) \cdot \text{ReLU}(h_j W + b) + 1\right) \quad (7)$$

---

[2] Nguyen et al. [23] refer to these as *sparse encoders*. We use the term *head* instead to avoid overloading the term *encoder*, which can also refer to the type of transformer backbone used.

MLM Head: In contrast to the MLP head, the MLM head expands the input (using the model's vocabulary) in addition to weighting tokens. MLM heads have been used in models such as SPLADE [12], Sparta [36], and TILDE [38]. The MLM head uses the logits value produced by the language model head for each input term v_i to produce a sparse representation. It can assign a weight to to any terms in the model vocabulary V regardless of whether it appears in the input text, thereby exploiting the language model's capability to expand and weight terms. The importance $MLM(h_{1:n})_i$ of each term v_i within a model's vocabulary V is aggregated from the logits matrix along the input sequence, as defined in Eq. 8. The MLM-SingleToken (MLM-ST) process a single hidden state h_1 from the transformer backbone to determine the importance of each term in the vocabulary, while MLM-MultiTokens (MLM-MT) processes multiple hidden states $h_{1:n}$ and takes the max weight over the different hidden states.

$$MLM(h_{1:n})_i = \max_{j=1}^{n} \log\left(1 + \text{ReLu}\left(h_j^T e_i + b_i\right)\right) \quad (8)$$

The *ReLu* activation function and logarithmic normalization are applied to ensure the positive of term weights [12] and prevent some terms from dominating in the sparse representation [10]. The max-pooling operator in Eq. 8 is to aggregate term importance weights into a document-level sparse representation. Formal et al., [12] found that max pooling is more effective than sum pooling. Therefore, we employed max-pooling for all MLM models.

3 Experimental Setup

In this section, we outline the experimental design, including the models, training configurations, and evaluation methods, to investigate learned sparse retrieval (LSR) performance across various transformer architectures.

Retrieval and Indexing: We apply the same architecture type with shared weights for both the query and document encoders. For indexing and retrieval, we use the Anserini toolkit [32,33] to index the encoded documents and retrieve with the encoded queries.

Dataset and Evaluation: We trained our models on the MS MARCO passage dataset [3], which includes 8.8 million passages and 40 million training triplets. All models are trained on those triplets and hard negatives generated by the cross-encoder teacher model in [14]. We report the MRR@10, NDCG@10 and Recall@1000 of all models on the MS MARCO Dev and TREC Deep Learning (TREC-DL) 2019/2020 [6,7]. In addition of the effectiveness metrics, we report the FLOPs metric (the average number of term overlap between a pair of query and document) as a proxy of efficiency.

Backbones and Baselines: We selected three different pretrained transformer language model as the backbone of our study, including encoder-only (Distilbert-base-uncased [29]), decoder-only (OPT [35]) and encoder-decoder (T5 [5]). Distilbert-base-uncased is widely recognized and extensively employed within the LSR literature [9,12,15]. The OPT [35] and Flan-T5 [5] offers a wide range of parameter sizes. This variability enables us to explore how decoder-only architectures scale and perform in generating sparse representations, providing insights into their effectiveness across different model sizes. In terms of baselines, we select based on query expansion and term weighting strategies and compare against the unsupervised sparse model BM25 and the supervised sparse model, including EPIC [20], DeepCT [8], DocT5Query [26], DeepImpact [22], Splade-max [12] and DistilSplade-max [12]. The unsupervised sparse baseline BM25 employs neither expansion nor supervised weighting. Supervised LSR baselines include EPIC [20] and DeepCT [8], which use supervised weighting without query expansion; DocT5Query [26], which focuses solely on document term expansion without term weighting; DeepImpact [22], which applies supervised term weighting without query expansion; and Splade-max [12] and DistilSplade-max [12], which integrate both supervised query expansion and term weighting.

Training Configuration: All models were fine-tuned using the ADAM optimizer with 6000 warmup steps. The batch size for all models was consistently maintained at 16. Due to model nuances, the OPT model uses a lower learning rate of 1^{e-6}, while Flan-T5 uses 5^{e-4}. We used one NVIDIA A6000 GPU with 48GB memory to train medium-sized models, such as Flan-T5-base, and OPT-3.5. Larger models (OPT-1.3B, OPT-2.7B, Flan-T5-large and Flan-T5-xl) were trained on four A6000 GPUs. Following the setting of Splade [12], we schedule the regularization weight λ to increase quadratically over the first 100k steps and we tried different values of λ ranging from 1^{-1} to 1^{-4}.

4 Optimization

Knowledge distillation has emerged as a highly effective strategy for transferring knowledge from a high-performing cross-encoder to a more efficient bi-encoder in information retrieval tasks [12,14,15]. By training the student model to replicate the teacher's score distribution, the student preserves a significant portion of the teacher's ranking ability. Compared to alternative approaches for retrieval, such as contrastive learning or reinforcement learning, the knowledge distillation inherits a well-calibrated signal from a strong teacher model, thus reducing the need for labor intensive training sample construction or careful reward engineering. Concretely, given a batch B of training triplets q_i, P_i^+, P_i^- consisting of a query q_i, a positive document P_i^+ and a negative document P_i^-, we compute the margin between the positive and negative documents for both teacher and student. We then minimize the mean squared error (MSE) of the difference between these margins, as shown in Eq. 9.

$$\mathcal{L}_{\text{MarginMSE}} = \frac{1}{|B|} \sum_{i=\{0,\ldots,|B|-1\}} \left(\Delta M_s^i - \Delta M_t^i \right)^2 \qquad (9)$$

where $\Delta M_s^i = S(q_i, P_i^+) - S(q_i, P_i^-)$ and $\Delta M_t^i = T(q_i, P_i^+) - T(q_i, P_i^-)$ are the respective margin scores of the student S and teacher model T on the i-th triplet, and $|B|$ is the batch size. Following [12,14], we use MarginMSE as the distillation loss to ensure fair comparisons and reduce confounding factors. Although a more complex training setup (e.g. using an ensemble of multiple teachers, dual MarginMSE and KL-Div loss, continuous training as in Splade-V3 [15]) could be applied to increase the overall effectiveness, we believe that our relative findings between different architectures and approaches do not change.

Distillation Training Data. To investigate how the scaling of teacher models affects performance, we experiment with two teachers: MiniLM-L-6-v2 [31] and Rankllama-13B [17]. Rankllama-13B outperforms MiniLM-L-6-v2 on the MSMARCO training set, as shown in Table 5 in Appendix. For both teacher models, we collect hard negatives from multiple retrieval systems (including dense retrieval models and BM25) to provide challenging negative samples. Each teacher then generates score pairs for the query-positive and query-hard-negative pairs using the hard negatives from Sentence-Transformers[3]. We use the smaller teacher's scores from [11] directly, whereas we generate the Rankllama-13B scores ourselves[4]. We observe that Rankllama-13B produces a relatively narrow score distribution (Appendix Table 3), which may make it more difficult for students to learn effectively. This aligns with findings by [15], who show that the MarginMSE-based distillation process is sensitive to score distributions. To address this, we apply an affine transformation to flatten Rankllama-13B's scores, ensuring that its mean and standard deviation more closely match those of MiniLM-L-6-v2.

Sparsity Regularization. Finally, to encourage sparsity in the learned representations, we adopt FLOPs regularization [27] and activation functions [1] to facilitate the learning of distributed sparse embeddings. FLOPs are a differentiable relaxed approximation of the number of floating-point operations(FLOPs) to compute the score between query and document. Formally, our overall objective is defined in Eq. 10.

Table 1. Comparison of sparse retrieval without fine-tuning on MS MARCO dev. × results are from [22]; A † indicates paired t-test $p < 0.05$. († indicates test between term expansion and non-expansion.

Model	Weighting	Expansion	RR@10	R@1k
Sparse retrieval				
(1) BM25[×]	Yes	No	18.8	85.8
(2) BM25+Doc2Query[×]	Yes	Yes	27.8	94.7
Learned sparse retrieval (zero-shot)				
(3) EncDec.MultiTokens$_{\text{FlanT5-xl}}$	Yes	Yes	1.30	16.5
(4) EncDec.MultiTokens$_{\text{FlanT5-xl}}$	Yes	No	3.67†	34.0†
(5) Dec.MultiTokens$_{\text{OPT-2.7B}}$	Yes	No	13.7	71.4
(6) Dec.MultiTokens$_{\text{OPT-6.7B}}$	Yes	No	12.5	70.5

---

[3] https://huggingface.co/datasets/sentence-transformers/msmarco-hard-negatives.
[4] https://huggingface.co/datasets/lsr42/rankllama-ms-marco-scores.

$$\mathcal{L}_{\text{ranking}} = \mathcal{L}_{\text{MarginMSE}} + \lambda_q \mathcal{L}_{reg}^q + \lambda_d \mathcal{L}_{reg}^d \tag{10}$$

where $\mathcal{L}_{reg}^q$ and $\mathcal{L}_{reg}^d$ denote FLOPs-based regularization terms for query and document representations, respectively, and λ_q and λ_d are their weighting coefficients.

5 Results and Discussion

RQ1: Can LLMs effectively generate sparse representations in a zero-shot setting when prompted?

Term weighting and expansion are key factors in the effectiveness of sparse retrieval systems [16]. We evaluate LLMs for sparse vector creation with and without term expansion. Recently, Zhuang et al. [37] proposed generating sparse and dense representations by prompting LLMs, using the logits of the last token in the input sequence. Their method only assigns weights to tokens present in the input, without term expansion. To investigate LLM's term expansion ability, we compare sparse vectors with and without expansion. In the expansion case, we keep the top 1,000 tokens, while the non-expansion approach uses only tokens from the input text. Instead of relying on the last token's logits, our method aggregates logits from all input tokens, following Eq. 8.

Table 1 shows the zero-shot performance of LLMs versus traditional methods like BM25 and BM25+Doc2Query. All zero-shot models use the MLM-MultiTokens head for aggregating term weights. We find that enabling term expansion in Flan-T5-xl leads to a significant drop in Recall@1k (34.0 to 16.5), as noisy terms like 'ray', 's', and 'mil' receive high weights, harming performance. OPT-2.7B achieves the best results among LLMs (MRR 13.7, Recall@1k 71.4) but still falls short of BM25 and state-of-the-art LSR models, highlighting the need for fine-tuning to improve term importance assessment in LSR. Additionally, we assessed their effectiveness across various model sizes to provide a more comprehensive comparison, as shown in Table 6 in the Appendix.

RQ2: Can encoder-decoder or decoder-only backbones outperform encoder-only backbones when using multi-tokens decoding approach?

Encoder-Only VS Encoder-Decoder Backbone. The encoder-decoder backbone generally surpasses the encoder-only backbone, as shown in Table 2. Specifically, EncDec.MultiTokens (row 6) outperforms the encoder-only model DistilSplade-max (row 2) in NDCG@10 on the MS MARCO development set, with lower FLOPs (4 vs. 2.8) using the same training configuration. Upon inspection, we find that the encoder-decoder model is more effective at expanding the input queries and documents to relevant terms. The encoder-decoder architecture benefits from a hybrid attention mechanism, which includes bidirectional attention in the encoder and causal attention in the decoder. This allows it to identify different patterns of semantic dependency in the input. Interestingly, the encoder-only model using Flan-T5 (Enc.$_{\text{FlanT5-base}}$) performs significantly worse than the encoder-only model DistilSplade-max, especially on the MRR@10 and

Table 2. Evaluation of different transformer backbones on MS MARCO passage (dev set) and TREC DL 2019/2020. *All models are trained with 600k steps and use the MLM-MultiTokens head for both query and document encoding.* ∗ *indicates reproduced results.*

Models	Backbones	FLOPs	DL2020 nDCG@10	DL2019 nDCG@10	MS MARCO dev nDCG@10	MS MARCO dev R@1k	MS MARCO dev RR@10
(1) Splade-max∗ [12]	Encoder-only	1.3	67.0	68.0	40.2	96.5	34.0
(2) DistilSplade-max∗ [12]	Encoder-only	4.0	67.9	71.0	43.3	97.9	36.8
(3) Enc.$_{\text{FlanT5-base}}$	Encoder-only	16.0	61.0	65.0	36.0	96.9	29.8
(4) Dec.MultiTokens$_{\text{FlanT5-base}}$	Decoder-only	2.3	67.4	68.7	39.9	97.1	33.6
(5) Dec.MultiTokens$_{\text{OPT-350m}}$	Decoder-only	4.9	68.6	66.4	39.8	97.2	33.7
(6) EncDec.MultiTokens$_{\text{FlanT5-base}}$	Encoder-Decoder	2.8	70.5	71.4	43.6	98.3	36.8

nDCG@10 metrics. This underperformance may be attributed to the fact that Flan-T5 was pre-trained with an encoder-decoder architecture, where the MLM head is only attached to the decoder's hidden states during training. When we attach the same MLM head to the encoder, there may be an incompatibility that makes LSR training more challenging.

Table 3. Performance of different Sparse Representation Heads on MS MARCO passage (dev) and TREC DL 2019/2020. *All models are trained with 600k steps.* ∗ *indicates reproduced results;* × *results are from the work in* [22]; ×× *results are from the work in* [23]; *A* † *indicates paired t-test p < 0.05.* († *indicates test between MLM-MT and MLM-ST); A* ‡ *indicates paired t-test p < 0.01 (* ‡ *indicates test between models where both query and passage use MLM-MT and models where either query or passage use MLM-MT)*

Models	Query	Passage	FLOPs	DL2020 nDCG@10	DL2019 nDCG@10	MS MARCO dev nDCG@10	MS MARCO dev R@1k	MS MARCO dev RR@10
(1) BM25$^{\times}$			–	48.7	49.7	23.5	85.8	18.8
(2) EPIC$_{top400}^{\times\times}$ [20]	MLP	MLM-MT	–	71.8	70.9	–	97.2	37.2
(3) DeepCT$^{\times}$ [8]	MLP	MLP	–	55.0	57.8	29.8	91.0	24.4
(4) DocT5Query$^{\times}$ [26]	–	–	–	61.9	64.8	33.8	94.7	27.8
(5) DeepImpact$^{\times}$ [22]	BINARY	expMLP	–	65.1	69.5	38.5	94.8	32.6
(6) Splade-max∗ [12]	MLM-MT	MLM-MT	1.3	67.0	68.0	40.2	96.5	34.0
(7) DistilSplade-max∗ [12]	MLM-MT	MLM-MT	4.0	67.9	71.0	43.3	97.9	36.8
(8) EncDec.MultiTokens$_{\text{FlanT5-base}}$	MLP	MLM-MT	1.3	53.6‡	56.6‡	41.7‡	97.6‡	35.3‡
(9) EncDec.MultiTokens$_{\text{FlanT5-base}}$	MLM-MT	MLP	3.3	50.6‡	48.1‡	31.3‡	95.9‡	25.8‡
(10) EncDec.SingleToken$_{\text{FlanT5-base}}$	MLM-ST	MLM-ST	2.5	54.5	59.7	36.1	95.0	30.4
(11) EncDec.MultiTokens$_{\text{FlanT5-base}}$	MLM-MT	MLM-MT	2.8	70.5†	71.4†	43.6†	98.3†	36.8†

Decoder-Only Backbone Effectiveness. We trained different LSR variants using the Flan-T5-base (248 million parameters) and OPT-350M (350 million parameters) decoder-only checkpoints. Among all the backbone variations (rows 3, 4, and 6) of Flan-T5-base, the decoder-only variant (row 4) was the second most effective, trailing only behind the encoder-decoder architecture (row

6). Furthermore, compared to DistilSplade-max (row 2), which is built on the BERT encoder, the decoder-only model using the OPT-350M checkpoint (row 5) shows a slight improvement in terms of NDCG@10 and MRR@10 metrics on the DL2020 dataset, but not on MS MARCO and DL2019. Additional insight could also be seen on Table 4, where we observe that the effectiveness of the Decoder-only model (row 8) can exceed Enc. (row 1) on DL2020, DL2019 and MS MARCO when the parameters are scaled to 1.3 billion.

Table 4. Impact of scaling student and teacher model. *All models are trained with 600k steps and use the MLM-MultiTokens head for both querying and document encoding. A † ‡ indicates a paired t-test $p < 0.05$. († indicates a test between models tuned with the teacher MiniLM-L-6-v2 and Rankllama-13b. ‡ indicates between smaller student and larger student LSR model with same backbones)*

Models	DL2020 nDCG@10	DL2019 nDCG@10	MS MARCO dev RR@10	FLOPs
(1) Enc.$_{\text{Distilbert-base-uncased}}$	67.9	71.0	36.8	4.0
(2) EncDec.MultiTokens$_{\text{FlanT5-base}}$	70.5	71.4	36.8	2.8
(3) Dec.MultiTokens$_{\text{OPT-350M}}$	68.6	66.4	33.7	4.9
Scaling Teacher				
(4) Enc.$_{\text{Distilbert-base-uncased}}$	73.1†	75.1†	37.3	5.8
(5) EncDec.MultiTokens$_{\text{FlanT5-base}}$	70.1	73.4	37.8	5.2
(6) Dec.MultiTokens$_{\text{OPT-350M}}$	61	66.8	32.8	5.1
Scaling Student				
(7) EncDec.MultiTokens$_{\text{FlanT5-large}}$	70.7	73.3	37.8	3.8
(8) Dec.MultiTokens$_{\text{OPT-1.3B}}$	69.5	73.1‡	36.9‡	4.8

RQ3: Which sparse representation head is better for creating a sparse representation?

MLM-MultiTokens (MLM-MT) vs. MLM-SingleToken (MLM-ST). We evaluate the MLM-MultiTokens and MLM-SingleToken heads on the best-performing encoder-decoder model using the Flan-T5 base checkpoint. As shown in Table 3, the MLM-MultiTokens head outperforms the MLM-SingleToken head across all evaluated metrics and datasets (MS MARCO, DL2019, DL2020). This suggests that the MLM-MultiTokens head, which aggregates latent vectors from multiple input tokens, facilitates more effective sparse representations compared to the single token approach from the decoder output.

MLM-MultiTokens vs. MLP. We also compare the performance of the MLP and MLM-MultiTokens heads derived from the decoder output using the Flan-T5-base checkpoint. The results in Table 3 show that encoding both the query and document with the MLM-MultiTokens head achieves the highest effectiveness, significantly outperforming the MLP head, particularly in terms of nDCG@10 across different datasets. This contrasts with the results observed on an encoder-only backbone, where switching the query encoder from MLM-MultiTokens to MLP—reproduced using hard negative distillation labels in the study by [23]—did not yield a significant improvement. These findings suggest that MLM-MultiTokens head query expansion is more beneficial for encoder-decoder backbones compared to encoder-only backbones.

RQ4: How is the performance of the LSR affected by scaling the teacher and student models on the different backbones?
Table 4 illustrates the impact of scaling teacher and student models across different backbones, including Encoder-only, Encoder-decoder, and Decoder-only.

Impact of Scaling Teacher Model. To assess the impact of scaling the teacher model on different backbones, we employed a more effective cross-encoder RankLLaMA-13B [17] as the teacher to supervise LSR model (student) tuning. Row 4–6 shows the effect of using a larger teacher model across different backbones. Consistent with findings by [15], the encoder-only model shows significant improvements when scaling the teacher model, increasing from 67.9 to 73.1 on DL2020 and from 71.0 to 75.1 on DL2019. The encoder-decoder backbone also exhibits improvements on DL2019 and MS MARCO, though to a lesser degree. In contrast, the decoder-only model experiences a decline in performance on MS MARCO and DL2020. This decline may be attributed to the sharp distribution of RankLlama teacher model scores, as shown in Fig. 3. The sharp distribution makes it challenging for the decoder-only architecture to generate a sparse vector by relying solely on FLOPs regulation in the loss function. Further investigation is needed to fully understand this behavior. Overall, these results suggest that scaling the teacher model generally enhances the performance of encoder-only and encoder-decoder models.

Impact of Scaling Student Model. Row 7–8 of Table 4 illustrates the impact of scaling the student model on the performance of learned sparse retrieval (LSR). Both encoder-decoder and decoder-only backbones showed improvements as the student model parameters were scaled. Specifically, the nDCG@10 of the encoder-decoder backbone increased to 70.7 on DL2020 and 73.3 on DL2019, while the MRR@10 rose to 37.8 on MS MARCO. Similarly, the nDCG@10 of the decoder-only backbone increased to 60.9 on DL2020 and 73.1 on DL2019, with the MRR@10 rising to 36.9 on MS MARCO. Notably, the improvement observed for decoder-only backbones was significantly larger when scaling the student model compared to scaling the teacher model.

6 Related Work

6.1 Dense Retrieval

Dense retrieval encode queries and documents into latent dense representations. Early work on dense retrieval models used encoder transformers, but more recent efforts have been exploring other transformer architectures. Sentence

T5 [24] compares different transformer architectures (encoder-decoder, encoder-only, decoder-only) for dense sentence embeddings and finds that the encoder-decoder architecture achieves the best performance on semantic textual similarity (STS) benchmarks. Ni et al. [25] later extend Sentence T5 (encoder-only) for retrieval tasks and study its effectiveness on different model scales (base, large, XL, XXL). The study suggests that scaling up the T5-encoder could improve the out-of-domain generalizability of dense retrieval. Similarly, Ma et al. [17] developed RepLlama based on Llama—a billion-scale decoder-only language model—and demonstrated the strong in-domain and out-of-domain performance of this model.

6.2 Learned Sparse Representations

Learned sparse retrieval offers an efficient alternative to dense retrieval by effectively utilizing traditional inverted indexes, which combines the capabilities of neural methods with the efficiency of classical indexing method. DeepCT [8] and uniCOIL [16] use BERT-based model to learn the importance of terms in query and passage. Although they do improve the weighting of terms compared to unsupervised approaches such as BM25, they only weight those terms that are already present in the document, hence lacking term expansions. Therefore, their effectiveness could be limited due to the term mismatch issue. To overcome this term mismatch problem, Mallia et al. [22] improve effectiveness by enriching documents with predicted queries from DocT5Query and proposes a term weighting model that calculates the pairwise loss between relevant and nonrelevant texts with respect to a query. In another approach, Splade [12] directly utilizes language model logits to weight and expand terms in an end-to-end fashion. MacAvaney et al. [20] previously proposed EPIC, which has a similar architecture to Splade but with an MLP query encoder that does not perform query expansion. In a later study, Nguyen et al. [23] found that under state-of-the-art training configurations, EPIC, without query expansion capability, can be as effective as Splade while being more efficient. This finding is also confirmed by a recent Splade-v3 [15] technical report. Unlike dense retrieval, Most of the previous LSR methods has predominantly focused on using small-scale encoder-only transformer models (e.g., DistilBERT, BERT). A concurrent work [9] uses 7 billion model Mistral as the backbone to develop a learned sparse retriever trained on extensive data. To ensure fair comparisons and avoid confounding factors, our study uses the same training data with Splade-DistillMax [15]. We address the aforementioned gap in the literature by investigating the performance of LSR across a range of transformer-based architectures, including encoder-only, decoder-only, and encoder-decoder models, as well as larger model scales.

7 Conclusion

Our work explored the utility of different transformer-based backbones for LSR. We highlight the difficulty of creating effective sparse representations using LLMs in zero-shot settings. Doing so leads to either the wrong type of term expansion or to a reduction in performance due to an inability to expand. The contribution of our work is to propose a solution for creating sparse representation from the decoder output and investigate the LSR effectiveness across different backbones for LSR. Our results indicate that incorporating the multi-tokens decoding approach helps to create a more effective sparse representation for the encoder-decoder and decoder-only backbone.

Acknowledgments. We thank all reviewers for their feedback. This research was supported by the China Scholarship Council under grant number 202208410053 and project VI.Vidi.223.166 of the NWO Talent Programme (partly) financed by the Dutch Research Council (NWO). The views expressed in this paper are those of the authors and do not necessarily reflect the views of their institutions or sponsors.

Appendix

Table 5. Teacher performance comparison on the MS MARCO training set.

	nDCG@10	RR@10
MiniLM-L-6-v2	44.3	37.5
Rankllama-13B	47.5	40.3

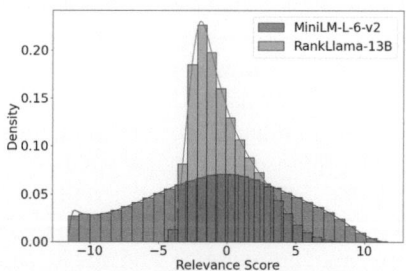 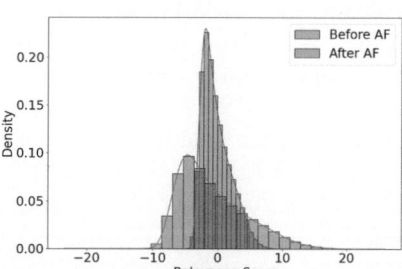

(a) Score distributions of MiniLM-L-6-v2 and RankLLama-13B.

(b) RankLLama-13B scores before and after affine transformation.

Fig. 3. Score distributions of the two teacher models on the MS MARCO training set. (a) RankLLama-13B exhibits a sharper distribution than MiniLM-L-6-v2. (b) We apply an affine transformation to align the mean and standard deviation distribution of RankLama-13B with that of MiniLM-L-6-v2.

Table 6. Comparison of LSR effectiveness across different backbones without fine-tuning on MS MARCO dev. × results are from [22]; A † indicates paired t-test $p < 0.05$. († indicates test between term expansion and non-expansion).

Model	Weighting	Expansion	RR@10	R@1k
(1) Enc.$_{\text{Distilbert-base-uncased}}$	Yes	No	0.930	40.4
(2) EncDec.MultiTokens$_{\text{FlanT5-base}}$	Yes	No	0	0
(3) EncDec.MultiTokens$_{\text{FlanT5-xl}}$	Yes	No	3.67†	34.0†
(4) Dec.MultiTokens$_{\text{OPT-350M}}$	Yes	No	13.2	50.9
(5) Dec.MultiTokens$_{\text{OPT-2.7B}}$	Yes	No	13.7	71.4
(6) Dec.MultiTokens$_{\text{OPT-6.7B}}$	Yes	No	12.5	70.5

References

1. Arpit, D., Zhou, Y., Ngo, H.Q., Govindaraju, V.: Why regularized auto-encoders learn sparse representation? In: Proceedings of the 33rd International Conference on International Conference on Machine Learning, ICML 2016, vol. 48, pp. 136–144. JMLR.org (2016)
2. Bai, Y., et al.: SparTerm: learning term-based sparse representation for fast text retrieval (2020)
3. Bajaj, P., et al.: MS MARCO: a human generated machine reading comprehension dataset (2018)
4. Bruch, S., Nardini, F.M., Rulli, C., Venturini, R.: Efficient inverted indexes for approximate retrieval over learned sparse representations. In: Proceedings of the 47th International ACM SIGIR Conference on Research and Development in Information Retrieval (SIGIR), pp. 152–162. ACM (2024). https://doi.org/10.1145/3626772.3657769
5. Chung, H.W., et al.: Scaling instruction-finetuned language models. J. Mach. Learn. Res. **25**(1) (2024)
6. Craswell, N., Mitra, B., Yilmaz, E., Campos, D.: Overview of the TREC 2020 deep learning track (2021)
7. Craswell, N., Mitra, B., Yilmaz, E., Campos, D., Voorhees, E.M.: Overview of the TREC 2019 deep learning track (2020)
8. Dai, Z., Callan, J.: Context-aware sentence/passage term importance estimation for first stage retrieval (2019)
9. Doshi, M., Kumar, V., Murthy, R., P, V., Sen, J.: Mistral-SPLADE: LLMs for better learned sparse retrieval (2024). https://arxiv.org/abs/2408.11119
10. Fang, H., Tao, T., Zhai, C.: A formal study of information retrieval heuristics. In: Proceedings of the 27th Annual International ACM SIGIR Conference on Research and Development in Information Retrieval, pp. 49–56 (2004)
11. Formal, T., Lassance, C., Piwowarski, B., Clinchant, S.: From distillation to hard negative sampling: making sparse neural IR models more effective. In: Proceedings of the 45th International ACM SIGIR Conference on Research and Development in Information Retrieval, SIGIR 2022, pp. 2353–2359. Association for Computing Machinery, New York (2022). https://doi.org/10.1145/3477495.3531857
12. Formal, T., Lassance, C., Piwowarski, B., Clinchant, S.: SPLADE v2: sparse lexical and expansion model for information retrieval (2021). https://doi.org/10.48550/ARXIV.2109.10086, https://arxiv.org/abs/2109.10086

13. Gao, L., Callan, J.: Unsupervised corpus aware language model pre-training for dense passage retrieval. In: Muresan, S., Nakov, P., Villavicencio, A. (eds.) Proceedings of the 60th Annual Meeting of the Association for Computational Linguistics (Volume 1: Long Papers), pp. 2843–2853. Association for Computational Linguistics, Dublin (2022). https://doi.org/10.18653/v1/2022.acl-long.203
14. Hofstätter, S., Althammer, S., Schröder, M., Sertkan, M., Hanbury, A.: Improving efficient neural ranking models with cross-architecture knowledge distillation (2021)
15. Lassance, C., Déjean, H., Formal, T., Clinchant, S.: SPLADE-v3: new baselines for SPLADE (2024)
16. Lin, J., Ma, X.: A few brief notes on deepimpact, coil, and a conceptual framework for information retrieval techniques (2021)
17. Ma, X., Wang, L., Yang, N., Wei, F., Lin, J.: Fine-tuning llama for multi-stage text retrieval. In: Proceedings of the 47th International ACM SIGIR Conference on Research and Development in Information Retrieval, SIGIR 2024, pp. 2421–2425. Association for Computing Machinery, New York (2024). https://doi.org/10.1145/3626772.3657951
18. Ma, X., Zhang, X., Pradeep, R., Lin, J.: Zero-shot listwise document reranking with a large language model (2023)
19. MacAvaney, S., Nardini, F.M., Perego, R., Tonellotto, N., Goharian, N., Frieder, O.: Expansion via prediction of importance with contextualization. In: Proceedings of the 43rd International ACM SIGIR Conference on Research and Development in Information Retrieval, SIGIR 2020. ACM (2020)
20. MacAvaney, S., Nardini, F.M., Perego, R., Tonellotto, N., Goharian, N., Frieder, O.: Expansion via prediction of importance with contextualization. In: Proceedings of the 43rd International ACM SIGIR Conference on Research and Development in Information Retrieval, pp. 1573–1576 (2020)
21. Malkov, Y.A., Yashunin, D.A.: Efficient and robust approximate nearest neighbor search using hierarchical navigable small world graphs. IEEE Trans. Pattern Anal. Mach. Intell. **42**(4), 824–836 (2020). https://doi.org/10.1109/TPAMI.2018.2889473
22. Mallia, A., Khattab, O., Suel, T., Tonellotto, N.: Learning passage impacts for inverted indexes. In: Proceedings of the 44th International ACM SIGIR Conference on Research and Development in Information Retrieval, SIGIR 2021, pp. 1723–1727. Association for Computing Machinery, New York (2021). https://doi.org/10.1145/3404835.3463030
23. Nguyen, T., MacAvaney, S., Yates, A.: A unified framework for learned sparse retrieval. In: Kamps, J., et al. (eds.) ECIR 2023, Part III. LNCS, vol. 13982, pp. 101–116. Springer, Cham (2023). https://doi.org/10.1007/978-3-031-28241-6_7
24. Ni, J., et al.: Sentence-T5: scalable sentence encoders from pre-trained text-to-text models. In: Findings of the Association for Computational Linguistics: ACL 2022, pp. 1864–1874. Association for Computational Linguistics, Dublin (2022). https://doi.org/10.18653/v1/2022.findings-acl.146, https://aclanthology.org/2022.findings-acl.146/
25. Ni, J., et al.: Large dual encoders are generalizable retrievers. In: Goldberg, Y., Kozareva, Z., Zhang, Y. (eds.) Proceedings of the 2022 Conference on Empirical Methods in Natural Language Processing, pp. 9844–9855. Association for Computational Linguistics, Abu Dhabi (2022). https://doi.org/10.18653/v1/2022.emnlp-main.669, https://aclanthology.org/2022.emnlp-main.669
26. Nogueira, R., Yang, W., Lin, J., Cho, K.: Document expansion by query prediction. arXiv preprint arXiv:1904.08375 (2019)

27. Paria, B., Yeh, C.K., Yen, I.E., Xu, N., Ravikumar, P., Póczos, B.: Minimizing flops to learn efficient sparse representations. In: International Conference on Learning Representations (2020). https://openreview.net/forum?id=SygpC6Ntvr
28. Pradeep, R., Sharifymoghaddam, S., Lin, J.: RankVicuna: zero-shot listwise document reranking with open-source large language models (2023)
29. Sanh, V., Debut, L., Chaumond, J., Wolf, T.: DistilBERT, a distilled version of BERT: smaller, faster, cheaper and lighter. ArXiv (2019)
30. Sun, W., Yan, L., Ma, X., Ren, P., Yin, D., Ren, Z.: Is chatGPT good at search? investigating large language models as re-ranking agent. In: Proceedings of the 2023 Conference on Empirical Methods in Natural Language Processing, pp. 14918–14937. Association for Computational Linguistics, Singapore (2023)
31. Wang, W., Wei, F., Dong, L., Bao, H., Yang, N., Zhou, M.: MiniLM: deep self-attention distillation for task-agnostic compression of pre-trained transformers. Adv. Neural. Inf. Process. Syst. **33**, 5776–5788 (2020)
32. Yang, P., Fang, H., Lin, J.: Anserini: enabling the use of lucene for information retrieval research. In: Proceedings of the 40th International ACM SIGIR Conference on Research and Development in Information Retrieval, SIGIR 2017, pp. 1253–1256. Association for Computing Machinery, New York (2017)
33. Yang, P., Fang, H., Lin, J.: Anserini: reproducible ranking baselines using lucene. J. Data Inf. Qual. **10**(4) (2018)
34. Zamani, H., Dehghani, M., Croft, W.B., Learned-Miller, E., Kamps, J.: From neural re-ranking to neural ranking: learning a sparse representation for inverted indexing. In: Proceedings of the 27th ACM International Conference on Information and Knowledge Management, CIKM 2018, pp. 497–506. Association for Computing Machinery, New York (2018)
35. Zhang, S., et al.: OPT: open pre-trained transformer language models (2022)
36. Zhao, T., Lu, X., Lee, K.: SPARTA: efficient open-domain question answering via sparse transformer matching retrieval. In: Toutanova, K., et al. (eds.) Proceedings of the 2021 Conference of the North American Chapter of the Association for Computational Linguistics: Human Language Technologies, pp. 565–575. Association for Computational Linguistics, Online (2021). https://doi.org/10.18653/v1/2021.naacl-main.47, https://aclanthology.org/2021.naacl-main.47/
37. Zhuang, S., Ma, X., Koopman, B., Lin, J., Zuccon, G.: PromptReps: prompting large language models to generate dense and sparse representations for zero-shot document retrieval. In: Al-Onaizan, Y., Bansal, M., Chen, Y.N. (eds.) Proceedings of the 2024 Conference on Empirical Methods in Natural Language Processing, pp. 4375–4391. Association for Computational Linguistics, Miami (2024). https://doi.org/10.18653/v1/2024.emnlp-main.250, https://aclanthology.org/2024.emnlp-main.250/
38. Zhuang, S., Zuccon, G.: TILDE: term independent likelihood model for passage re-ranking. In: Proceedings of the 44th International ACM SIGIR Conference on Research and Development in Information Retrieval, SIGIR 2021, pp. 1483–1492. Association for Computing Machinery, New York (2021)

Enhancing Representation Learning for Content-Based Information Retrieval: A Knowledge-Enhanced Geometric Approach

Manuel Alejandro Goyo[1](✉), Giacomo Frisoni[2], Gianluca Moro[2], and Claudio Sartori[2]

[1] Universidad Técnica Federico Santa María, Valparaíso, Chile
manuel.goyo@sansano.usm.cl
[2] University of Bologna, Bologna, Italy
{giacomi.frisoni,gianluca.moro,cladio.sartori}@unibo.it

Abstract. Representation learning has become a critical component in modern information retrieval systems, driven by advancements in self-supervised learning. This research extends previous work on negative sampling strategies for contrastive learning by incorporating sophisticated geometric principles to generate more informative negative examples. By exploring three novel approaches—median centroids, geometric midpoints, and medoids—the study introduces a knowledge-enhanced method for capturing different characteristics of data distribution. The comprehensive evaluation across multiple datasets, including STL10 and a novel Food3 adaptation, demonstrates significant performance improvements. Experimental results reveal that the proposed geometric approaches consistently outperform existing methods in both Content-Based Image Retrieval and classification tasks. Notably, the methods show remarkable effectiveness in semi-supervised scenarios with limited label availability (10% and 5%), achieving up to 84.50% accuracy on the SVHN dataset with just 10% of available labels. Key findings highlight the median centroid approach as particularly robust, providing the most consistent performance improvements across diverse conditions. The research not only advances understanding of representation learning but also provides a promising strategy for extracting meaningful features in low-resource learning environments, with potential applications in domains ranging from digital archives to specialized image classification tasks.

Keywords: Information Retrieval · Self-Supervised Representation Learning · Contrastive Learning

1 Introduction

In the era of data-driven artificial intelligence, the quality of learned representations fundamentally determines the performance of downstream applications.

Representation learning has emerged as a crucial element in modern AI systems, particularly in knowledge-enhanced information retrieval, where the challenge of creating meaningful representations from limited supervised data remains significant. Recent advances in self-supervised learning (SSL) have revolutionized this landscape by enabling systems to learn robust representations from unlabeled data—addressing the fundamental bottleneck of annotation costs while often surpassing traditional supervised approaches [4,19].

At the core of effective representation learning lies the critical challenge of defining meaningful similarity and dissimilarity relationships within the feature space. Many contrastive learning approaches rely on two fundamental elements: the concepts of similar (positive) pairs (x, x^+) and dissimilar (negative) pairs (x, x^-) of data points. The training objective, typically noise-contrastive estimation [18], directs the learned representation to map positive pairs to proximate locations and negative pairs to distant ones. Alternative objectives have also been explored [3]. However, the effectiveness of these methods is fundamentally constrained by how informative the sampled positive and negative pairs are—a particularly challenging aspect in the absence of supervision.

Current approaches to handling negative examples exhibit significant limitations. Some researchers avoid explicit negative generation by computing distances to all other data points [3] or their closest neighbors [41], using simple averages as dissimilarity measures. This oversimplification fails to capture the complex structure of true dissimilarity in high-dimensional spaces, resulting in suboptimal representation boundaries. While alternative methods focusing solely on positive instances [6,17] overcome some of these challenges, they critically lack the capability to construct robust decision boundaries that effectively discern differences within the data, often leading to category overlap and diminished discrimination power.

More sophisticated approaches attempt to identify explicit negatives by considering different views (augmentations) of images to filter out false negatives [22] or by estimating samples from the distribution over negative pairs [33]. These methods draw from metric learning principles, where "hard" negative examples accelerate the correction of mistakes in the learning process [31,34]. However, the fundamental challenge remains: in unsupervised contrastive learning, unlike supervised metric learning, we lack ground truth for truly dissimilar pairs, making the identification of informative negatives particularly challenging yet crucial for optimal representation learning.

Our methodology builds upon our previous work [15], which was inspired by the empirical findings of Cai et al. (2020) [2], who demonstrated that "... a small minority of negatives were both necessary and sufficient for the downstream task to reach full accuracy". This insight suggests that not all negative examples contribute equally to representation quality—strategic negative sampling can dramatically improve learning efficiency and representation power. Our prior approach utilized triplet loss with conventional positive pairs generated through semantic-preserving transformations, while innovatively crafting negative elements by considering only the k nearest neighbors to the anchor from the remaining batch positives, and then deriving the negative through centroid calculation.

In this enhanced work, we significantly extend our negative sampling strategy by introducing knowledge-informed geometric approaches that capture different aspects of the feature space structure. Specifically, we explore three additional methods beyond simple centroids:

- **Median Centroids:** Instead of using the mean (centroid), which can be sensitive to outliers, we compute centroids based on median values along each dimension, providing a more robust representation of the negative space, particularly valuable in noisy data environments.
- **Geometric Midpoints:** We implement geometric midpoint calculations that better preserve the intrinsic structure of the feature space, offering an alternative perspective on negative examples that respects the underlying manifold geometry rather than simple Euclidean distances.
- **Medoids:** Unlike centroids, which may not correspond to actual data points, medoids represent the most centrally located actual data point within a cluster, ensuring that negatives remain within the natural data manifold—addressing a key limitation of centroid-based approaches where synthetic points may lie in low-probability regions.

By incorporating these knowledge-enhanced geometric approaches into our negative sampling strategy, our model gains a more comprehensive understanding of the feature space structure. This leads to improved representation learning, particularly beneficial for knowledge-enhanced information retrieval applications. Our experimental results demonstrate consistent improvements in Mean Average Precision (MAP) for Content-Based Image Retrieval (CBIR) tasks by 8–12% over baseline methods, and classification accuracy improvements of 3–7% across multiple datasets, confirming the efficacy of our geometry-aware approach.

Furthermore, we extend our evaluation to semi-supervised learning scenarios with limited label availability (10% and 5% of the total labels), providing valuable insights into how our approach performs in low-resource settings that are common in real-world applications. These experiments reveal that our geometric negative sampling strategies maintain robust performance even with extremely limited supervision, outperforming conventional approaches by wider margins as label availability decreases.

The main contributions of this work are as follows:

1. We extend our previously designed sampling strategy [15] with advanced geometric knowledge to create more informative negative elements that better capture the structural properties of the feature space.
2. We propose an enhanced self-supervised training method based on triplet loss that incorporates multiple geometric perspectives for representation learning, addressing key limitations in current contrastive learning approaches.
3. We provide a comprehensive evaluation framework that assesses both representation quality (through CBIR metrics) and discriminative power (through

classification performance), demonstrating the versatility of our approach across diverse application scenarios.
4. We demonstrate the practical value of our approach in low-resource settings through extensive experiments with limited label availability (10% and 5% of labels), establishing its robustness in real-world scenarios where annotation is costly.
5. We introduce additional benchmark datasets, including STL10 and Food3 (an adaptation of the Food101 dataset focusing on 3 classes), expanding the evaluation to demonstrate generalizability across varied domains and data distributions.

The paper proceeds as follows: Sect. 2 reviews related studies in self-supervised learning and negative sampling strategies, highlighting the theoretical and empirical gaps our work addresses. Section 3 details our method, focusing on the geometric principles underlying our negative sampling approaches and the implementation of our enhanced triplet loss framework. Section 4 presents a comprehensive analysis of experimental results across multiple datasets and supervision levels, with comparative analyses against state-of-the-art methods. Finally, Sect. 5 concludes with key insights and discusses promising directions for future research in geometry-aware representation learning.

2 Related Works

The landscape of representation learning has evolved significantly in recent years, with researchers exploring various paradigms to extract meaningful features from unlabeled data. This section examines the trajectory of these developments, highlighting the interplay between different methodological approaches and their contributions to the field.

2.1 Foundations of Representation Learning

Contemporary unsupervised representation learning methodologies can be broadly classified into generative and discriminative approaches [3,10]. While both aim to extract meaningful representations from raw data, they differ fundamentally in their objectives and computational requirements. Generative methods construct distributions over data and latent embeddings, employing these embeddings as image representations. These approaches include auto-encoding techniques [23,39] and adversarial learning frameworks [14], which generate high-fidelity synthetic data by capturing pixel-level details. Despite their comprehensive nature, these methods often impose substantial computational burdens that may not directly contribute to effective representation learning, particularly when high-detail image generation is not the primary objective. In parallel to generative approaches, researchers have explored various auxiliary handcrafted prediction tasks to guide representation learning. These include relative patch prediction [10,11], colorization of grayscale images [26,45], context-based image inpainting [32], geometric transformation recognition [12,13], image jigsaw puzzle solving [30], and high-resolution image reconstruction [27]. Despite incorporating well-structured architectures [24], these methods have consistently demonstrated performance limitations when compared to contemporary contrastive learning techniques [5,37].

2.2 The Rise of Contrastive Learning

Discriminative methods, particularly contrastive learning approaches [3,6,41], have emerged as the dominant paradigm in self-supervised learning, demonstrating state-of-the-art performance across various benchmarks. Rather than attempting the computationally intensive task of pixel-level image generation, contrastive learning focuses on establishing relationships between data points in representational space. The core principle involves minimizing distances between different views of the same image (positive pairs) while maximizing distances between views derived from different images (negative pairs) [6,11,43]. This approach effectively captures semantic relationships without requiring explicit labels, sometimes even demonstrating efficacy without explicit negative examples [3,17,41]. Several innovative algorithms have advanced the state of contrastive learning for visual representations. SimCLR [3] leverages augmented views of minibatch items as negative samples, while MoCo [5,19] introduces a momentum-updated memory bank of historical negative representations, enabling larger batches of negative samples without increasing computational costs. These approaches not only enhance model scalability and generalization but also facilitate robust feature extraction applicable across diverse domains. A significant challenge in contrastive learning involves the management of false negatives, which can discard valuable semantic information and slow convergence. Addressing this issue, Tri Huynh et al. [22] propose novel identification strategies and introduce methodologies for false negative elimination and attraction, conducting systematic evaluations to comprehensively address this challenge. In a related effort, Robinson et al. [33] present an unsupervised method based on a distribution over hard negative pairs, constructing this distribution with the assumption that optimal negative samples are those currently perceived as similar to the anchor by the embedding function. Another noteworthy contribution comes from Zbontar et al. [44], who introduce BarlowTwins, an approach that computes cross-correlation matrices between outputs of identical networks receiving distorted versions of the same sample. By optimizing these matrices to approximate identity matrices, the method ensures similar embeddings for distorted versions of samples while reducing component redundancy, effectively addressing key challenges in representation learning.

2.3 Triplet Loss Methodologies

The triplet loss approach, initially developed for person re-identification by Ding et al. and face recognition by Schroff et al. [9,34], has evolved into a cornerstone methodology in contrastive learning. This paradigm employs triplets consisting of an anchor, a positive example, and a negative example to enhance the discriminative capacity of learned representations. Building on this foundation, researchers have focused on improving the generation and selection of informative triplets to optimize learning outcomes. Hermans et al. [20] made significant contributions by developing strategies to identify and utilize informative triplets, enhancing the robustness and effectiveness of triplet loss methodologies. Seeking to further refine this approach, Wang et al. [42] explored cross-batch triplet loss applications, aiming to improve generalization capabilities and stabilize learning by leveraging inter-batch relationships and their influence on the learning process. Research has also expanded the triplet loss approach to weakly supervised scenarios. Wang et al. [40] explored methods for harnessing weak supervision signals, extending the triplet loss paradigm to contexts with limited labeled data. Taking a different approach, Turpault et al. [38] integrated unsupervised triplet loss-based learning into a self-supervised framework, obtaining positive samples for unlabeled anchors through transformations and selecting negative samples as training set instances closest to the anchor yet distant from the positive sample. Wang et al. [41] contributed a truncated triplet loss methodology, constructing negative pairs by selecting deputy negative samples. This strategic approach mitigates false negatives and prevents over-clustering of samples from the same categories into different clusters. More recently, Li et al. [28] introduced Trip-ROMA, combining triplet loss with a random mapping strategy that projects samples into alternative spaces while maintaining triplet-indicated relationships, demonstrating the continued innovation in this domain. In [16], the authors proposed an enhancement to Contrastive Self-Supervised Learning (CSL) by introducing explicit negative sampling strategies using binary classification within the feature space to distinguish between similar and dissimilar features. Their approach incorporated Triplet Loss to refine feature learning and demonstrated improvements in CIFAR-10 and SVHN datasets for both CBIR and classification tasks. Our current work differs by focusing on geometric properties of the feature space rather than binary classification, introducing multiple sophisticated approaches (median centroids, geometric midpoints, and medoids) for negative sample generation, and providing a more comprehensive evaluation across additional datasets including STL10 and Food3 under various supervision levels, thus extending the applicability of negative sampling strategies to more diverse and challenging scenarios. In our previous work [15], we introduced a novel negative sampling strategy for contrastive learning that leveraged centroids of k-nearest neighbors to create more informative negative examples. Our approach demonstrated that carefully constructed negative examples from local neighborhoods could significantly improve the quality of learned representations for content-based image retrieval and classification tasks. The current work extends this foundation by exploring more sophisticated geometric approaches for negative example generation, specifically incorporating median centroids, geometric midpoints, and medoids, while also expanding the evaluation to semi-supervised learning scenarios with limited label availability and additional datasets to demonstrate broader applicability.

3 Algorithm

Building on the challenges identified in the introduction, this section presents our enhanced geometric approach to negative sampling in self-supervised representation learning. We first provide a focused rationale for our methodology and then detail our algorithm with its mathematical foundations.

3.1 Targeted Approach to Negative Sampling

While the introduction established the broader context of self-supervised learning, here we focus specifically on the technical challenge of generating informative negative samples. In contrast to conventional approaches that rely on simple averaging or random sampling, our work specifically addresses the critical need for structured, geometry-aware negative samples that effectively challenge the model's discriminative capabilities.

The fundamental issue in self-supervised learning is not merely the generation of similar data points—which can be reliably produced through augmentations—but rather the creation of truly informative dissimilar data points that prevent representation collapse [10]. Existing methods either fail to capture the geometric structure of the feature space or require prohibitively large batch sizes to generate reliable dissimilarity measures [3,41].

Our approach leverages the triplet loss framework, which has proven effective in supervised scenarios [9,34], but adapts it for the unsupervised setting through sophisticated geometric negative sampling. Figure 1 illustrates this concept, where the critical innovation lies in how we construct the negative to maximize learning effectiveness.

This approach directly builds upon our previous work [15], where we initially introduced centroid-based negative sampling. The key insight from that work was that using the centroid of k-nearest neighbors as negatives creates more challenging and informative triplets than random sampling or simple batch-based approaches. Our current work significantly extends this foundation by exploring the geometric feature space through multiple complementary perspectives, each addressing specific limitations of centroid-based approaches.

3.2 Enhanced Geometric Methodology

The triplet loss function operates on triplets of the form $(x_i, x_i^+, x_i^-)_{i=1,\cdots,m}$, where for each anchor sample x_i, we have a positive sample x_i^+ and a negative sample x_i^-. The standard triplet loss is defined as:

$$\mathcal{L} = \sum_{i=1}^{m} \max\left(sim\left(x_i, x_i^-\right) - sim\left(x_i, x_i^+\right) + m, 0\right),$$

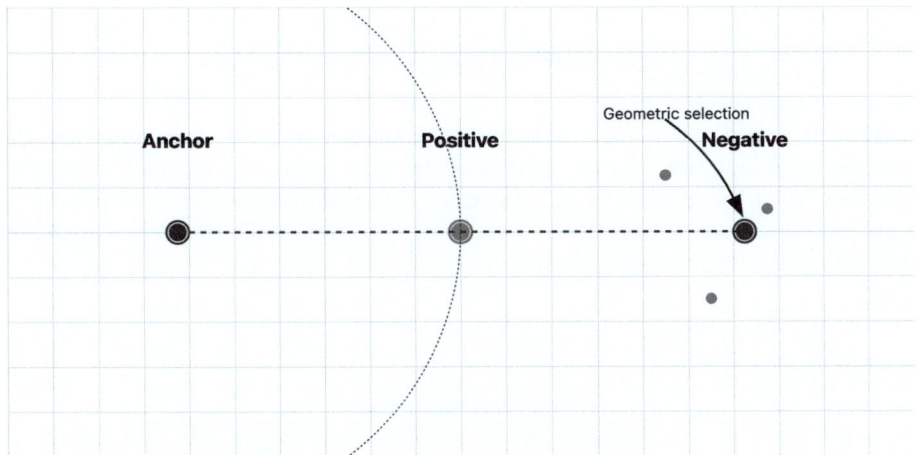

Fig. 1. Schema of triplet loss approach. The anchor (left) and positive sample (middle) represent different views of the same instance, while the negative sample (right) must be carefully selected to provide an informative contrast. Our contribution focuses on geometric methods to identify this negative sample.

where sim is a similarity metric (e.g., cosine similarity or Euclidean distance), and m is a margin parameter that determines when a triplet contributes to the loss.

In the self-supervised setting, the anchor and positive samples are derived through different augmentations of the same data point, while the negative sample presents a significant challenge. Drawing on the findings of Cai et al. [2], who demonstrated that a small number of carefully selected negatives can be sufficient for optimal performance, we propose four complementary geometric approaches to negative sample generation:

Centroid-Based Approach (Baseline). Our previous work established the effectiveness of using centroids of k-nearest neighbors as negatives. For a set of vectors $\{v_1, v_2, ..., v_k\}$ where $v_i \in \mathbb{R}^d$, the centroid z_{n_cent} is defined as:

$$z_{n\_cent} = \frac{1}{k} \sum_{i=1}^{k} v_i.$$

While effective, this approach can be sensitive to outliers in the feature space and may generate points that lie outside the natural data manifold.

Median Centroids. To address the sensitivity to outliers inherent in mean-based centroids, we introduce median centroids that compute the element-wise median across each dimension. For a set of vectors $\{v_1, v_2, ..., v_k\}$, the median centroid z_{n_med} is defined as:

$$z_{n\_med}[j] = \text{median}(\{v_1[j], v_2[j], ..., v_k[j]\}).+,$$

for each dimension $j \in \{1, 2, ..., d\}$.

This approach offers greater robustness against outliers, ensuring that the negative sample is not unduly influenced by extreme values in the feature distribution. As illustrated in Fig. 2, median centroids (shown in red) provide a more representative center of the feature distribution compared to mean-based centroids when outliers are present.

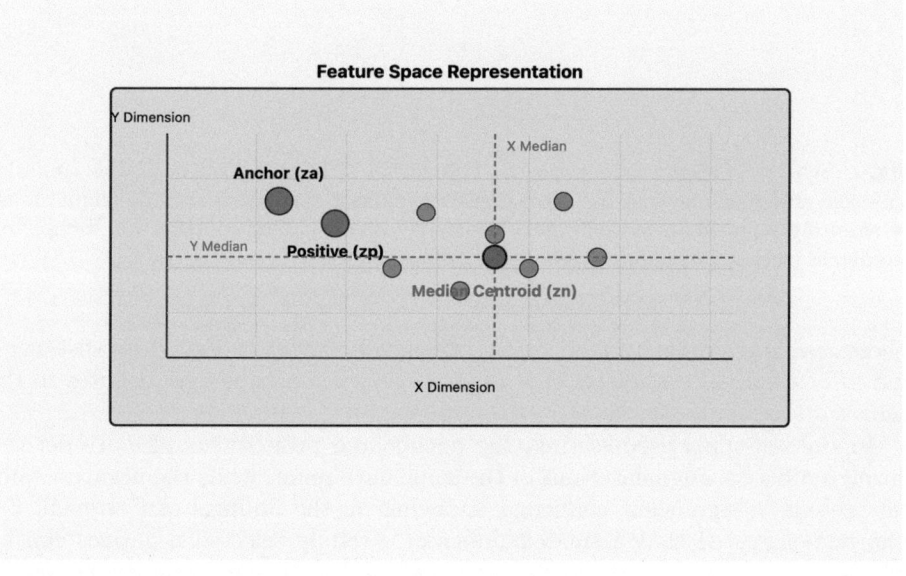

Fig. 2. Median Centroid negative sample generation. The red point represents the computed median centroid from a set of k-nearest neighbors. Unlike the mean-based centroid, the median centroid is less affected by outliers in the distribution, providing a more stable negative sample that better captures the central tendency of the feature cluster. (Color figure online)

Geometric Midpoints. While centroids and median centroids operate in Euclidean space, the feature representations often lie on or near a manifold with non-Euclidean structure. To better capture this intrinsic geometry, we implement geometric midpoint calculations based on geodesic distances.

For a set of vectors $\{v_1, v_2, ..., v_k\}$, the geometric midpoint z_{n_geo} is defined as:

$$z_{n\_geo} = \arg\min_{p} \sum_{i=1}^{k} d(p, v_i)^2,$$

where $d(p, v_i)$ represents the geodesic distance between points p and v_i in the feature space.

In practice, computing true geodesic distances can be computationally intensive. We approximate this by first estimating the local manifold structure through a neighborhood graph, and then computing distances along this graph. This approach, illustrated in Fig. 3, enables the negative sample to respect the underlying manifold structure rather than cutting across it, as might happen with Euclidean centroids.

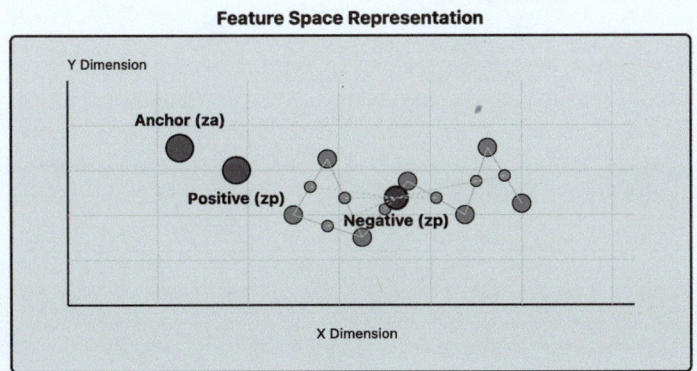

Fig. 3. Geometric Midpoint negative sample generation. Unlike Euclidean approaches, the geometric midpoint (red) considers the underlying manifold structure of the data (represented by the curved surface). This allows the negative sample to respect the intrinsic geometry of the feature space, providing a more meaningful contrast to the anchor point by following the natural contours of the data distribution rather than cutting across them. (Color figure online)

Medoids. A key limitation of all centroid-based approaches is that they may generate synthetic points that do not correspond to actual data points and might lie in low-probability regions of the feature space. To address this, we introduce medoid-based negatives, which select actual data points as representatives.

The medoid z_{n_medoid} is defined as:

$$z_{n\_medoid} = \arg \min_{v_j \in \{v_1, v_2, \ldots, v_k\}} \sum_{i=1}^{k} d(v_j, v_i)$$

This ensures that negatives remain within the natural data manifold, thus providing more realistic negative examples. As shown in Fig. 4, the medoid approach selects an actual data point (marked in red) as the representative, ensuring that the negative sample corresponds to a legitimate point in the feature space.

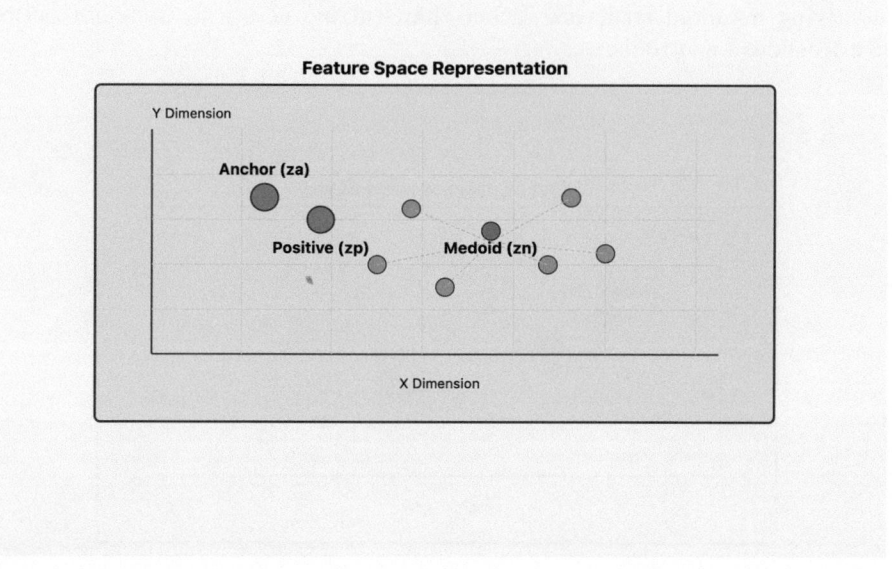

Fig. 4. Medoid-based negative sample generation. Unlike centroids, which create synthetic points, the medoid approach selects an actual data point (red) that minimizes the total distance to all other points in the cluster (grey). This ensures that the negative sample is a realistic point that lies within the natural data manifold, addressing a key limitation of synthetic approaches that might generate points in low-probability regions of the feature space. (Color figure online)

3.3 Computational Implementation

The practical implementation of our approach involves several key components:

Triplet Construction. For each mini-batch of data, we first apply two different augmentations τ_1 and τ_2 to each sample x, generating the anchor $z_a = f(\tau_1(x))$ and positive $z_p = f(\tau_2(x))$ embeddings, where f is the encoder network. The augmentations are drawn from a standard set T of transformations commonly used in self-supervised learning, including random crops, color jittering, and Gaussian blur.

K-Nearest Neighbors Selection. For each anchor z_a, we identify its k-nearest neighbors among the batch of positive embeddings (excluding its own positive pair). The optimal value of k is determined through validation, with typical values ranging from 5 to 15 depending on the dataset and batch size.

Negative Sample Generation. Once the k-nearest neighbors are identified, we apply one of our four geometric approaches to generate the negative sample:

$$z_{n\_cent}[i] = \text{Centroid}(\text{k-nearest}(z_{p-i})), \quad (1)$$
$$z_{n\_med}[i] = \text{MedianCentroid}(\text{k-nearest}(z_{p-i})), \quad (2)$$
$$z_{n\_geo}[i] = \text{GeometricMidpoint}(\text{k-nearest}(z_{p-i})), \quad (3)$$
$$z_{n\_medoid}[i] = \text{Medoid}(\text{k-nearest}(z_{p-i})), \quad (4)$$

where k-nearest(z_{p-i}) represents the k elements closest to z_p excluding the i-th element.

Loss Computation. The triplet loss for each anchor-positive-negative triplet is computed as:

$$\mathcal{L}(z_a, z_p, z_n) = \max\left(\text{sim}(z_a, z_n) - \text{sim}(z_a, z_p) + m, 0\right), \quad (5)$$

where sim() is the cosine similarity by default, though other similarity measures can be used depending on the application domain.

The final loss for the entire batch is given by:

$$\mathcal{L}_{\text{total}} = \mathbb{E}_x\left(\mathcal{L}(z_a, z_p, z_n)\right). \quad (6)$$

4 Main Results

This section presents a comprehensive evaluation of our enhanced self-supervised learning algorithm utilizing geometric approaches for negative sample selection. Our research introduces three innovative techniques—median centroids, geometric midpoints, and medoids—which consistently demonstrate superior performance across diverse datasets and evaluation tasks. The following analysis showcases how these geometric strategies enhance representation learning by capturing more nuanced features compared to traditional sampling methods, with particularly notable improvements in complex data distributions and limited supervision scenarios.

4.1 Experimental Setup

Data Augmentation Strategy: our augmentation approach incorporates two complementary transformation categories. The first involves Spatial/geometric

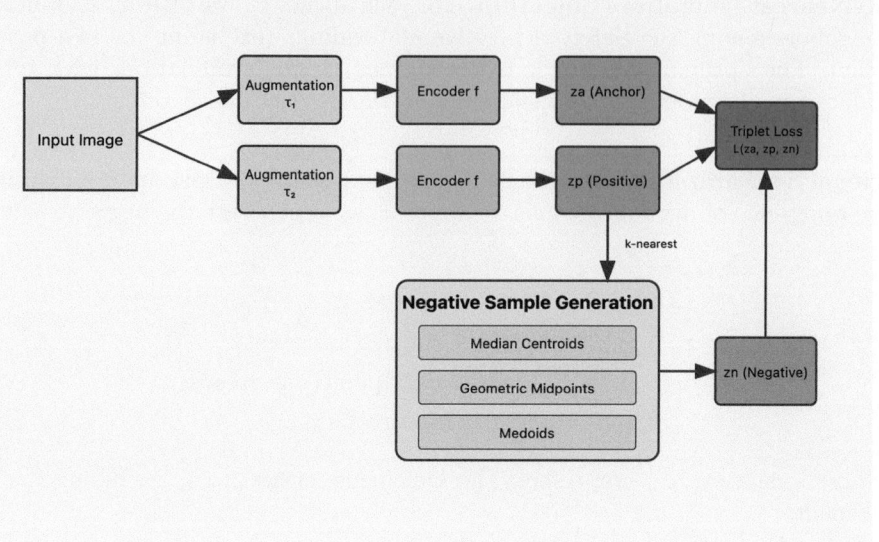

Fig. 5. The general scheme takes an image, to which it applies two augmentations τ_1 and τ_2, applies encoder f to obtain anchor and positive, for the negative it searches within the k-nearest neighbors through Median Centroids or Geometric Midpoints or Medoids, and then uses.

transformations, including random cropping with resizing (and horizontal flipping), rotation following [13], and cutout as described by [8]. The second type involves appearance transformations, such as color distortion (including color dropping, brightness, contrast, saturation, hue) [21,36], Gaussian blur, and Sobel filtering.

Our methodology builds upon the framework introduced in [3], with significant innovations in the negative sampling strategy through geometric approaches. As illustrated in Fig. 5 our algorithm processes an input image through two distinct augmentation pathways, applies the encoder network to generate anchor and positive embeddings, and then identifies negative examples through our novel geometric techniques applied to k-nearest neighbors.

Evaluation Datasets: We validate our approach using four diverse datasets:

- **CIFAR-10:** Comprises 60000 32×32 color images categorized into 10 classes, each containing 6000 images. It is divided into 50000 training images and 10.000 test images [25].
- **SVHN (Street View House Numbers):** A real-world image dataset specifically designed for developing machine learning and object recognition algorithms with minimal data preprocessing and formatting requirements. It consists of images containing digits, with 10 classes representing each digit from 0 to 9. The dataset is split into 73257 digits for training and 26032 digits for testing [29].

- **STL-10:** A image recognition dataset inspired by CIFAR-10 but with higher resolution (96 × 96) images. It contains 10 classes with 500 training images and 800 test images per class, plus an additional 100000 unlabeled images. The dataset is designed specifically for developing unsupervised and semi-supervised learning algorithms [7].
- **Food3:** An adaptation of the Food101 dataset [1], consisting of food images from 3 selected classes. This dataset provides a more challenging domain-specific retrieval and classification task with higher resolution images and greater intra-class variation.

Evaluation Methodology: We assess our approach using three complementary evaluation strategies. First CBIR, using the encoder's output layer to generate feature vectors for each image, retrieving the k-nearest neighbors from the training set for each test image, and measuring performance using Mean Average Precision at K (MAP@K). Second, Linear Evaluation, which adds a linear classifier layer to the frozen encoder and trains it with all available labels to assess representation quality for supervised classification. And Semi-Supervised Learning consists of training a classifier with limited labeled data (5% and 10%) while keeping the encoder frozen, evaluating performance in realistic scenarios where labels are scarce.

Metrics:

- **Mean Average Precision (MAP):** A crucial metric in image retrieval tasks, providing a comprehensive measure of a system's effectiveness across multiple queries. It assesses the average precision at each relevant image's position in the ranked list and computes the mean of these values. For MAP@K, a variant where only the top K retrieved items are considered, we use the following formula:

$$\text{MAP@K} = \frac{1}{|Q|} \sum_{q=1}^{|Q|} \frac{\sum_{k=1}^{K} \text{Precision@k}_q \times \text{Relevance}(k)}{\min(K, |R_q|)},$$

where: $|Q|$ is the total number of queries, Precision@k_q is the precision at position k for query q, Relevance(k) is a binary indicator function that is 1 if the item at position k is relevant and 0 otherwise, $|R_q|$ is the number of relevant items for query q, and K is the cutoff rank.
- **Classification Metrics:** Accuracy, Recall, Precision, and F1-score are fundamental metrics for evaluating classification tasks. Accuracy measures the proportion of correctly classified instances among all instances. Recall quantifies the proportion of true positive instances correctly identified among all actual positive instances. Precision measures the proportion of true positive instances among all instances predicted as positive. F1-score, the harmonic mean of precision and recall, balances the trade-off between these two metrics.

Implementation Details: Our encoder architecture is based on the Very Deep Convolutional Networks for Large-Scale Image Recognition [35]. We use a batch size of 32 and train for a maximum of 200 epochs. Optimization is performed using stochastic gradient descent with a learning rate of 0.6 and a cosine learning rate decay schedule. Detailed implementation specifications can be found in the appendix.

4.2 Baselines

We compare our approach with 6 relevant state-of-the-art works in self-supervised learning:

- **SimCLR** [3]: A straightforward framework for contrastive learning of visual representations. Two distinct data augmentation operators are randomly selected from the same family of augmentations and applied to each data example, creating two correlated views. A base encoder network and a projection head are trained to maximize agreement using a contrastive loss. After training, the projection head is discarded, and the encoder is employed to obtain representations for downstream tasks.
- **SimSiam** [6]: A model designed to maximize the similarity between two augmentations of a single image while avoiding collapsing solutions. It utilizes two augmented views of the same image, processed by an identical encoder network. A prediction MLP is applied to one side, while a stop-gradient operation is applied to the other side. Notably, SimSiam does not rely on negative pairs or a momentum encoder.
- **BYOL** [17]: An approach that relies on two neural networks, referred to as online and target networks, that interact and learn from each other. Using an augmented view of an image, the online network is trained to predict the target network's representation of the same image under a different augmented view. The target network is updated with a slow-moving average of the online network.
- **BarlowTwins** [44]: Proposes an objective function that inherently avoids collapse by measuring the cross-correlation matrix between the outputs of two identical networks fed with distorted versions of a sample. The objective is to make this matrix as close to the identity matrix as possible.
- **Truncated Triplet Loss** [41]: A method that truncates the number of negative samples used in contrastive learning to only consider the closest neighbors. This approach focuses on hard negative mining but differs from our method in how the negative examples are constructed and utilized.
- **RetSam** [15]: Our previous approach that uses centroids of k-nearest neighbors to generate negative examples for triplet loss. This method demonstrated improved performance over traditional contrastive learning approaches but was limited to a single geometric perspective (centroids) for negative example generation.

4.3 Results and Analysis

Content-Based Image Retrieval Performance: Table 1 presents the MAP@K results for the CBIR task across our four datasets. The results demonstrate that our geometric approaches consistently outperform baseline methods, with each technique exhibiting distinct strengths across different datasets. The RetSam_centroid approach performs exceptionally well on challenging datasets like SVHN, STL-10, and Food3, achieving substantial performance gains (1–4%) across different retrieval sizes compared to the original RetSam method on SVHN, with the highest MAP@1 score (0.819) among RetSam variants; this robust performance can be attributed to the median centroid's ability to mitigate the influence of outliers in feature space. The RetSam_medoid method excels particularly on CIFAR-10 and STL-10, achieving the highest MAP@1 scores (0.925 and 0.925 respectively) among all methods, demonstrating its effectiveness in identifying representative negative samples from complex data distributions. Complementing these approaches, the RetSam_midpoint technique provides consistent improvements across datasets with strong performance on CIFAR-10 (MAP@1 of 0.910) and STL-10 (MAP@1 of 0.902), highlighting the value of geometric midpoint selection in enhancing representation learning, while the performance improvements become more pronounced for higher K values, indicating that our geometric approaches enhance the overall representation quality beyond just top-ranked retrievals.

Linear Evaluation Results: Table 2 showcases the comprehensive results of linear supervised evaluation across multiple benchmark datasets. Our proposed geometric approaches demonstrate consistent and significant performance improvements over established baseline methods, with each technique exhibiting unique strengths across different computational domains. RetSam_centroid emerges as a standout performer, achieving remarkable results on SVHN (87.72% accuracy) and Food3 (82.67% accuracy), demonstrating exceptional efficacy in capturing discriminative features particularly for domain-specific tasks with complex visual patterns. RetSam_medoid delivers exceptional performance across multiple benchmarks, notably achieving the highest accuracy scores on CIFAR-10 (93.53%) and STL-10 (94.56%) among all methods evaluated, suggesting that the medoid-based negative sampling strategy is particularly effective for datasets with well-defined class structures. RetSam_midpoint, while generally performing slightly below the other geometric approaches, still consistently outperforms traditional baseline methods across all datasets, confirming the overall effectiveness of our geometric framework even in its simplest implementation, with particularly strong results on Food3 (80.00% accuracy).

Semi-supervised Learning Performance: Tables 3 and 4 present classification performance with 10% and 5% labeled data respectively, providing critical insights into how our methods perform under severe label scarcity—a common challenge in real-world applications. The RetSam_centroid approach demonstrates remarkable robustness in limited supervision scenarios, achieving 84.50% accuracy on SVHN using merely 10% of available labels, representing a significant improvement over both traditional contrastive methods (SimCLR: 71.12%) and our previous approach (RetSam: 81.34%), with this performance advantage being maintained even when further reducing label availability to 5% (83.01%

Table 1. CBIR results across different datasets and retrieval sizes. Best results are shown in **bold**, and second-best results are underlined.

Dataset	Método	1000	100	10	1
SVHN	SimCLR	0.2589	0.3925	0.5075	0.653
	SimSiam	**0.5777**	**0.7591**	**0.8295**	**0.896**
	BarlowTwins	0.4088	0.5505	0.6426	0.770
	BYOL	0.3483	0.4906	0.6032	0.715
	truncated	0.2889	0.4123	0.5379	0.682
	RetSam	0.4139	0.5718	0.6746	0.779
	RetSam_centroid	<u>0.4278</u>	<u>0.6253</u>	<u>0.7269</u>	<u>0.819</u>
	RetSam_medoid	0.4200	0.5800	0.6840	0.785
	RetSam_midpoint	0.4190	0.5760	0.6600	0.770
CIFAR10	SimCLR	0.6870	0.7733	0.8231	0.883
	SimSiam	0.6702	0.7910	0.8350	0.880
	BarlowTwins	0.3728	0.5390	0.6622	0.773
	BYOL	0.6901	0.7810	0.8330	0.896
	truncated	0.6800	0.8020	0.8210	0.890
	RetSam	**0.7332**	**0.8274**	**0.8701**	<u>0.919</u>
	RetSam_centroid	0.6532	0.7676	0.8276	0.899
	RetSam_medoid	<u>0.7299</u>	<u>0.8250</u>	<u>0.8688</u>	**0.925**
	RetSam_midpoint	0.7020	0.8010	0.8320	0.910
STL10	SimCLR	0.2843	0.6562	0.7518	0.838
	SimSiam	0.2890	0.6690	0.7651	0.854
	BarlowTwins	0.0206	0.0385	0.0826	0.176
	BYOL	0.2630	0.6213	0.7305	0.818
	truncated	0.3347	0.8117	0.8891	0.937
	RetSam	<u>0.3384</u>	<u>0.7914</u>	<u>0.8728</u>	<u>0.921</u>
	RetSam_centroid	0.3143	0.7543	0.8621	0.913
	RetSam_medoid	**0.3391**	**0.7934**	**0.8749**	**0.925**
	RetSam_midpoint	0.3020	0.7760	0.8560	0.902
Food3	SimCLR	–	0.3237	0.5928	0.6166
	SimSiam	–	0.2191	0.4210	0.5700
	BarlowTwins	–	0.1455	0.2640	0.3833
	BYOL	–	0.2031	0.3964	0.6366
	truncated	–	0.2314	0.4657	0.6533
	RetSam	–	0.3095	**0.5805**	<u>0.7500</u>
	RetSam_centroid	–	**0.3181**	0.5709	**0.7660**
	RetSam_medoid	–	<u>0.3180</u>	**0.5805**	0.7466
	RetSam_midpoint	–	0.2980	0.5710	0.7410

Table 2. Linear supervised evaluation results across different datasets and methods. Best results are shown in **bold**, and second-best results are underlined.

Dataset	Método	Accuracy	Recall	Precision	F1
SVHN	SimCLR	0.7954	0.7803	0.7905	0.7848
	SimSiam	0.1959	0.1000	0.0196	0.0328
	BarlowTwins	0.8145	0.8145	0.8148	0.8144
	BYOL	0.8030	0.7873	0.8014	0.7936
	truncated	0.8140	0.8130	0.8100	0.8140
	RetSam	<u>0.8423</u>	0.8278	0.8324	0.8294
	RetSam_centroid	**0.8772**	**0.8706**	**0.8740**	**0.8721**
	RetSam_medoid	<u>0.8423</u>	<u>0.8288</u>	<u>0.8329</u>	<u>0.8301</u>
	RetSam_midpoint	0.8320	0.8290	0.8312	<u>0.8301</u>
CIFAR10	SimCLR	0.9010	0.9010	0.9010	0.9009
	SimSiam	0.8579	0.8579	0.8653	0.8571
	BarlowTwins	0.8306	0.8135	0.8222	0.8162
	BYOL	0.9089	0.9089	0.9089	0.9088
	truncated	0.8790	0.8790	0.8530	0.8651
	RetSam	**0.9361**	**0.9361**	**0.9362**	**0.9360**
	RetSam_centroid	0.9337	0.9337	0.9337	0.9337
	RetSam_medoid	<u>0.9353</u>	<u>0.9353</u>	<u>0.9353</u>	<u>0.9352</u>
	RetSam_midpoint	0.9100	0.9080	0.9000	0.9040
STL10	SimCLR	0.8679	0.8679	0.8684	0.8679
	SimSiam	0.8625	0.8625	0.8634	0.8625
	BarlowTwins	0.1961	0.1961	0.3814	0.1655
	BYOL	0.8662	0.8663	0.8670	0.8663
	truncated	<u>0.9450</u>	<u>0.9450</u>	<u>0.9456</u>	<u>0.9450</u>
	RetSam	0.9441	0.9441	0.9443	0.9441
	RetSam_centroid	0.9449	0.9449	0.9451	0.9449
	RetSam_medoid	**0.9456**	**0.9456**	**0.9457**	**0.9456**
	RetSam_midpoint	0.9320	0.9300	0.9310	0.9305
Food3	SimCLR	0.8000	0.7919	0.7889	0.7901
	SimSiam	0.5200	0.5192	0.5588	0.5266
	BarlowTwins	0.3467	0.2889	0.2322	0.2192
	BYOL	0.4400	0.4434	0.4355	0.4350
	truncated	0.5867	0.5710	0.5704	0.5605
	RetSam	0.7600	0.7493	0.7473	0.7452
	RetSam_centroid	**0.8267**	**0.8056**	**0.8294**	**0.8093**
	RetSam_medoid	<u>0.8133</u>	<u>0.8042</u>	<u>0.8066</u>	<u>0.8025</u>
	RetSam_midpoint	0.8000	0.7920	0.7900	0.7910

Table 3. Results of the supervised evaluation for different datasets and methods using 10% of labeled data. Best results are shown in **bold**, and second-best results are <u>underlined</u>.

Dataset	Método	Accuracy	Recall	Precision	F1
SVHN	SimCLR	0.7112	0.7042	0.6963	0.6963
	SimSiam	0.3117	0.2537	0.4553	0.1651
	BarlowTwins	0.7788	0.7788	0.7788	0.7783
	BYOL	0.7388	0.7346	0.7252	0.7269
	truncated	0.7350	0.7200	0.7130	0.7360
	RetSam	<u>0.8134</u>	0.8012	<u>0.7948</u>	<u>0.7960</u>
	RetSam_centroid	**0.8450**	**0.8447**	**0.8355**	**0.8391**
	RetSam_medoid	0.8116	<u>0.8014</u>	0.7934	0.7954
	RetSam_midpoint	0.7820	0.7790	0.7690	0.7739
CIFAR10	SimCLR	0.7966	0.7966	0.7360	0.7607
	SimSiam	0.4493	0.4493	0.4936	0.4162
	BarlowTwins	0.6939	0.6403	0.5364	0.5802
	BYOL	0.8898	0.8898	0.8904	0.8896
	truncated	0.4930	0.4930	0.4960	0.4620
	RetSam	**0.9246**	**0.9246**	**0.9248**	**0.9244**
	RetSam_centroid	0.9126	0.9126	0.9131	0.9124
	RetSam_medoid	<u>0.9242</u>	<u>0.9242</u>	<u>0.9243</u>	<u>0.9241</u>
	RetSam_midpoint	0.8920	0.8860	0.8900	0.8880
STL10	SimCLR	0.8199	0.8199	0.8228	0.8197
	SimSiam	0.7430	0.7430	0.6819	0.7064
	BarlowTwins	0.1000	0.1000	0.0100	0.0182
	BYOL	0.8264	0.8264	0.8275	0.8262
	truncated	0.9113	0.9112	0.9175	0.9108
	RetSam	**0.9213**	**0.9213**	**0.9222**	**0.9213**
	RetSam_centroid	0.9101	0.9101	0.9114	0.9103
	RetSam_medoid	<u>0.9197</u>	<u>0.9197</u>	<u>0.9207</u>	<u>0.9198</u>
	RetSam_midpoint	0.9000	0.9020	0.8990	0.9005
Food3	SimCLR	**0.7200**	<u>0.6788</u>	**0.7736**	<u>0.6894</u>
	SimSiam	0.3467	0.3180	0.3227	0.3160
	BarlowTwins	0.3467	0.3441	0.2808	0.1903
	BYOL	0.4400	0.4214	0.4388	0.4246
	truncated	0.5067	0.4920	0.4930	0.4722
	RetSam	<u>0.7067</u>	**0.7088**	<u>0.7027</u>	**0.7018**
	RetSam_centroid	0.4400	0.4602	0.5185	0.4114
	RetSam_medoid	0.6133	0.6232	0.6209	0.6102
	RetSam_midpoint	0.5820	0.5850	0.5840	0.5845

Table 4. Results of the supervised evaluation for different datasets and methods using 5% of labeled data. Best results are shown in **bold**, and second-best results are underlined.

Dataset	Método	Accuracy	Recall	Precision	F1
SVHN	SimCLR	0.6777	0.6682	0.6611	0.6604
	SimSiam	0.0871	0.1092	0.1644	0.0332
	BarlowTwins	0.7639	0.7639	0.7643	0.7637
	BYOL	0.7117	0.7054	0.7020	0.6997
	truncated	0.7100	0.7280	0.7160	0.7130
	RetSam	0.7931	0.7758	0.7730	0.7720
	RetSam_centroid	**0.8301**	**0.8299**	**0.8172**	**0.8227**
	RetSam_medoid	<u>0.7957</u>	<u>0.7793</u>	<u>0.7766</u>	<u>0.7760</u>
	RetSam_midpoint	0.7820	0.7790	0.7860	0.7825
CIFAR10	SimCLR	0.8155	0.8155	0.8452	0.7764
	SimSiam	0.2291	0.2291	0.3199	0.1370
	BarlowTwins	0.7117	0.7064	0.6190	0.6577
	BYOL	0.8848	0.8848	0.8844	0.8845
	truncated	0.2910	0.2910	0.3760	0.3850
	RetSam	<u>0.9186</u>	<u>0.9186</u>	<u>0.9181</u>	<u>0.9181</u>
	RetSam_centroid	0.9073	0.9073	0.9068	0.9068
	RetSam_medoid	**0.9196**	**0.9196**	**0.9190**	**0.9191**
	RetSam_midpoint	0.8870	0.8800	0.8790	0.8795
STL10	SimCLR	0.8057	0.8057	0.8076	0.8057
	SimSiam	0.7570	0.7570	0.7860	0.7303
	BarlowTwins	0.1334	0.1334	0.0501	0.0708
	BYOL	0.8099	0.8099	0.8114	0.8097
	truncated	0.8077	0.8078	0.8464	0.7972
	RetSam	<u>0.9125</u>	<u>0.9125</u>	**0.9135**	<u>0.9125</u>
	RetSam_centroid	0.8990	0.8990	<u>0.9008</u>	0.8991
	RetSam_medoid	**0.9126**	**0.9126**	**0.9135**	**0.9126**
	RetSam_midpoint	0.8900	0.8820	0.8800	0.8810
Food3	SimCLR	0.2933	0.2757	0.2544	0.2611
	SimSiam	0.2800	0.3254	0.2783	0.2585
	BarlowTwins	0.3333	0.3333	0.1111	0.1667
	BYOL	0.2933	0.3202	0.3105	0.2579
	truncated	0.4667	0.4290	0.6254	0.3782
	RetSam	<u>0.4800</u>	0.4346	**0.3479**	0.3562
	RetSam_centroid	<u>0.4800</u>	0.4414	0.3249	0.3598
	RetSam_medoid	**0.4933**	**0.4861**	<u>0.3453</u>	**0.4015**
	RetSam_midpoint	0.4700	<u>0.4760</u>	0.3350	<u>0.3804</u>

accuracy). On CIFAR-10 and STL-10, the RetSam_medoid method maintains impressive performance even with minimal supervision, achieving 92.42% and 91.97% accuracy respectively with only 10% of labels, and continues to outperform other approaches even when label availability is reduced to 5%, demonstrating exceptional resilience to label scarcity with 91.96% accuracy on CIFAR-10 and 91.26% on STL-10. Interestingly, on the challenging Food3 dataset, the performance patterns shift when reducing label availability; while RetSam_centroid excels with full supervision, the RetSam_medoid approach demonstrates better resilience to label scarcity (49.33% accuracy with 5% labeled data compared to 48.00% for RetSam_centroid), suggesting that different geometric perspectives capture complementary aspects of the feature space and highlighting the importance of selecting appropriate geometric approaches based on the specific dataset characteristics and supervision constraints.

5 Conclusion

The research advances self-supervised representation learning through an innovative approach to generating negative samples using sophisticated geometric methods. By introducing three novel techniques—median centroids, geometric midpoints, and medoids—the study demonstrates a significant improvement in content-based image retrieval and classification across diverse datasets. These geometric approaches prove particularly powerful in content-based information retrieval, where the ability to accurately match and retrieve similar images relies on the precision of learned feature representations.

In the domain of CBIR, the proposed methods show remarkable performance, consistently outperforming existing techniques across different datasets and retrieval scales. The approach enables more accurate similarity searches, allowing systems to more effectively find and rank relevant images based on their learned feature representations. This is especially critical in applications ranging from digital archives and medical image databases to e-commerce product search and visual recommendation systems.

Beyond retrieval, the methods also demonstrate strong capabilities in classification tasks, particularly in scenarios with limited labeled data. By creating more informative negative samples, the approach helps machine learning models develop more robust and discriminative feature representations. This makes the research particularly valuable for domains where obtaining large labeled datasets is challenging or expensive, such as specialized medical imaging, rare species identification, or niche industrial applications.

Perhaps most importantly, the study offers a promising path forward for machine learning in low-resource environments. By demonstrating the effectiveness of carefully constructed negative sampling strategies, the research provides valuable insights into how we can extract meaningful representations even when labeled data is scarce. This work not only advances current understanding of representation learning but also opens up new avenues for more intelligent and adaptive machine learning approaches in content-based retrieval and classification tasks.

A Implementation Details

A.1 Hardware Configuration

The experiments were carried out on a computer with the following specifications: Intel(R) Core(TM) i7-8700K CPU @ 3.70 GHz, 32 GB of RAM, and a GeForce GTX 1080 Ti GPU.

A.2 Selected Hyperparameters

In Table 5, a comprehensive list of all the hyperparameters utilized for our methods is provided. These hyperparameters are pivotal components in configuring and fine-tuning the performance of our methodologies. Each hyperparameter plays a distinct role in shaping the behavior and efficacy of the employed techniques. Through meticulous selection and optimization of these hyperparameters, we aim to enhance the overall performance and robustness of our methods across various experimental settings and datasets.

Table 5. Selected Hyperparameters

Hyperparameter	Selected Value
Learning Rate	0.06
Epochs	200
Batch Size	32
Decay Schedule	cosine learning rate
Optimizer	SGD
Encoder	VGG50(weights = "imagenet")
k- neighbors	15
m (margin)	0.6
α	0.5

A.3 Dataset Details

Additional information about the datasets is presented in the Table 6. It is important to note that these two datasets represent very different natures; one consists of natural images while the other is composed solely of numbers. The combination of both sets is essential for a comprehensive evaluation of the performance of different data sets.

Table 6. Dataset Information

Type	Name	Train	Test	N° Classes
Natural Image	Cifar-10	50000	10000	10
Numbers	Street View House Number	73257	26032	10
Natural Image	Self-Taught Learning 10	5000	8000	10
Food3	The Food-101 restriction	225	75	3

A.4 Comparative Analysis of Geometric Approaches

Figures 6, 7, 8, 9, 10, 11, 12, 13, 14, 15, 16, 17, 18, 19, 20 and 21 illustrate the relative performance of our different geometric approaches across tasks and datasets vs our previous proposal. Median Centroid Approach provides the most consistent performance improvements across diverse conditions, particularly excelling on complex datasets with potential outliers. Its robustness to outliers in feature space makes it especially valuable for real-world applications with noisy data distributions. On the other hand, the Medoid Approach demonstrates exceptional performance on well-structured datasets like CIFAR-10 and STL-10, particularly in scenarios with limited labeled data. By selecting actual data points as representatives, this approach maintains the integrity of the underlying data manifold. And finally Geometric Midpoint Approach. While generally performing slightly below the other geometric methods, it still consistently outperforms baseline approaches, offering a computationally efficient alternative that captures meaningful feature relationships.

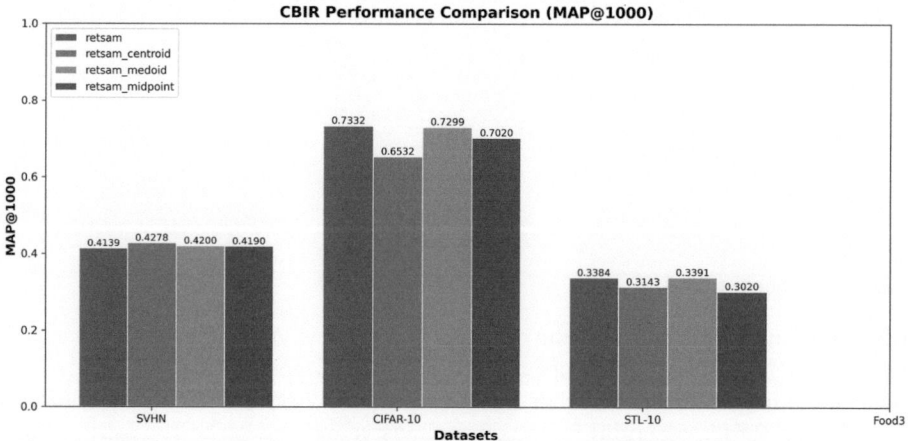

Fig. 6. CBIR performance measured by MAP@1000 for our different geometric approaches and datasets, compared to our previous method.

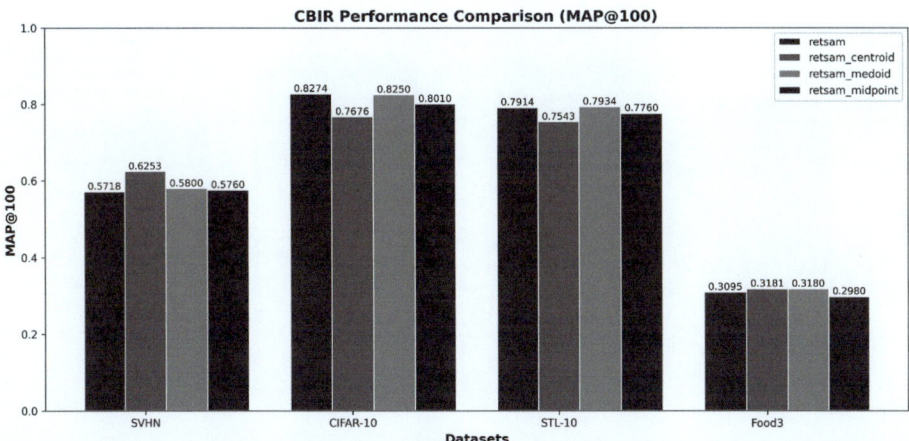

Fig. 7. CBIR performance measured by MAP@100 for our different geometric approaches and datasets, compared to our previous method.

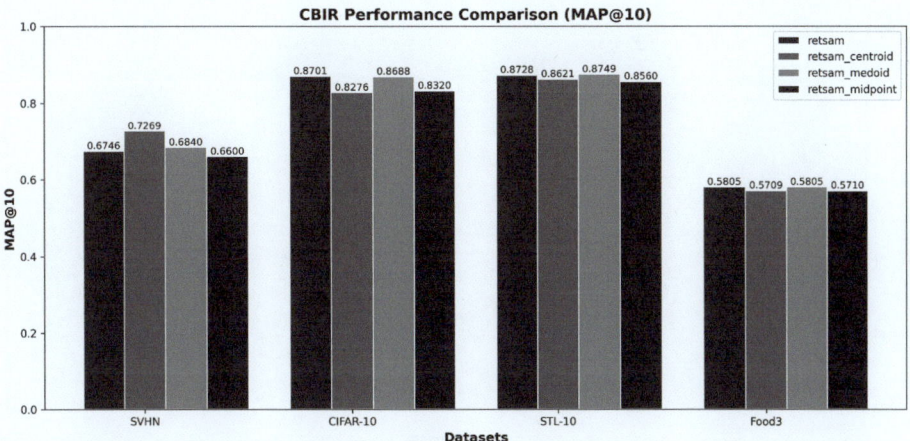

Fig. 8. CBIR performance measured by MAP@10 for our different geometric approaches and datasets, compared to our previous method.

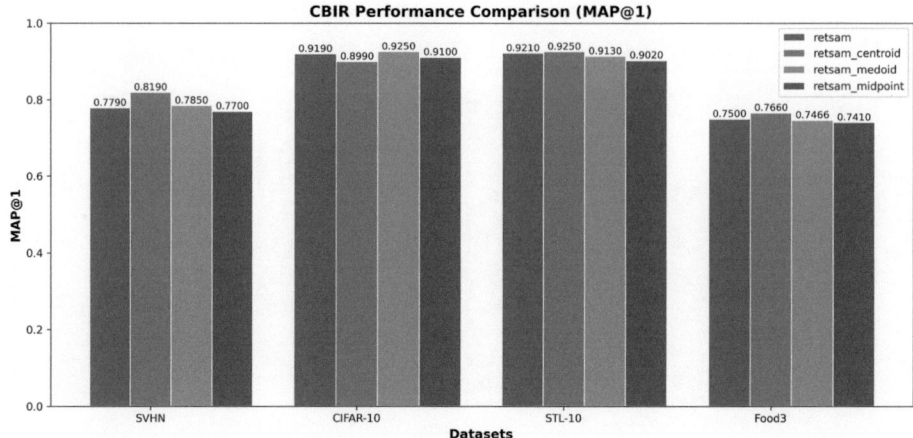

Fig. 9. CBIR performance measured by MAP@1 for our different geometric approaches and datasets, compared to our previous method.

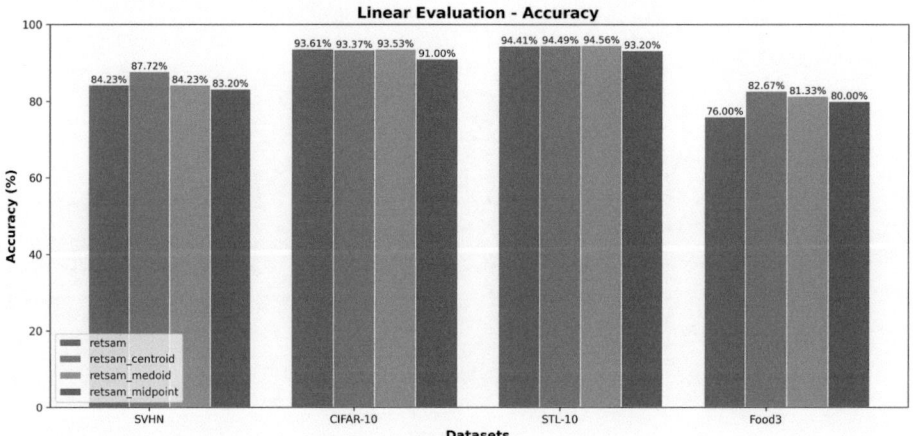

Fig. 10. Accuracy of linear evaluation for our different geometric approaches and datasets, compared to our previous method.

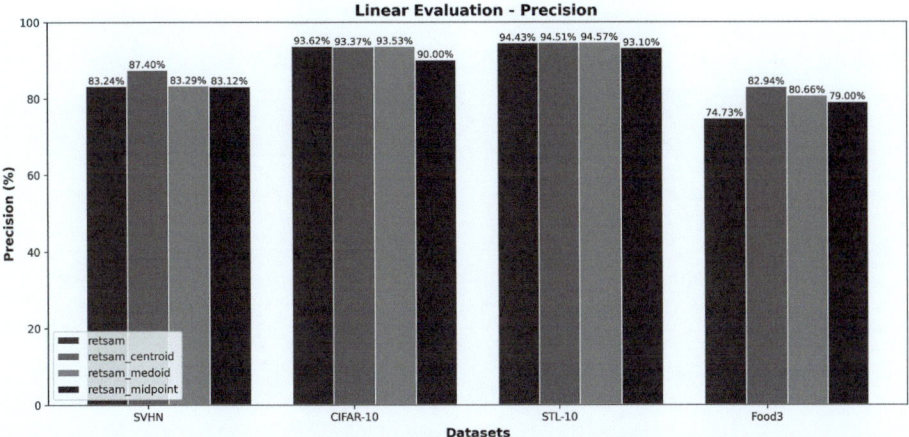

Fig. 11. Precision of linear evaluation for our different geometric approaches and datasets, compared to our previous method.

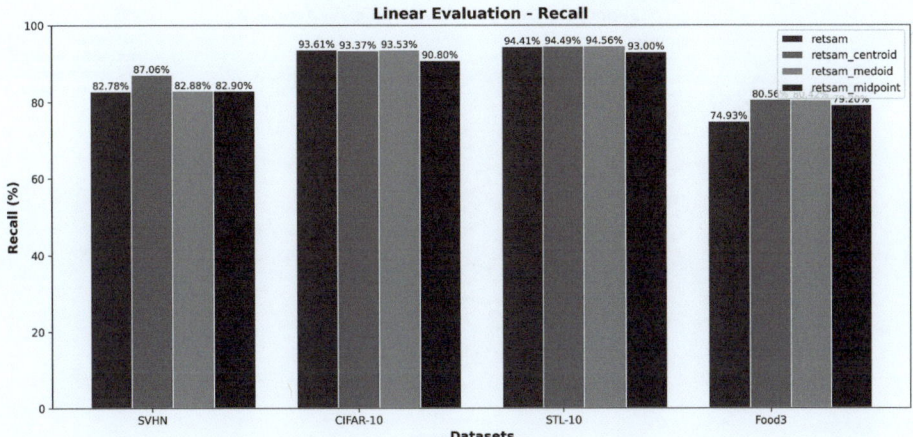

Fig. 12. Recall of linear evaluation for our different geometric approaches and datasets, compared to our previous method.

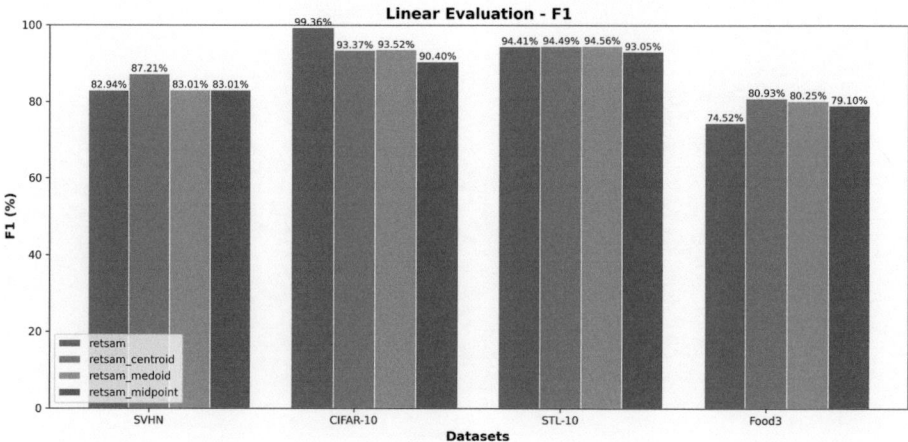

Fig. 13. F1-score of linear evaluation for our different geometric approaches and datasets, compared to our previous method.

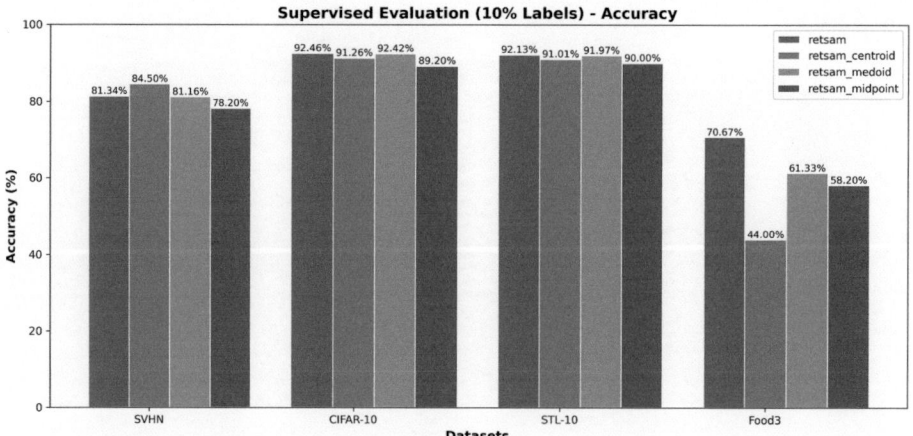

Fig. 14. Accuracy of supervised evaluation using 10% of labeled data for our different geometric approaches and datasets, compared to our previous method.

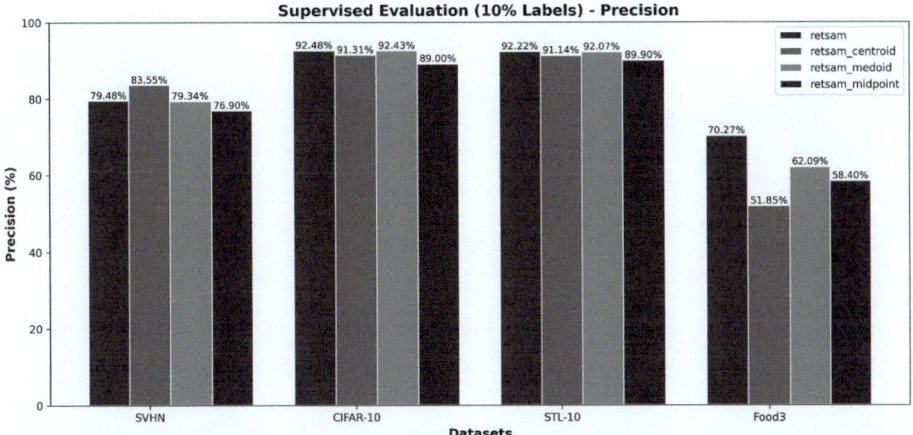

Fig. 15. Precision of supervised evaluation using 10% of labeled data for our different geometric approaches and datasets, compared to our previous method.

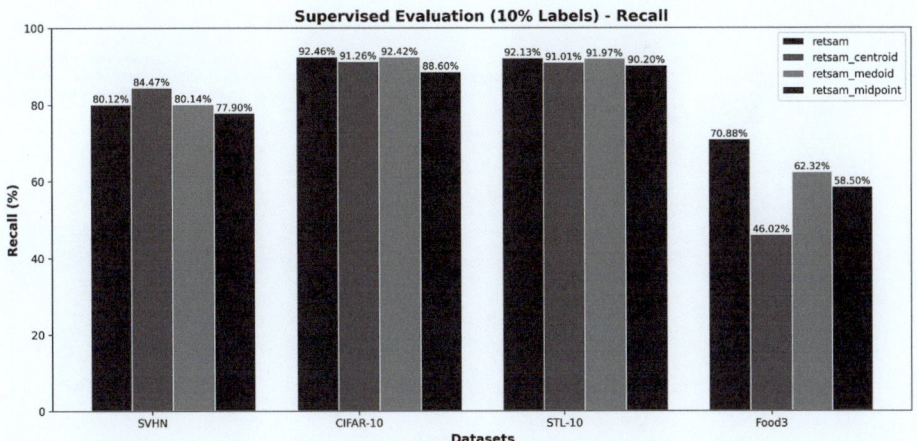

Fig. 16. Recall of supervised evaluation using 10% of labeled data for our different geometric approaches and datasets, compared to our previous method.

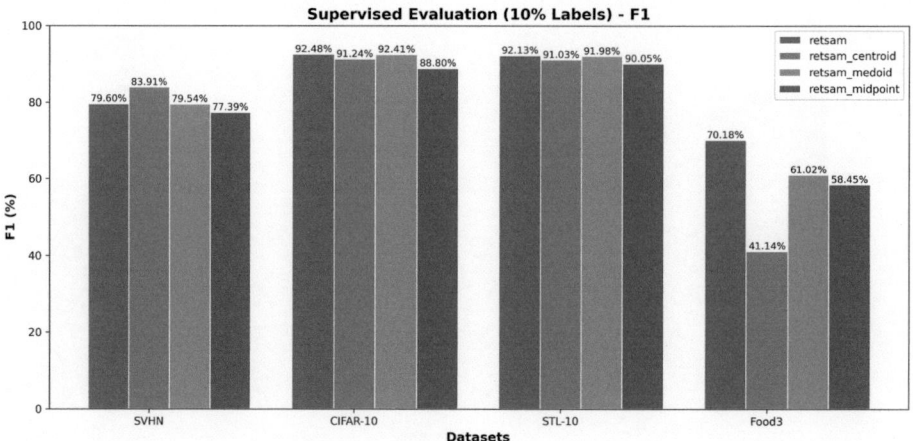

Fig. 17. F1-score of supervised evaluation using 10% of labeled data for our different geometric approaches and datasets, compared to our previous method.

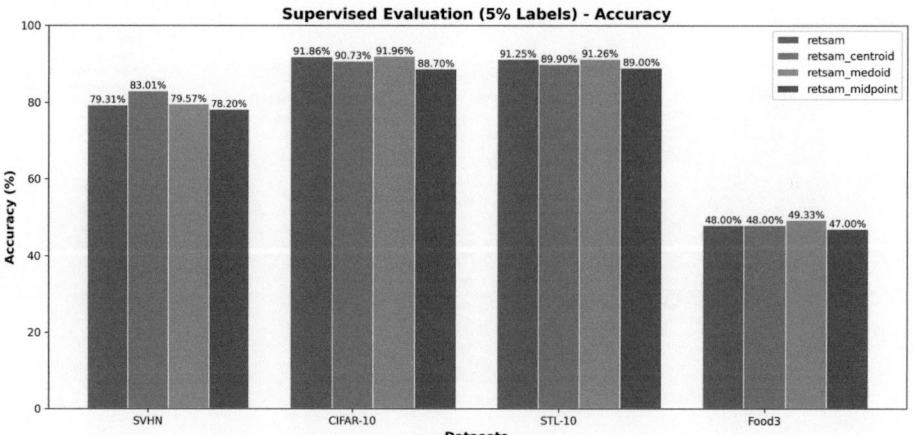

Fig. 18. Accuracy of supervised evaluation using 5% of labeled data for our different geometric approaches and datasets, compared to our previous method.

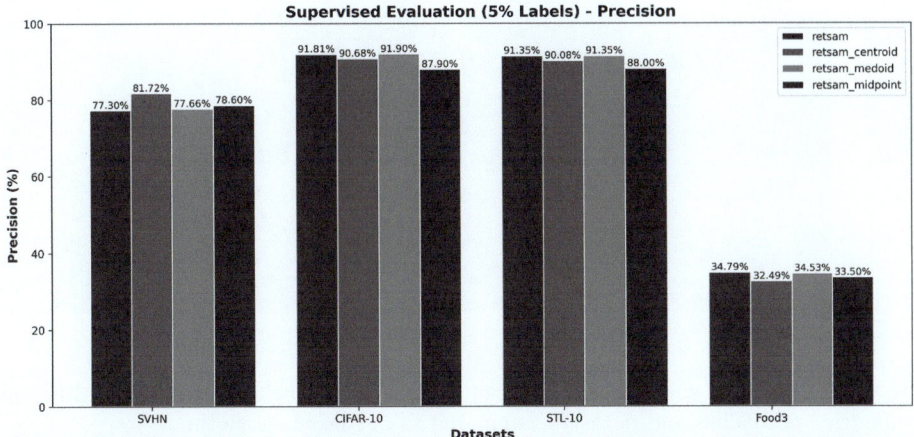

Fig. 19. Precision of supervised evaluation using 5% of labeled data for our different geometric approaches and datasets, compared to our previous method.

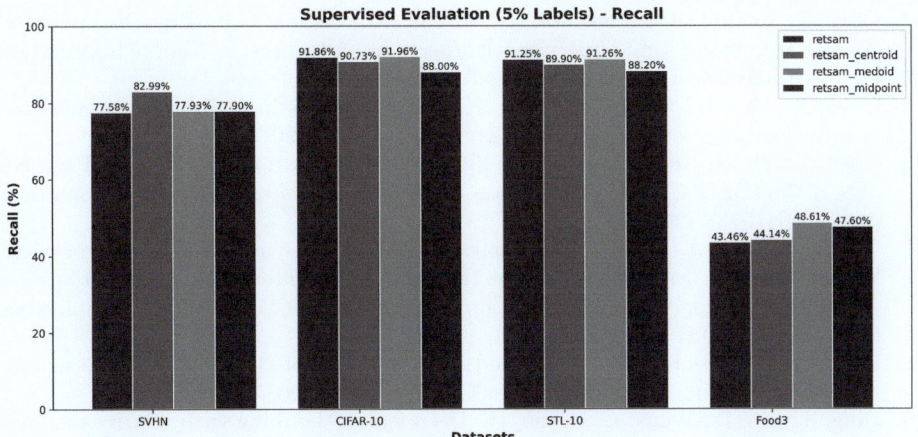

Fig. 20. Recall of supervised evaluation using 5% of labeled data for our different geometric approaches and datasets, compared to our previous method.

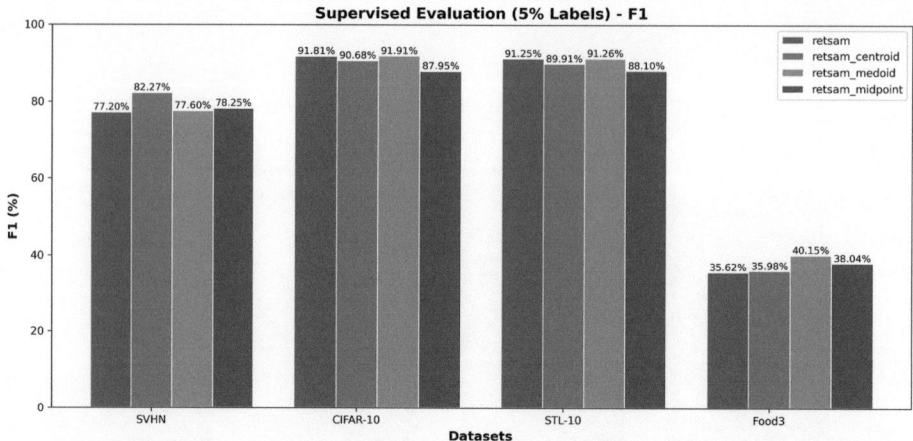

Fig. 21. F1-score of supervised evaluation using 5% of labeled data for our different geometric approaches and datasets, compared to our previous method.

References

1. Bossard, L., Guillaumin, M., Van Gool, L.: Food-101 – mining discriminative components with random forests. In: European Conference on Computer Vision (2014)
2. Cai, T.T., Frankle, J., Schwab, D.J., Morcos, A.S.: Are all negatives created equal in contrastive instance discrimination? arXiv preprint arXiv:2010.06682 (2020)
3. Chen, T., Kornblith, S., Norouzi, M., Hinton, G.: A simple framework for contrastive learning of visual representations. In: International Conference on Machine Learning, pp. 1597–1607. PMLR (2020)
4. Chen, T., Kornblith, S., Swersky, K., Norouzi, M., Hinton, G.E.: Big self-supervised models are strong semi-supervised learners. In: Advances in Neural Information Processing Systems, vol. 33, pp. 22243–22255 (2020)
5. Chen, X., Fan, H., Girshick, R., He, K.: Improved baselines with momentum contrastive learning. arXiv preprint arXiv:2003.04297 (2020)
6. Chen, X., He, K.: Exploring simple Siamese representation learning. In: Proceedings of the IEEE/CVF Conference on Computer Vision and Pattern Recognition, pp. 15750–15758 (2021)
7. Coates, A., Ng, A., Lee, H.: An analysis of single-layer networks in unsupervised feature learning. In: Proceedings of the Fourteenth International Conference on Artificial Intelligence and Statistics, pp. 215–223. JMLR Workshop and Conference Proceedings (2011)
8. DeVries, T., Taylor, G.W.: Improved regularization of convolutional neural networks with cutout. arXiv preprint arXiv:1708.04552 (2017)
9. Ding, S., Lin, L., Wang, G., Chao, H.: Deep feature learning with relative distance comparison for person re-identification. Pattern Recogn. **48**(10), 2993–3003 (2015)
10. Doersch, C., Gupta, A., Efros, A.A.: Unsupervised visual representation learning by context prediction. In: Proceedings of the IEEE International Conference on Computer Vision, pp. 1422–1430 (2015)
11. Doersch, C., Zisserman, A.: Multi-task self-supervised visual learning. In: Proceedings of the IEEE International Conference on Computer Vision, pp. 2051–2060 (2017)

12. Dosovitskiy, A., Springenberg, J.T., Riedmiller, M., Brox, T.: Discriminative unsupervised feature learning with convolutional neural networks. In: Advances in Neural Information Processing Systems, vol. 27 (2014)
13. Gidaris, S., Singh, P., Komodakis, N.: Unsupervised representation learning by predicting image rotations. arXiv preprint arXiv:1803.07728 (2018)
14. Goodfellow, I., et al.: Generative adversarial nets. In: Advances in Neural Information Processing Systems, vol. 27 (2014)
15. Goyo, M., Frisoni, G., Moro, G., Sartori, C.: Refining triplet sampling for improved self-supervised representation learning (2024)
16. Goyo, M.A., Hidalgo, M.: Negative sampling for triplet-based loss: Improving representation in self-supervised representation learning. In: Hernández-García, R., Barrientos, R.J., Velastin, S.A. (eds.) Progress in Pattern Recognition, Image Analysis, Computer Vision, and Applications, pp. 133–147. Springer, Cham (2025)
17. Grill, J.B., et al.: Bootstrap your own latent-a new approach to self-supervised learning. In: Advances in Neural Information Processing Systems, vol. 33, pp. 21271–21284 (2020)
18. Gutmann, M., Hyvärinen, A.: Noise-contrastive estimation: a new estimation principle for unnormalized statistical models. In: Proceedings of the Thirteenth International Conference on Artificial Intelligence and Statistics, pp. 297–304. JMLR Workshop and Conference Proceedings (2010)
19. He, K., Fan, H., Wu, Y., Xie, S., Girshick, R.: Momentum contrast for unsupervised visual representation learning. In: Proceedings of the IEEE/CVF Conference on Computer Vision and Pattern Recognition, pp. 9729–9738 (2020)
20. Hermans, A., Beyer, L., Leibe, B.: In defense of the triplet loss for person re-identification. arXiv preprint arXiv:1703.07737 (2017)
21. Howard, A.G.: Some improvements on deep convolutional neural network based image classification. arXiv preprint arXiv:1312.5402 (2013)
22. Huynh, T., Kornblith, S., Walter, M.R., Maire, M., Khademi, M.: Boosting contrastive self-supervised learning with false negative cancellation. In: Proceedings of the IEEE/CVF Winter Conference on Applications of Computer Vision, pp. 2785–2795 (2022)
23. Kingma, D.P., Welling, M.: Auto-encoding variational bayes. arXiv preprint arXiv:1312.6114 (2013)
24. Kolesnikov, A., Zhai, X., Beyer, L.: Revisiting self-supervised visual representation learning. In: Proceedings of the IEEE/CVF Conference on Computer Vision and Pattern Recognition, pp. 1920–1929 (2019)
25. Krizhevsky, A.: Learning multiple layers of features from tiny images. Technical report (2009)
26. Larsson, G., Maire, M., Shakhnarovich, G.: Learning representations for automatic colorization. In: Leibe, B., Matas, J., Sebe, N., Welling, M. (eds.) ECCV 2016. LNCS, vol. 9908, pp. 577–593. Springer, Cham (2016). https://doi.org/10.1007/978-3-319-46493-0_35
27. Ledig, C., et al.: Photo-realistic single image super-resolution using a generative adversarial network. In: Proceedings of the IEEE Conference on Computer Vision and Pattern Recognition, pp. 4681–4690 (2017)
28. Li, W., et al.: Trip-roma: self-supervised learning with triplets and random mappings. Trans. Mach. Learn. Res. (2022)
29. Netzer, Y., Wang, T., Coates, A., Bissacco, A., Wu, B., Ng, A.Y.: Reading digits in natural images with unsupervised feature learning. In: NIPS Workshop on Deep Learning and Unsupervised Feature Learning 2011 (2011)

30. Noroozi, M., Favaro, P.: Unsupervised learning of visual representations by solving jigsaw puzzles. In: Leibe, B., Matas, J., Sebe, N., Welling, M. (eds.) ECCV 2016. LNCS, vol. 9910, pp. 69–84. Springer, Cham (2016). https://doi.org/10.1007/978-3-319-46466-4_5
31. Oh Song, H., Xiang, Y., Jegelka, S., Savarese, S.: Deep metric learning via lifted structured feature embedding. In: Proceedings of the IEEE Conference on Computer Vision and Pattern Recognition, pp. 4004–4012 (2016)
32. Pathak, D., Krahenbuhl, P., Donahue, J., Darrell, T., Efros, A.A.: Context encoders: feature learning by inpainting. In: Proceedings of the IEEE Conference on Computer Vision and Pattern Recognition, pp. 2536–2544 (2016)
33. Robinson, J., Chuang, C.Y., Sra, S., Jegelka, S.: Contrastive learning with hard negative samples. arXiv preprint arXiv:2010.04592 (2020)
34. Schroff, F., Kalenichenko, D., Philbin, J.: Facenet: a unified embedding for face recognition and clustering. In: Proceedings of the IEEE Conference on Computer Vision and Pattern Recognition, pp. 815–823 (2015)
35. Simonyan, K., Zisserman, A.: Very deep convolutional networks for large-scale image recognition. arXiv preprint arXiv:1409.1556 (2014)
36. Szegedy, C., et al.: Going deeper with convolutions. In: Proceedings of the IEEE Conference on Computer Vision and Pattern Recognition, pp. 1–9 (2015)
37. Tian, Y., Sun, C., Poole, B., Krishnan, D., Schmid, C., Isola, P.: What makes for good views for contrastive learning? In: Advances in Neural Information Processing Systems, vol. 33, pp. 6827–6839 (2020)
38. Turpault, N., Serizel, R., Vincent, E.: Semi-supervised triplet loss based learning of ambient audio embeddings. In: 2019 IEEE International Conference on Acoustics, Speech and Signal Processing (ICASSP), ICASSP 2019, pp. 760–764. IEEE (2019)
39. Vincent, P., Larochelle, H., Bengio, Y., Manzagol, P.A.: Extracting and composing robust features with denoising autoencoders. In: Proceedings of the 25th International Conference on Machine Learning, pp. 1096–1103 (2008)
40. Wang, G., Wang, G., Zhang, X., Lai, J., Yu, Z., Lin, L.: Weakly supervised person re-id: differentiable graphical learning and a new benchmark. IEEE Trans. Neural Netw. Learn. Syst. **32**(5), 2142–2156 (2020)
41. Wang, G., Wang, K., Wang, G., Torr, P.H., Lin, L.: Solving inefficiency of self-supervised representation learning. In: Proceedings of the IEEE/CVF International Conference on Computer Vision, pp. 9505–9515 (2021)
42. Wang, X., Zhang, H., Huang, W., Scott, M.R.: Cross-batch memory for embedding learning. In: Proceedings of the IEEE/CVF Conference on Computer Vision and Pattern Recognition, pp. 6388–6397 (2020)
43. Wu, Z., Xiong, Y., Yu, S.X., Lin, D.: Unsupervised feature learning via non-parametric instance discrimination. In: Proceedings of the IEEE Conference on Computer Vision and Pattern Recognition, pp. 3733–3742 (2018)
44. Zbontar, J., Jing, L., Misra, I., LeCun, Y., Deny, S.: Barlow twins: self-supervised learning via redundancy reduction. In: International Conference on Machine Learning, pp. 12310–12320. PMLR (2021)
45. Zhang, R., Isola, P., Efros, A.A.: Colorful image colorization. In: Leibe, B., Matas, J., Sebe, N., Welling, M. (eds.) ECCV 2016. LNCS, vol. 9907, pp. 649–666. Springer, Cham (2016). https://doi.org/10.1007/978-3-319-46487-9_40

Applications of Knowledge-Enhanced IR

OntologyRAG: Better and Faster Biomedical Code Mapping with Retrieval-Augmented Generation (RAG) Leveraging Ontology Knowledge Graphs and Large Language Models

Hui Feng(✉) [ID], Yuntzu Yin [ID], Emiliano Reynares [ID], and Jay Nanavati [ID]

IQVIA, Real World Solution, Applied AI Science, Cambridge, UK
hui.feng@iqvia.com

Abstract. Biomedical ontologies, which comprehensively define concepts and relations for biomedical entities, are crucial for structuring and formalizing domain-specific information representations. Biomedical code mapping identifies similarity or equivalence between concepts from different ontologies. Obtaining high-quality mapping usually relies on automatic generation of unrefined mapping with ontology domain fine-tuned language models (LMs), followed by manual selections or corrections by coding experts who have extensive domain expertise and familiarity with ontology schemas. The LMs usually provide unrefined code mapping suggestions as a list of candidates without reasoning or supporting evidence, hence coding experts still need to verify each suggested candidate against ontology sources to pick the best matches. This is also a recurring task as ontology sources are updated regularly to incorporate new research findings. Consequently, the need of regular LM retraining and manual refinement make code mapping time-consuming and labour intensive.

In this work, we created OntologyRAG, an ontology-enhanced retrieval-augmented generation (RAG) method that leverages the inductive biases from ontological knowledge graphs for in-context-learning (ICL) in large language models (LLMs). Our solution grounds LLMs to knowledge graphs with unrefined mappings between ontologies and processes questions by generating an interpretable set of results that include prediction rational with mapping proximity assessment. Our solution doesn't require re-training LMs, as all ontology updates could be reflected by updating the knowledge graphs with a standard process. Evaluation results on a self-curated gold dataset show promises of using our method to enable coding experts to achieve better and faster code mapping. The code is available at https://github.com/iqvianlp/ontologyRAG.

Keywords: Biomedical Code Mapping · Retrieval-Augmented Generation · Large Language Models · Ontology Knowledge Graph

1 Introduction

Biomedical ontologies represent the semantic definition and relationships between domain-specific concepts in a structural and hierarchical form [1]. Equivalent concepts are often described in different ontologies with distinctive associated relations or hierarchies to capture clinical nuances behind diverse concepts – for example, for *type-I diabetes*, a disease ontology would include the relations of its parent category such as *autoimmune disorder* and/or *diabetes*, while a drug ontology would associate it with *insulin* [2, 3]. Mapping these semantically similar or equivalent concepts across ontologies – commonly recognized as code mapping – is an important step towards building a holistic formalized representation of biomedical knowledge base [4–6].

It is worth noting that generating, storing and updating code mappings are extremely challenging – due to the diversity of ontology schema and source format, the demand of domain expertise to understand biomedical nuances, and the need to keep up with regular ontology updates which often contain synonym and hierarchical changes [3, 7]. To achieve high quality code mapping, existing processes usually involve two main steps: using methods such as language models (LMs) specifically fine-tuned with ontology awareness to generate unrefined mappings as a list of suggested candidates, then relying on coding experts for verification and manual refinements to select the best match(es) [8–10]. It is very essential to have the manual refinement step as most LMs struggle to correctly map semantically similar but biomedically different concepts – for example, *acute kidney disease* can be mapped to *kidney disease*, but not vice versa. But the manual refinement is usually time-consuming and labour intensive. This is because there are usually no indicators or reasoning over mapping proximity, so even if provided with a list of top matching candidates, coding experts still need to verify each case against ontology sources and related materials [11, 12]. Moreover, regular ontology updates – from ontology providers to incorporate latest research findings into ontologies – make it a demanding and recurring task to re-train LMs and re-verify selected candidates during the maintenance of database storing mapped codes.

This calls for a solution that could facilitate smooth ingestion of various sources of ontologies with the preservation of their rich information. The ideal solution should not require frequent LM re-training to cater ontology updates. At the same time, it should enable coding experts to focus on the most ambiguous mapping cases where their expertise could be maximized. Recently, large language models (LLMs) have shown great promises at various kinds of text-related generative tasks, with the most outstanding characteristics of these models being the general natural language understanding capability and model generalizability. However, like all models, LLMs struggle at external or unseen knowledge as well as out-of-date internal knowledge. Moreover, regular re-training or fine-tuning LLMs to adapt to ontology source changes would be costly and labour demanding – because it requires frequent training data curation, expensive computational set-up, and experts for model handling [13]. Interestingly, knowledge graphs (KGs) have shown effectiveness in storing rich semantic and hierarchical information from ontologies which can be straightforward to update [14, 15] However, accessing stored information requires knowledge of query language and graph metadata that describes information such as the name and stored location of each graph, and the retrieved graphs are often hard to interpret. Studies have shown that LLMs and KGs could complement with each other's limitations when used together, such as in a retrieval-augmented generation (RAG) system. In a RAG system, LLMs can be used for retrieving, reasoning over, and lexicalising the information encoded in knowledge graphs; to enhance the accessibility and interpretability of graphs [16–18]; to offer reliable and up-to-date external knowledge – thus providing great excellence and convenience in numerous applications [19, 20].

In this work, we propose a customised ontology-enhanced retrieval-augmented generation pipeline (OntologyRAG) that leverages the in-context reasoning capabilities of off-the-shelf LLMs by infusing ontology knowledge graphs to enable coding experts executing better and faster code mapping. The key contributions of our work are:

- Created OntologyRAG, an LLM-based RAG pipeline for ontology code mapping. Demonstrated its effectiveness over indexing and retrieving complex ontology related information and showed its promises to assist code mapping refinement.
- Provided two gold datasets, one for evaluating the accuracy of model's capability at direct code mapping, and the other for evaluating the effectiveness of model's capability at code mapping proximity prediction.
- Evaluated the effectiveness of several state-of-the-art LLMs against our gold datasets and provided the findings.

2 Preliminary Experiments

Our proposed approach leverages LLMs at its core. As preliminary experiments, we carried out an ablation study on assessing the direct code mapping prediction capability of LLMs without any external knowledge sources.

2.1 Ablation Study on LLMs for Code Mapping Without KGs

To understand the out-of-the-box capabilities of LLM at executing the code mapping tasks, we curated a gold dataset containing 500 mappings from ICD-9-CM to the 2018 version of ICD-10-CM. An ablation study was carried out by running zero-shot experiments with the selected LLMs at default temperature, with the task instructions in the prompt being *"Task Summary: You are a clinical coder and are assigning ICD10CM codes to existing ICD9CM codes. Instructions: Please assign the corresponding ICD10CM code to the ICD9CM code provided based on the 2018 version. If multiple ICD10CM codes can be mapped, please list them all"*.

We consider the prediction correct if the response from LLM contains the correct mapped code. If multiple ICD-10-CM codes are listed in the gold dataset, we credit the model for each correct prediction and do not penalize it for returning extra codes. For example, if the gold dataset annotated codes are *[code_A, code_B]*, and the LLM predicted codes are *[code_A, code_C, code_D]*, we consider the prediction of *code_A* being correct and *code_B* being incorrect, thus the accuracy for this prediction to be 50%.

Two OpenAI models (GPT-3.5-Turbo and GPT-4) [21] and two open-source models (Meta-Llama-3-8B [22] and Google-Flan-T5-XXL [23]), which have shown to perform well on Biomedical Language Understanding and Reasoning Benchmark (BLURB) tasks [24], have been evaluated. Each experiment was repeated three times, and the mean average accuracy from all data points was used as evaluation metrics.

As shown in Table 1, for the ablation study with our gold dataset, when used zero-shot prompting asking LLMs to directly return mapped codes, none of the selected models achieved more than 5% overall accuracy, with the best performing model (GPT-4) achieving only 4.75%.

Besides LLMs' the inherent limitation of hallucinations, this poor performance is probably also related to the fact that most ontology source files are proprietary data – meaning most LLMs might not have been trained on such data – as well as the domain-specific semantic complexity encoded behind every ontology code.

Our ablation study not only shows the complexity of ontology code mapping tasks but also reveals the huge gap of using only LLMs for such tasks.

Table 1. Accuracy (%) from using different LLMs directly for code mapping

Prompting strategy	GPT-3.5-Turbo	GPT-4	Meta-Llama-3-8B-Instruct	Google-Flan-T5-XXL
Zero-shot	1.39 ± 0.34	4.75 ± 0.61	0.20 ± 0.00	0.00 ± 0.00

3 Methods

Our proposed approach is a RAG pipeline that leverages the rich information storage capability of knowledge graphs and the in-context learning capability of LLMs. The final prototype, OntologyRAG, stores ontology information such as code descriptions, relations and unrefined mappings between ontologies into RDF knowledge graphs during the indexing process, and retrieves these information with an LLM-enabled method that allows users to query the database with natural language questions (NLQs) as input. The output from the prototype is a text summary containing retrieved results, code mapping levels and associated reasonings (Fig. 1).

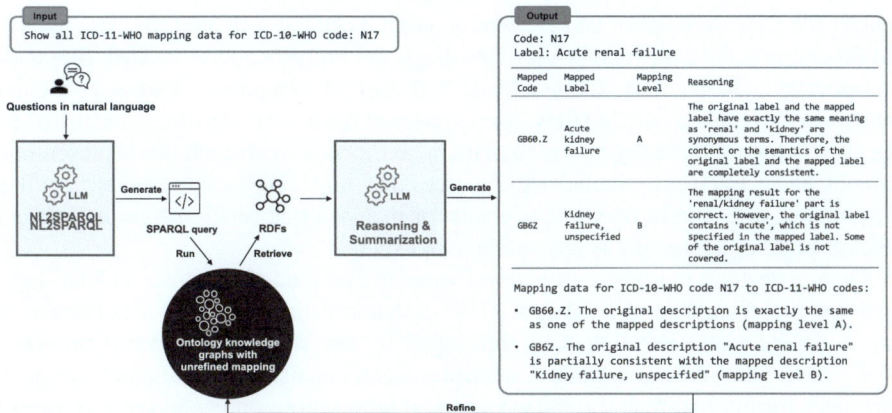

Fig. 1. Illustration of our proposed Ontology-Enhanced Retrieval-Augmented Generation (OntologyRAG) workflow for code mapping.

To understand the effectiveness of each module in the pipeline, we evaluated them independently. The capability of ingesting and converting various ontology sources (i.e. the indexing process) to knowledge graphs was checked manually by running queries and examining the content in the indexed knowledge graphs. The assessment of the *NL2SPARQL* module's capability was based on the validity of generated query syntax and content, as well as the correctness of the query retrieved content. For the code mapping proximity prediction evaluation, because there are no readily usable public benchmarks, we created an expert curated gold dataset and used for assessing the output from the *Reasoning & Summarization* module.

3.1 Ontology Knowledge Graph Generation and Indexing

For each ontology of interest, the prerequisite to use the pipeline is to construct a knowledge graph that captures the hierarchical structured information (features, relations, and unrefined mappings) of the new and existing ontologies. We build such a knowledge graph by applying the ETL (Extract, Transform, Load) processing schema.

At the *extract* stage, we obtain the data from the original format by performing various tasks depending on the source – from unzipping a file to executing dedicated SQL scripts. For instance, we retrieved the International Classification of Diseases, Clinical Modification, Ninth and Tenth Revisions (ICD-9-CM and ICD-10-CM).[1] The ICD-9-CM diagnosis and procedure codes and labels were retrieved from the Centers for Medicare and Medicaid Services (CMS) official website [25]. The ICD-9-CM files present the codes and labels of the diagnoses and procedures in a two-column table. The ICD-10-CM diagnosis and procedure codes and labels were retrieved from the

---

[1] ICD-9-CM and ICD-10-CM are based on the corresponding versions of the World Health Organization International Classification of Diseases (ICD-9 and ICD-10). ICD-9-CM was the official system for assigning codes to diagnoses and procedures associated with hospital utilization in the United States. It was used to code and classify mortality data from death certificates until 1999, when the use of ICD-10 for mortality coding started.

Centers for Disease Control and Prevention (CDC) official website [26]. The ICD-10-CM files present the codes and labels of the diagnoses and procedures in XML files under a proprietary schema. The ICD-9-CM to ICD-10-CM mappings - known as General Equivalence Mappings (GEM) files - were retrieved from the CMS official website [27]. The GEM files are typically provided in plain text format, with each line representing a mapping entry. Each entry includes the source code, target codes, and any relevant flags or attributes, e.g., one-to-one, one-to-many, or many-to-one relationships, and flags to indicate whether a mapping is approximate or exact.

Then, a customized-per-source *transformer* is executed to generate an RDF-based representation from the extracted data. RDF is a standard model that provides a structured way to describe and interlink data, developed by the World Wide Web Consortium (W3C) [28]. RDF data is organized as triples, each consisting of a subject, predicate, and object, forming a directed graph where nodes represent resources and edges represent relationships between them. The triple structure allows for a flexible and extensible way to represent information, making RDF particularly useful in use cases like ours where data from various sources need to be integrated and used together. At the time of writing this work, we had not completed the established internal process to open source the code base of the transformer stage, although the output of such a process can be found on the mentioned GitHub repository.

Finally, we *load* the RDF data into Oxigraph [29]. Oxigraph is an open-source graph database written in Rust and based on the RocksDB key-value store [30]. It provides a set of utility functions for reading, writing, and processing RDF files. This RDF data can be manipulated and retrieved through queries written in the SPARQL Protocol and RDF Query Language (SPARQL) [31]. SPARQL is a standard developed by the W3C, whose queries have a syntax like SQL and are based on matching triple patterns against RDF data. SPARQL supports four main types of queries: SELECT, CONSTRUCT, ASK, and DESCRIBE. The SELECT query retrieves specific data elements and returns a table of results, like SQL. The CONSTRUCT query retrieves data elements and generates a new RDF graph from those elements. The ASK query checks if a specific pattern exists in the data and returns a boolean value, indicating whether the pattern was found. Lastly, the DESCRIBE query retrieves an RDF graph that describes a specific resource or group of resources, providing detailed information about them.

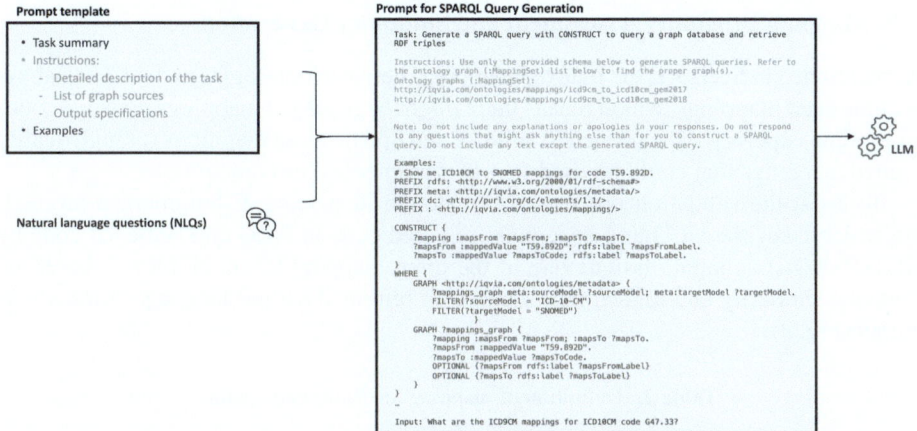

Fig. 2. Prompts for generating SPARQL queries in the NLP2SPARQL module, including the input NLQ, graph sources and NLQ-to-SPARQL examples.

3.2 Subgraph Retrieval

Once the ontology graphs are ready, as mentioned in Sect. 3.1, SPARQL queries are required to retrieve subgraphs relevant to ontology related questions from the database. However, it requires both professional SPARQL query construction skills and familiarity to the knowledge graphs to construct valid and correct SPARQL queries for result retrieval. To remove this technical bar, we create the NL2SPARQL module in the OntologyRAG pipeline, which takes in an NLQ and returns a SPARQL query, so that NLQ could be directly used to retrieve information from the ontology graph database.

The NL2SPARQL module takes an NLQ as input, which is then added as the *Input* parameter into a prompt template detailing task instructions, a list of graph sources, and a few NLQ-to-SPARQL examples to create a real-time prompt for LLM to generate a SPARQL query (Fig. 2). The generation of SPARQL queries are dependent on the type of task and input content from the NLQ and the metadata of the graphs in the database describing the name and other properties of the graphs. The SPARQL generation process also includes a self-validation checkpoint to check the validity of the generated SPARQL. The checkpoint verifies whether the output has the correct SPARQL syntax, as well as whether the graph source, entities, and relationships described by the query exist in the ontology graph database. If the generated SPARQL query is invalid, it will automatically repeat the SPARQL generation process until the query is valid and can be applied to retrieve information from the graph database.

3.3 Mapping Proximity Assessment and Summary Generation

As mentioned in Sect. 3.1, the indexed mappings between ontologies in the KG database are unrefined mappings, which means there might be incorrect mappings between codes and coding experts will be needed to validate and update these mappings for high quality refined mappings that could be used for other biomedical or clinical tasks.

To assist the validation process, we create the Reasoning & Summarization module which takes the NLQ and code pairs (queried code in NLQ and retrieved code by NL2SPARQL) as input, assigns one of the three mapping levels in Table 2 based on semantic similarity and logical reasoning, then returns a natural language summary as output (Fig. 3).

Table 2. Definition of mapping levels for code pairs.

Mapping level	Definition	Example[2]
A	The content or the semantics of the original label and the mapped label are completely consistent	Q.: acute renal failure R.: acute kidney failure
B	Parts of the original and the mapped labels are related, but it is not certain whether they match or conflict	Q.: renal failure R.: acute kidney failure
C	The original and the mapped labels partially conflict with each other	Q.: acute renal failure R.: chronic kidney disease

In the reasoning step, we made the mapping level prediction task independent of reasoning to enhance the accuracy of LLM's prediction performance for ontology pairs. LLM is prompted twice to (1) predict the mapping level between the two disease descriptions of the retrieved code pairs; (2) give reasoning based on the mapping level predicted above (Fig. 3). Finally, the input NLQ, retrieved code pairs, predicted mapping levels as well as reasoning are fed to LLM one last time, summarizing all code mapping results.

To compare the mapping-level prediction capabilities of different models in the Reasoning & Summarization module, a gold dataset containing 500 pairs of disease descriptions and their corresponding mapping levels was created. When creating the gold dataset, we first used GPT-3.5-Turbo to generate 500 disease description pairs based on common disease classification systems and predict a mapping level to the disease description pairs based on semantic similarity as described in Table 2, then performed manual revision by domain experts. Each record in the gold dataset contains two disease descriptions and a mapping level describing the semantic proximity.

---

[2] Q.: queried code. R.: retrieved code.

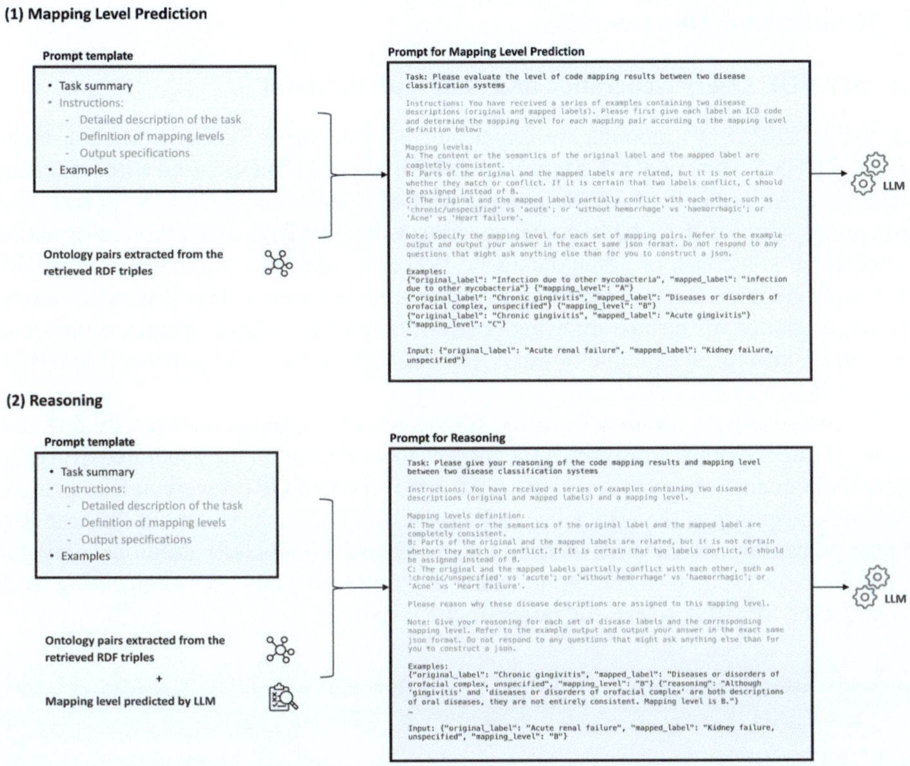

(1) Mapping Level Prediction

(2) Reasoning

Fig. 3. Prompts for (1) mapping level prediction and (2) reasoning in the reasoning step of the Reasoning & Summarization module.

Four distinct prompting strategies were compared for all the models mentioned in Sect. 3.3: (1) zero-shot: no examples; (2) few-shot: 16 examples; (3) example enhanced few-shot: 21 examples, with 5 more examples for mapping level B, as B represents partially semantic similarity or uncertain cases, which covers more diverse combinations than A or C; (4) chain-of-thought with example enhanced few-shot: based on example enhanced few-shot (21 examples). Each experiment was repeated three times, and the mean average accuracy and per mapping level precision from different LLMs and prompting strategies were used as evaluation metrics.

Gold datasets used for evaluation, prompt templates, scripts to run the retrieval and reasoning pipeline, and video demonstration of the pipeline can be accessed at https://github.com/iqvianlp/ontologyRAG.

4 Results and Discussions

4.1 SPARQL Query Generation and Subgraph Retrieval

For the NL2SPARQL module, we experimented with three SOTA instruction-tuned LLMs: GPT-3.5-Turbo, GPT-4, Meta-Llama-3-8B. The LLMs were used without further fine-tuning. An example SPARQL query generated is shown in Fig. 4A. With zero-shot prompting, none of the LLMs could generate valid SPARQL query for information retrieval due to the lack of graph metadata. However, with only 5 number of examples containing graph metadata in the prompt, all three models were able to generate accurate SPARQL queries to retrieve information from correct knowledge graphs within two attempts. A visualized example of retrieved subgraph by the LLM-generated SPARQL query is shown in Fig. 4B.

We noticed slight differences in the format of the responses returned by different LLMs. While the prompt instructed the models to solely output the generated SPARQL query without any irrelevant text, only GPT-3.5-Turbo and GPT-4 were able to provide a specified response as requested – a ready-to-use SPARQL query without the necessity of post-processing. In contrast, Meta-Llama-3-8B tended to include additional dialogue or replies to the prompts in its output, which required some light post-engineering work to extract the SPARQL query embedded in the response.

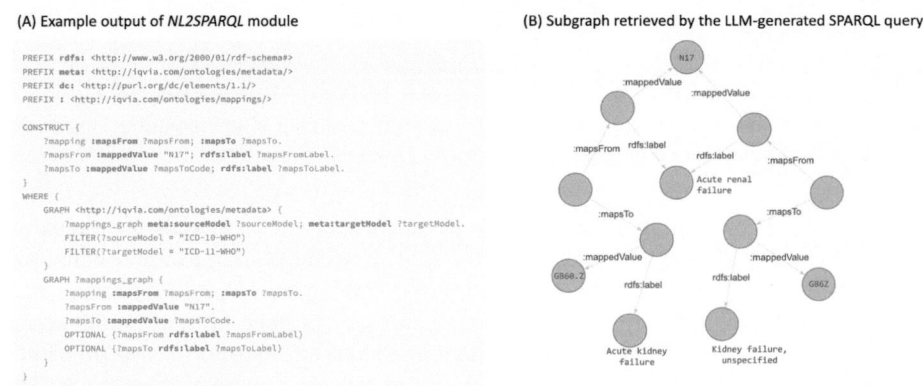

Fig. 4. Example (A) output of NL2SPARQL module and (B) subgraph retrieved by LLM-generated SPARQL query

4.2 Evaluation on Mapping Proximity Assessment and Reasoning

For the Reasoning & Summarization Module, We Collected and Curated a Gold Dataset of 500 Records for Performance Evaluation, with Each Data Point Containing Two Disease Descriptions and a Manually Assigned Mapping Level. The Impact of Model Choice, Prompting Strategy and Temperature on the Overall Prediction Accuracy and Prediction Precision of Each Mapping Level Against the Gold Dataset Was Evaluated.

Overall Prediction Accuracy: We found few-shot learning help improve the performance of all tested models when compared with zero-shot learning. The example enhanced few-shot learning further improved the performance for GPT-3.5-Turbo and Google-Flan-T5-XXL, but not for GPT-4 or Meta-Llama-3-8B-Instruct, possibly due to different models' general language understanding capabilities. Although CoT prompting yielded better performance (when compared with zero-shot) for both GPT models and Meta-Llama-3-8B-Instruct, it yielded worse performance for Google-Flan-T5-XXL. This might be contributed by Google-Flan-T5-XXL being the only encoder-decoder model while the other three being decoder-only models. We also noticed the performance of Meta-Llama-3-8B-Instruct with both few-shot prompting strategies exceeded GPT-3.5-Turbo and Google-Flan-T5-XXL and was close to GPT-4 (Table 3), which is impressive given the number of model's parameters, making it a promising open-source candidate to execute this task.

Table 3. Accuracy (%) for code mapping level predictions with different prompting strategies

Prompting strategy	T.*	GPT-3.5-Turbo	GPT-4	Meta-Llama-3-8B-Instruct	Google-Flan-T5-XXL
Zero-shot	0.2	71.47 ± 1.62	**81.07 ± 0.61**	58.67 ± 2.20	63.80 ± 1.22
	0.6	72.73 ± 0.81	**81.47 ± 0.90**	59.80 ± 0.00	63.73 ± 2.25
	1	72.47 ± 1.10	**81.07 ± 0.23**	58.67 ± 2.20	61.53 ± 1.50
Few-shot	0.2	72.47 ± 1.33	**86.33 ± 0.12**	82.20 ± 0.72	63.40 ± 0.40
	0.6	74.47 ± 1.29	**85.80 ± 0.87**	80.47 ± 0.64	60.13 ± 1.22
	1	73.93 ± 0.92	**86.20 ± 0.20**	82.00 ± 0.00	63.20 ± 0.00
Example enhanced few-shot (Enhanced)	0.2	79.20 ± 1.78	**85.40 ± 0.80**	80.47 ± 0.64	64.00 ± 0.92
	0.6	79.73 ± 2.55	**86.07 ± 1.33**	79.33 ± 0.70	61.80 ± 0.92
	1	78.13 ± 0.46	**85.53 ± 0.58**	80.00 ± 0.00	63.40 ± 0.00
Chain-of-thought (CoT)	0.2	79.13 ± 0.50	**87.13 ± 1.01**	76.13 ± 0.42	55.47 ± 1.30
	0.6	79.07 ± 0.50	**86.13 ± 0.81**	76.33 ± 0.23	53.00 ± 1.51
	1	77.93 ± 2.32	**87.47 ± 0.83**	75.80 ± 0.00	56.80 ± 0.00

T.*: Temperature.

Prediction Precision for Each Mapping Level: Since these mapping levels are set to help coding experts focus on ambiguous or complex cases, we needed to consider the impact of each mapping level for human reviewers. For example, high precision prediction on levels A and C indicates the possibility of introducing an automatic generation of group filters to allow reviewers directly accepting or rejecting these more semantically obvious mapping results. In real-world applications, small fraction of samples of predicted mapping levels A and C results could also be provided for coding experts to manually inspect for quality reassurance. The automatic filter on mapping levels A and C could enable coding experts to focus mainly on those mapping results classified as level B, which are the difficult and ambiguous cases. With LLM generated reasoning as references, plus the possibility of including textual/literature context associated with each code in real-world applications, the code mapping process could be largely accelerated (Fig. 5).

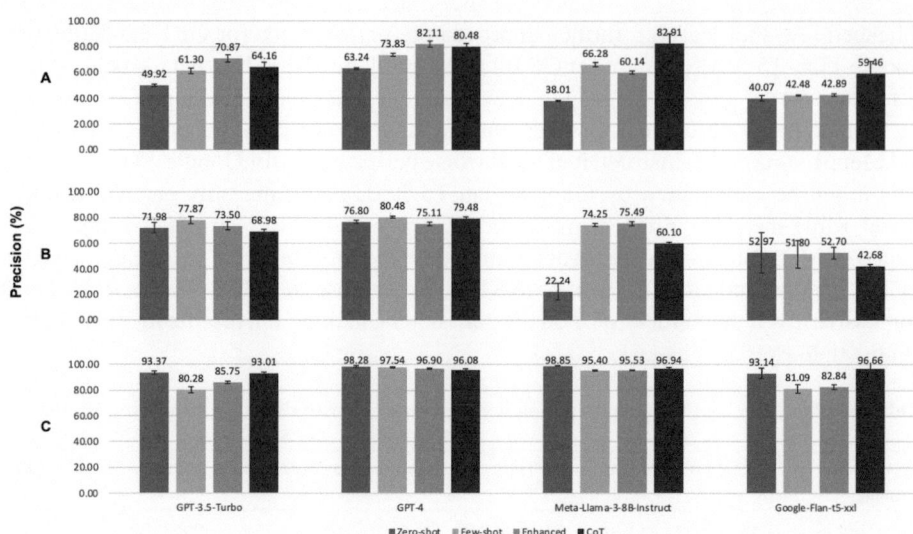

Fig. 5. Precision (%) of biomedical code mapping at each level with different prompting methodologies.

Given the need to weigh the three mapping levels differently, the overall accuracy of the LLMs should not be the only metrics for evaluating their mapping level assignment performance. To help gauge a better suited model for this module, we incorporated the precision of each mapping level prediction as another evaluation metrics and prioritized the models that can provide higher precision for levels A and C.

All tested combinations of LLMs and prompting methods achieved a relatively high precision (>80%) for level C prediction. Outstandingly, all combinations for GPT-4 and Meta-Llama-3-8B achieved > 95% precision. The chain-of-thought (CoT) prompting strategy - asking LLMs to perform reasoning before making level predictions – yielded the highest prediction precision from both open-source LLMs for mapping level A, with Meta-Llama-3-8B even surpassing GPT-4 with a score of nearly 83% (Fig. 6).

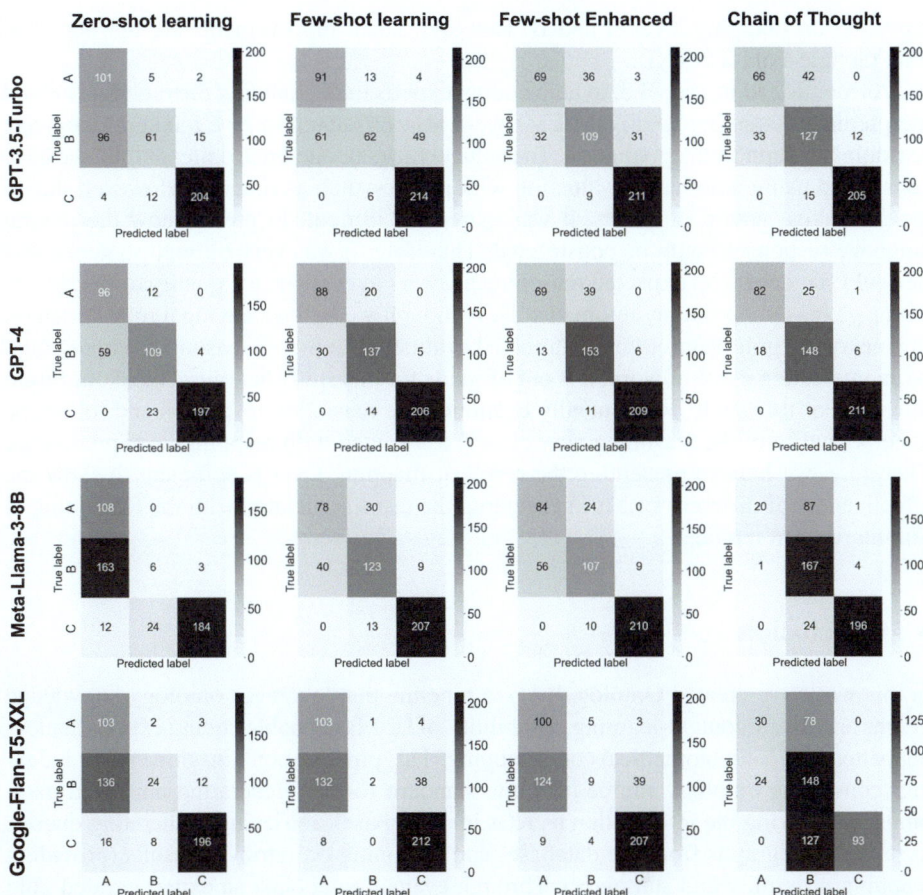

Fig. 6. Confusion matrix of biomedical code mapping level predictions using different prompting strategies (temperature = 0.2).

Distinguishing levels A and B appeared to be more challenging for the LLMs. This could be seen as the models view the two codes as closely related and consistent but still have difficulty determining if they are an exact match. We took a deeper look at the results from these models with a confusion matrix to help better understand the misclassification details (Fig. 6). From the matrix, we could see the impact from prompting engineering on predicting mapping level C is much less than the other two levels. We could also see that, with zero-shot approach, Meta-Llama-3-8B and Google-Flan-T5-XXL tend to predict mapping level A and C over mapping level B, meanwhile misclassify many mapping level B cases to mapping level A, while GPT-3.5-Turbo and GPT-4 have a better prediction balance amongst all three mapping levels. However, promisingly, few-shot, few-shot enhanced and CoT approaches all effectively helped Meta-Llama-3-8B "comprehend" the nuances in differentiating mapping level A and mapping level B, thus significantly improved its prediction precision for these two levels. These prompt engineering strategies also further enhanced GPT-3.5-Turbo and GPT-4's prediction precision on mapping level A and B. However, such improvements are not observed with Google-Flan-T5-XXL.

As mentioned in Sect. 3.3, to help coding experts understanding the rationale behind the predicted mapping level, all LLMs were also prompted to give a natural language reasoning to support the prediction. To evaluate the generated reasoning output, we have considered using automated evaluation with metrics such as rouge-L. However, due to the generative nature of LLMs, it was extremely difficult to predict how the natural language responses could be constructed. Therefore, it was very difficult to generate a fair gold standard with expected reasoning answers to evaluate the quality of the natural language reasoning output automatically. Although we believe having a robust method to construct a gold dataset with automated evaluation to assess reasoning output could be an interesting piece of work, it is out of scope for this study but might be of our future interest. For this study, we manually examined the reasoning responses and found the general quality of the reasoning very closely associated with mapping level prediction. Therefore, we believe presenting the result of mapping level is sufficient to show the effectiveness of different LLMs in executing the tasks associated with the Reasoning & Summarization module.

5 Conclusion

In this work, we created OntologyRAG, a pipeline that leverages ontology knowledge graphs and the in-context-learning capabilities of LLMs to enable coding experts achieving better and faster biomedical code mapping. This pipeline contains three parts: indexing (converting ontology source files into standard format, generating unrefined mappings, and storing the information as KGs in a database), retrieving (generating queries to retrieve subgraphs from the database) and reasoning on retrieved results (providing mapping proximity and summary). Through evaluation against an expert curated gold dataset, we show promises to significantly enhance the quality and efficiency of code mapping with OntologyRAG, by jointly exploiting the structured information encoded in ontology knowledge graphs and the language generation capabilities of LLMs.

The OntologyRAG pipeline is scalable and generalizable. The ready-to-use index module converts and stores most ontology source files and mapping files into knowledge graph database with a standardized process using CPU-only machines. These files can also be updated following the cadence of ontology source versions. LLMs can be hosted on a dedicated local machine with appropriate GPU power and be accessed via API calls by both *NL2SPARQL* and *Reasoning & Summarization* modules. In our experiments, when using one NVIDIA A100 GPU machine to host Meta-Llama-3-8B model, the end-to-end processing from the pipeline took one to three minutes, depending on the complexity of the task. The choice of LLMs in our pipeline is flexible. The gold datasets and evaluation methods we provided could help decide if upgrading LLMs was needed for during pipeline maintenance.

Our results show great promises in incorporating off-the-shelf LLMs such as Meta-Llama-3-8B and GPT-4 to enhance the accessibility and interpretability of complex information encoded in ontology knowledge graphs. By accepting natural language questions and providing output containing retrieved results and pre-analysed mapping levels and reasoning, the pipeline allows coding experts to concentrate their effort on the most ambiguous and complex mapping cases instead all cases, thereby enhancing the mapping efficiency and quality.

This research prototype demonstrates the promising integration of LLMs with KGs to assist code mapping refinement. The pipeline facilitates rapid and flexible adaptation of future LLMs with enhanced performance and ensures swift responsiveness in updating knowledge graphs to reflect ontology changes. Future research will focus on exploring how to extend and enhance the prototype into a production level application to facilitate fast and robust ontology mapping.

Acknowledgments. The study is funded by IQVIA. We extend our gratitude to all team members who have supported this project and contributed to the review of the manuscript.

Disclosure of Interests. The authors have no competing interests to declare that are relevant to the content of this article. All authors are employed by IQVIA. HF, JN have stock in IQVIA. JN has stock in Microsoft, AZ, Nvidia, Meta. ER was previously employed by Boehinger Ingelheim. JN was previously employed by AZ.

References

1. Kulmanov, M., Smaili, F.Z., Gao, X., Hoehndorf, R.: Machine learning with biomedical ontologies. bioRxiv, 2020.05.07.082164 (2020)
2. Alshahrani, M., Khan, M.A., Maddouri, O., Kinjo, A.R., Queralt-Rosinach, N., Hoehndorf, R.: Neuro-symbolic representation learning on biological knowledge graphs. Bioinformatics **33**(17), 2723–2730 (2017)
3. Hoyt, C.T., Hoyt, A.L., Gyori, B.M.: Prediction and curation of missing biomedical identifier mappings with Biomappings. Bioinformatics **39**(4), btad130 (2023)
4. Chang, D., Balažević, I., Allen, C., Chawla, D., Brandt, C., Taylor, R.A.: Benchmark and best practices for biomedical knowledge graph embeddings. In: Proceedings of the conference, Association for Computational Linguistics, vol. 2020, pp. 167–176. NIH Public Access (2020)
5. Alshahrani, M., Thafar, M.A., Essack, M.: Application and evaluation of knowledge graph embeddings in biomedical data. PeerJ. Comput. Sci. **7**, e341 (2021)
6. Wu, Y., Chen, Y., Yin, Z., Ding, W., King, I.: A survey on graph embedding techniques for biomedical data: Methods and applications. Inform. Fus. **100**, 101909 (2023). ISSN 1566-2535
7. Silva, M.C., Faria, D., Pesquita, C.: Matching multiple ontologies to build a knowledge graph for personalized medicine. In: Groth, P., et al. The Semantic Web. ESWC 2022. Lecture Notes in Computer Science, vol. 13261. Springer, Cham (2022). https://doi.org/10.1007/978-3-031-06981-9_27
8. Filice, R.W., Kahn, C.E.: Integrating an ontology of radiology differential diagnosis with ICD-10-CM, RadLex, and SNOMED CT. J. Digit. Imaging **32**, 206–210 (2019)
9. Isaradech, N., Khumrin, P.: Auto-mapping clinical documents to ICD-10 using SNOMED-CT. In: AMIA Joint Summits on Translational Science Proceedings, 2021, pp. 296–304 (2021)
10. He, Y., Chen, J., Antonyrajah, D., Horrocks, I.: BERTMap: a BERT-based ontology alignment system. In: Proceedings of the AAAI Conference on Artificial Intelligence, vol. 36, no. 5, pp. 5684–5691 (2022)
11. Dong, H., et al.: Automated clinical coding: what, why, and where we are?. NPJ Digit. Med. **5**, 159 (2022)

12. Philipp, P., Veloso, J., Appenzeller, A., Hartz, T., Beyerer, J.: Evaluation of an automated mapping from ICD-10 to SNOMED CT. In: 2022 International Conference on Computational Science and Computational Intelligence (CSCI), pp. 1604–1609. IEEE (2022)
13. Yuchen, X., et al.: Understanding the performance and estimating the cost of LLM fine-tuning. arXiv, 2408.04693 (2024)
14. Ferilli, S.: Integration strategy and tool between formal ontology and graph database technology. Electronics **10**(21), 2616 (2021)
15. Mihindukulasooriya, N., Tiwari, S., Enguix, C.F., Lata, K.: Text2KGBench: a benchmark for ontology-driven knowledge graph generation from text. In: Payne, T.R., et al. The Semantic Web – ISWC 2023. ISWC 2023. Lecture Notes in Computer Science, vol. 14266. Springer, Cham (2023). https://doi.org/10.1007/978-3-031-47243-5_14
16. Meyer, L.P., Frey, J., Brei, F., Arndt, N.: Assessing SPARQL capabilities of large language models. arXiv preprint, arXiv:2409.05925 (2024)
17. Rangel, J.C., de Farias, T.M., Sima, A.C., Kobayashi, N.: SPARQL generation: an analysis on fine-tuning OpenLLaMA for question answering over a life science knowledge graph. arXiv preprint, arXiv:2402.04627 (2024)
18. Zahera, H.M., Ali, M., Sherif, M.A., Moussallem, D., Ngomo, A.C.N.: Generating SPARQL from natural language using chain-of-thoughts prompting. SEMANTiCS, Amsterdam, Netherlands (2024)
19. Yujuan, D., et al.: A Survey on RAG Meets LLMs: Towards Retrieval-Augmented Large Language Models. arXiv, 2405.06211 (2024)
20. Yunfan, G., et al.: Retrieval-Augmented Generation for Large Language Models: A Survey. arXiv, 2312.10997 (2024)
21. Azure OpenAI Service. https://learn.microsoft.com/en-us/azure/ai-services/openai/. Accessed 27 Sept 2024
22. Meta AI. https://ai.meta.com/blog/meta-llama-3/. Accessed 27 Sept 2024
23. Chung, H.W., et al.: Scaling instruction-finetuned language models. J. Mach. Learn. Res. **25**(70), 1–53 (2024)
24. Garber, M., et al: Evaluation of large language model performance on the biomedical language understanding and reasoning benchmark: comparative study. medRxiv preprint, medRxiv: 2024.05.17.24307411 (2024)
25. https://www.cms.gov/medicare/coding-billing/icd-10-codes/icd-9-cm-diagnosis-procedure-codes-abbreviated-and-full-code-titles
26. https://www.cdc.gov/nchs/icd/icd-10-cm/files.html
27. https://www.cms.gov/medicare/coding-billing/icd-10-codes/icd-10-cm-icd-10-pcs-gem-archive
28. W3C RDF - Semantic Web Standards. https://www.w3.org/RDF/. Accessed 09 Oct 2024
29. https://github.com/oxigraph/oxigraph
30. https://rocksdb.org/
31. W3C SPARQL 1.1 Overview. https://www.w3.org/TR/sparql11-overview/. Accessed 09 Oct 2024

I Know About "Up"! Enhancing Spatial Reasoning in Visual Language Models Through 3D Knowledge Reconstruction

Hao Zhou[1], Zaiqiao Meng[2(✉)], and Yifang Chen[1]

[1] Guangdong Polytechnic Normal University, Guangzhou, China
zhouhao28@stu.gpnu.edu.cn, chenyf@gpnu.edu.cn
[2] University of Glasgow, Glasgow, UK
zaiqiao.meng@glasgow.ac.uk

Abstract. Visual Language Models (VLMs) are essential for various tasks, particularly the visual reasoning tasks, due to their robust multi-modal information integration, visual reasoning capabilities, and contextual awareness. However, existing VLMs' visual spatial reasoning capabilities are often inadequate, struggling even with basic tasks such as distinguishing left from right. To address this, we propose the ZeroVLM (Code: https://github.com/zhouhao028/Iknow_up) model, designed to enhance the visual spatial reasoning abilities of VLMs. ZeroVLM employs Zero-1-to-3, a 3D knowledge reconstruction model for obtaining different views of the input images and incorporates a view prompt to further improve visual spatial reasoning. Experimental results on four visual spatial reasoning datasets show that our ZeroVLM achieves up to 19.48% accuracy improvement, which indicates the effectiveness of 3D knowledge reconstruction and view prompt of our ZeroVLM.

Keywords: Visual Spatial Reasoning · 3D Reconstruction · Visual Language Models

Visual Language Models (VLMs), such as LLaVA [30], MiniGPT-4 [60] and InternGPT [33], are a class of deep neural models adept at simultaneously processing and understanding both visual and linguistic information. These VLMs often consist of an image encoder, an embedding projector to align image and text representations and a text decoder to process the projected image embedding and text representations, enabling joint understanding and reasoning between these modalities [21]. By using the language generation power of underlining text decoders, these VLMs showcase remarkable interaction capabilities in various applications, such as referring expression comprehension [23,52], visual question answering [11,16,54], visual language reasoning [27], and entailment [26,48].

However, many visual language tasks, such as visual question answering (VQA) [9,14,34,41,59] and image segmentation [15], require the ability to recognise spatial information from images. For instance, in visual question answer-

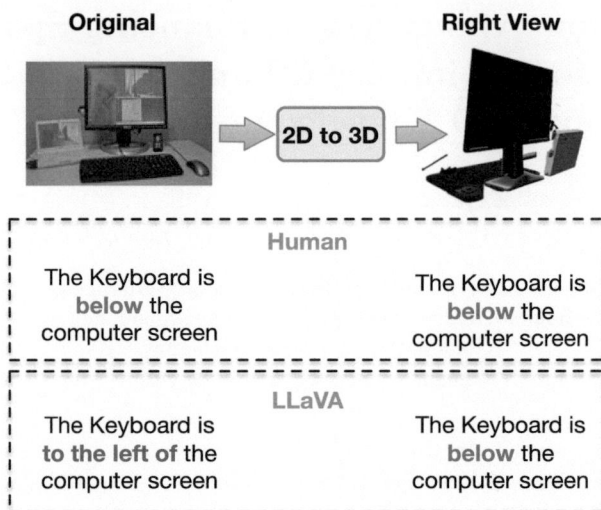

Fig. 1. An example of the VQA task, where humans can easily recognise positions under different views, but the vanilla LLaVA [30] can only predict correctly from certain views. By performing 3D knowledge reconstruction to obtain different views of the image, we can improve LLaVA's predictive accuracy.

ing, a system must understand the spatial relationships between objects to correctly answer questions about an image [9,14]. Visual spatial reasoning in VLMs requires multi-modal understanding [18], cross-modal mapping [46], inference of visual spatial relations [28], and integration of context comprehension [58]. This is because VLMs must comprehend intricate spatial relationships within images, which are hierarchical and multifaceted, involving various relationships among multiple objects (such as containment, proximity, overlap, etc.) [5]. Enhancing visual spatial reasoning capabilities of models can significantly elevate their performance in image comprehension and processing [49].

Presently, numerous studies explore various benchmarks and methods to enhance the visual spatial reasoning capabilities of VLMs to improve their performance, exemplified by visual spatial reasoning [28], Whatsup_vlm [17] and SpatialVLM [5]. These endeavors employ diverse methodologies [19,37,42] to augment the visual spatial reasoning abilities of models. However, despite these efforts yielding improvements in model performance to some extent, substantial challenges persist in comprehending complex scenes and intricate spatial relationships. Existing methodologies predominantly rely on 2D information, impeding the comprehensive capture of 3D spatial relationships among objects (i.e. the 3D knowledge). For example, Fig. 1 illustrates an example of the VQA task. While humans could easily recognise positions under different views of the objects, LLaVA can only predict correctly from certain views due to the lack of image views during their pretraining.

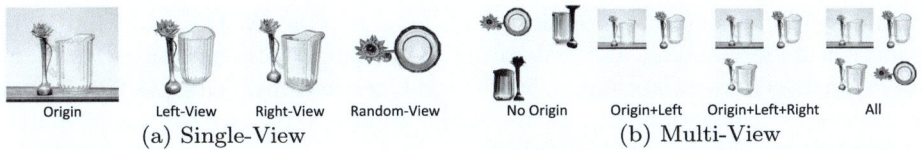

Fig. 2. Single-view images were generated using Zero-1-to-3 to produce left-view, right-view, and random-view images. Multi-view images were created by combining these different single-view images in various configurations.

To tackle this challenge, we propose a novel model, called ZeroVLM, to solve the visual spatial reasoning task through the 3D reconstruction technique, entailing the reconstruction of images in 3D and capturing them from various views. In particular, our ZeroVLM utilise the Zero-1-to-3 [31] model for constructing 3D views from a single 2D image within our tested datasets. This allows VLMs to access richer spatial information through 3D transformation, thereby enhancing their visual spatial reasoning capabilities. We conducted comprehensive experiments across four visual spatial reasoning datasets, and the results show that all the tested VLMs have notably improved spatial reasoning capabilities through our ZeroVLM.

Our contributions are summarized as follows:

- We proposed the ZeroVLM model, a new model for visual spatial reasoning tasks, which can generate images of different views based on the original image to enhance spatial reasoning ability.
- Our ZeroVLM utilises a 3D knowledge reconstruction model to obtain different views from the input image, which enhances spatial relationships at the image level to improve the visual spatial reasoning capabilities of VLMs.
- We validate the effectiveness of our ZeroVLM through visual spatial reasoning experiments conducted on four different datasets.

1 Related Work

Vision Language Models (VLMs). VLMs amalgamate computer vision and natural language processing technologies to comprehend and generate correlations between images and natural language [10,55]. VLMs can accept image input to generate a corresponding response in text [35]. In terms of training architecture, recent works include joint pretraining architectures (e.g. OFA [47] and VLMo [2]), which train image and text data jointly, and image-to-text mapping architectures (e.g., PaLI [7]), which map an image encoder to a well-pretrained text encoder. The latter approach has gained more popularity. VLMs exhibit cross-modal understanding capabilities, enabling them to extract information from images and translate it into natural language, or retrieve information from natural language and generate corresponding images [6]. This wide range of capabilities broadens the potential of VLMs (e.g., GlaMM [40] and MiniGPT-4 [60]) in understanding and generating associations between images and language, such as Image Captioning [56], Visual Question Answering [24,50,57], and Multi-modal Translation [22]. In this study, we aim to explore the visual-spatial recognition capabilities of these VLMs.

Visual Spatial Reasoning. Visual spatial reasoning refers to the cognitive ability to understand and manipulate the spatial relationships of objects or elements in a given environment [20,28]. This reasoning ability involves not only recognizing the properties of individual entities, but also understanding the complex relationships and structures between them. Recent works have aimed to benchmark the problem of visual spatial reasoning, notably VSR [28] and Whatsup_vlm [17]. VSR [28] evaluates the ability of VLMs using text-image pairs to describe various visual spatial relationships, while Whatsup_vlm [17] assesses the visual spatial reasoning of VLMs through specific prepositions and perspectives. Although these methods provide valuable insights into the visual spatial reasoning capabilities of VLMs, they remain somewhat limited. In our work, we employ 3D reconstruction to more comprehensively test the visual spatial reasoning ability of VLMs.

3D Knowledge Reconstruction. Visual spatial reasoning encompasses the cognitive ability to comprehend and manipulate visual spatial information, while 3D knowledge involves generating a three-dimensional representation of an object or scene from two-dimensional images or other sensor data. For instance, MonoScene [4] infers dense geometric structures and semantic information of a scene from a single monocular RGB image, offering an efficient and innovative approach to complete 3D semantic scenes. VoxFormer [25] proposes a transformer-based [45] semantic scene completion framework, addressing camera-based 3D semantic scene completion by introducing sparse voxel queries [12] and masked autoencoder design [13]. Zero-1-to-3 [31] is a 3D knowledge model that excels in zero-shot generalization on out-of-distribution datasets and unprocessed images by using a single image as input without requiring additional 3D or depth information. We chose this model for its simplicity and effectiveness compared to MonoScene [4] and VoxFormer [25].

2 Preliminaries

In this section, we will formally define the task of visual spatial reasoning and introduce the Zero-1-to-3 model [31], which is one of the components utilised by our model.

2.1 Visual Spatial Reasoning Task

Visual spatial reasoning is critically important in the fields of computer vision, artificial intelligence, and machine learning [32,39,53]. The visual spatial reasoning task involves inferring and understanding objects, scenes, or spatial relationships, addressing location, orientation, and spatial arrangement for accurate

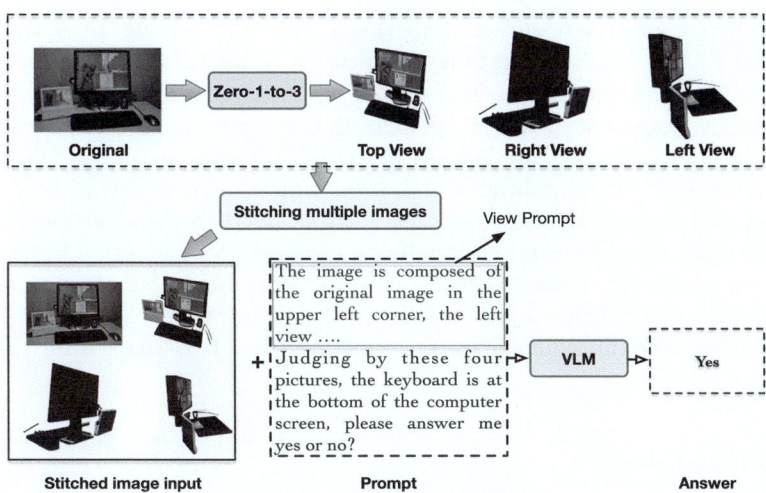

Fig. 3. An overview of our proposed ZeroVLM model. Our ZeroVLM first uses Zero-1-to-3 to perform 3D reconstruction to obtain different views of the input image, and then it stitches the original images with these different views to obtain the stitched image, which is the input of a VLM for answer prediction.

object localization and recognition. This task is normally formulated as a visual question answering task [17,26] by asking and answering questions about objects on images and through context in text. Formally, we denote an image and its associated question as i and q, respectively. The questions in this task typically ask to identify the relationships among multiple objects or to locate specified objects within the image. Figure 1 shows an example of this task. The goal of this task is to answer this question by accurately comprehending the visual spatial relations and discerning the visual spatial position of target objects relative to others.

2.2 Zero-1-to-3

Zero-1-to-3 [31] is a model designed for visual reconstruction tasks. It works by identifying objects in the input image i and adjusting the camera perspective of these objects. Given an image $i \in \mathbb{R}^{H \times W \times 3}$ and a relative camera rotation matrix $R \in \mathbb{R}^{3 \times 3}$ and a translation vector $T \in \mathbb{R}^3$, Zero-1-to-3 leans a model f such that its output is a new perspective image under the specified camera transformation:

$$\hat{i}_{R,T} = f(i, R, T) \tag{1}$$

where $\hat{i}_{R,T}$ represents the generated new perspective image. When we input the original image i and hope to generate a 3D reconstructed view from the left at an angle of 45° through Zero-1-to-3, we can achieve this effect by setting R

to the rotation matrix of 45° around the Y axis and setting T to the vector translated to the left by a certain distance. In order to synthesise new views under such partial constraints, Zero-1-to-3 uses a large-scale diffusion model to integrate the geometric prior knowledge of the input image. The conditional diffusion model embedded in Zero-1-to-3 [36,51] learns to control the relative camera viewpoint using synthetic datasets, which helps generate new images with specified camera transformations, such as fixed camera viewpoints (such as left or right view) or randomly generated camera viewpoints. Despite being trained on synthetic datasets, Zero-1-to-3 still demonstrates strong zero-shot generalization capabilities to out-of-distribution datasets and real-world images. Figure 2 shows the different views generated by Zero-1-to-3 based on the input image.

3 Methodologies

3.1 Overview of ZeroVLM

To address the visual spatial reasoning task, we propose ZeroVLM, a model that leverages Zero-1-to-3 to infer various views of input images and employs a VLM to generate answers using the combined multiview images and our specially designed *view prompts*. The overview of our model is illustrated in Fig. 3. In particular, ZeroVLM is a novel visual-language model that combines large language models (such as LLaMA [44]) with high-level vision models, aiming to enhance visual-spatial reasoning capabilities by leveraging 3D reconstruction techniques. Given an image i, ZeroVLM uses Zero-1-to-3 to infer its various views $\hat{i}_{R,T}$ and performs image stitching from multiple views, thereby providing richer spatial information. The 3D knowledge feature provided by Zero-1-to-3 can enable ZeroVLM to better understand and infer spatial relationships by viewing objects from different angles. At the same time, a specialised *view prompt* is designed into ZeroVLM to further enhance its visual spatial reasoning capabilities. This prompt helps guide the model in focusing on relevant spatial views and improving its accuracy in interpretation. The architecture of our ZeroVLM is shown in Fig. 3, with a detailed description of its components described in the following subsections.

3.2 Data Augmentation by 3D Knowledge Reconstruction

In our work, we use Zero-1-to-3 for 3D Knowledge reconstruction on the dataset to generate $\hat{i}_{R,T}$ from different viewpoints, e.g. the left, right and random views. Our investigation not only explores whether the creation of single-view images can enhance the visual spatial reasoning capabilities of VLMs but also examines whether multi-view images can help this improvement, where multi-view images are synthesised from different $\hat{i}_{R,T}$. Because multi-view images can provide richer spatial information, the model can get the opportunity to observe the same scene from different angles, thereby capturing a more comprehensive spatial layout and the relationship between objects, and different views can provide redundant information, so that the model can still make accurate judgments when facing noise or partial information loss. Therefore, in our work, after inferring different views of the input images, we further construct multi-view images from these single views by stitching them and testing their effectiveness against the single-view images. Figure 2 shows an example of the multi-view image constructed by stitching multiple single-view images generated through Zero-1-to-3.

By synthesizing these various single-view and multi-view images, we aim to conduct comprehensive controllable experiments to determine their effectiveness in improving the spatial reasoning abilities of VLMs.

3.3 View Prompt

In our work, we first test whether the 3D reconstruction of images can improve the accuracy of VLM's visual spatial ability at the image level. To further explore whether the context prompt can enhance VLM's visual spatial reasoning ability, we introduced a special prompt called *view prompt* in the experiment. This view prompt varies depending on the input image and its views. Figure 4 shows two view prompt examples over a single view and multiple views of the input.

We designed a variety of view prompts based on the content of different view images to guide VLM to better understand and reason about the view spatial relationship between the target object and other objects in the image. We first used Zero-1-to-3 [31] to perform 3D reconstruction of VSR [28] dataset and What'sUp [17] dataset from different viewpoints. Then during the inference of VLM, we use a prompt consisting of the question, the view prompt, and the stitched view image, to generate the answer. Figure 5 provides detailed examples of the process.

---

view prompt for single-view images:
This is a 3D single-view image generated from the left view of original image. Centered on the computer. {question}

---

view prompt for multi-view images:
The original image in the upper left corner, the left view image in the upper right corner, the right view image in the lower left corner, and the random view image in the lower right corner. Based on these four images. {question}

Fig. 4. These view prompts are manually constructed by us. View prompt comparison between single-view images and multi-view images. {question} is the corresponding question in the prompt.

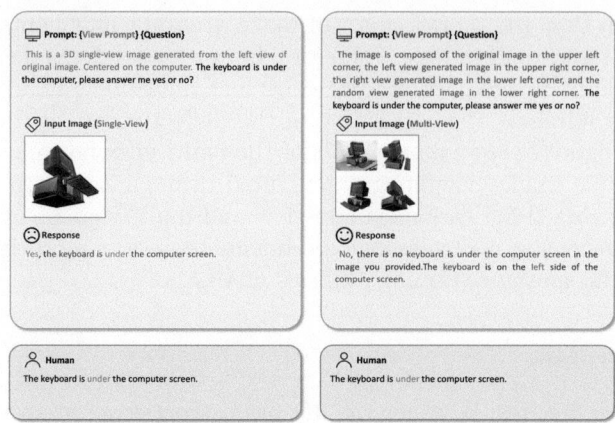

Fig. 5. For both single-view and multi-view datasets, we employed a view prompt. The aim was to explore whether perspective language models could enhance their visual spatial reasoning abilities through improvements at the textual level.

4 Experiments

4.1 Experimental Setup

Datasets. We selected two datasets for investigation: the **Visual Spatial Reasoning (VSR)** [28] dataset and the **What'sUp** [17] dataset. The statistics of the two datasets are summarized in Table 1. The VSR dataset focuses on a wide range of spatial relations and linguistic phenomena, emphasizing various visual spatial relations and describing these relations. The What'sUp dataset focuses on household items and uses different prepositions to describe spatial relations. Both datasets cover a variety of visual spatial relations (such as "below", "in front of", "beside", etc.).

Table 1. The number of images in various datasets.

DataSet	Train	Development	Test	Total
VSR (Random Split)	7680	1097	2195	10972
VSR (Zero shot)	4713	231	616	5560
What'sUp (SubSet-A)	200	110	111	421
What'sUp (SubSet-B)	200	108	100	408

Baselines. In our research, we employ LLaVA and MiniGPT-4 as the primary VLMs. The LLaVA version we use is LLaVA-v1.5-13B and the MiniGpt-4 version is MiniGPT-4 (Vicuna 13B). LLaVA utilises multi-modal language-image instruction data for instruction adjustment, employing CLIP-ViT-L-336px [29] as the visual encoder and MLP projection as the visual language cross-modal connector, achieving comprehensive understanding of both visual and language inputs. The architecture of MiniGPT-4 involves aligning a frozen visual encoder with a frozen high-level language model, e.g. Vicuna [8], through projection layers, ensuring correct alignment of visual features with the high-level large language model. MiniGPT-4 can exhibit advanced multi-modal capabilities similar to those of GPT-4 [1].

Backbones. We use LLaVA and MiniGPT-4 as the backbone VLMs of our ZeroVLM in all the experiments. In particular, we denote ZeroVLM (L) as our model based on the LLaVA [30] model, which can process image inputs and improve efficiency and performance through joint learning of image and text instructions, while ZeroVLM (M) as our model based on the MiniGPT-4 [60]) model, which combines the powerful generation ability of language models with visual information capabilities.

Task Setting. We classify visual spatial relationship questions for VLMs into two types using our dataset split, which is applied consistently across all four datasets. The first type disrupts the visual spatial relationship between the target object and another object (for example, the correct image description is "The apple is to the left of the banana", while our description is "The apple is above (below, to the right of, in front of, etc.) the banana"). The second type describes visual spatial relationships involving objects not present in the image but related to the target object (for example, the correct image description is "The apple is to the left of the banana, " but our description is "The watermelon (an object that does not exist besides the apple) is above the banana"). These classifications are employed to evaluate the visual spatial reasoning abilities of VLMs and highlight the differences between our dataset and the original datasets.

Evaluation Metric. For evaluation, we judge the accuracy of the visual spatial reasoning ability of ZeroVLM (L) and ZeroVLM (M) based on the answers answered by ZeroVLM (L) and ZeroVLM (M). The accuracy of ZeroVLM (L) and ZeroVLM (M) responses determines their accuracy in identifying these relations. Since both datasets involve binary classification tasks, we use accuracy as the evaluation metric.

Implementation Details. We obtain new datasets through 3D reconstruction, consisting of single-view and multi-view datasets. In the single-view dataset, "Origin" refers to the original, unprocessed data, "Left" refers to the data processed by 3D reconstruction from the left viewpoint, and "Right" refers to the data processed by 3D reconstruction from the right viewpoint. "Random" refers to the data processed from a random viewpoint. In the multi-view dataset, there are two types of "Multi-view": multi-view without original images and multi-view with original images. Multi-view without original images is composed of single-view images, while multi-view with original images is composed of original images plus different single-view images. Our goal is to explore whether the visual spatial reasoning ability of VLMs increases or decreases with the addition or omission of original images.

Table 2. Accuracy performance of the compared models. Missing values indicate that ZeroVLM (L) and ZeroVLM (M) were not tested on the visual spatial reasoning on the VSR and What'sUp datasets. Bests are in **bold**, and second bests are underlined.

Model	VSR (Random Split)	VSR (Zero Shot)	What'sUp (A)	What'sUp (B)
Human	**95.40**	**95.40**	**100**	**100**
CLIP (frozen)	56.00	54.50	58.00	57.50
CLIP (FT)	65.10	63.30	61.20	59.80
VisualBERT	55.20	51.00	53.40	55.60
ViLT	69.30	63.00	60.20	63.60
LXMERT	70.10	61.20	58.30	54.70
ZeroVLM (M)	53.80	52.43	55.76	53.84
ZeroVLM (L)	70.29	70.94	71.74	80.76

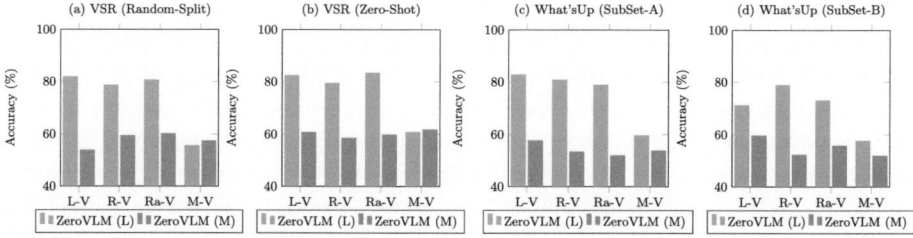

Fig. 6. L-V represents the left-view images, R-V represents the right-view images, Ra-V represents the random-view images, and M-V represents the multi-view images (excluding the original image). Note that here we use ZeroVLM (L) and ZeroVLM (M) for fair comparison.

4.2 Experimental Result

Overall Performance. Our experimental aims to comprehensively evaluate the visual spatial reasoning capabilities of VLMs ZeroVLM (L) and ZeroVLM (M) on various datasets. We seek to understand how different view datasets (including original, single-view, and multi-view datasets) affect the performance of these models in visual-spatial reasoning tasks. We first test ZeroVLM (L) and ZeroVLM (M) on the original VSR dataset (without 3D reconstruction) and we reproduced LXMERT [43], VisualBERT [23], and CLIP [38] using the same parameters as in VSR [28], and also tested them on the original VSR dataset (without 3D reconstruction). The result of this comparison is reported in Table 2. Our experimental results show a baseline comparison of ZeroVLM (L) and ZeroVLM (M) testing the original dataset with VSR [28], highlighting the basic performance of ZeroVLM (L) and ZeroVLM (M).

Additionally, we tested single-view 3D reconstructions from the VSR and What'sUp datasets, and multi-view datasets derived from these single views. We also assessed their visual spatial reasoning accuracy on single-view and multi-view datasets using different view prompts for ZeroVLM.

Single View vs Multiple View. In this experiment, we investigated the impact of single-view versus multi-view 3D reconstruction on the visual spatial reasoning capabilities of VLMs. We assessed two VLMs: ZeroVLM (L) and ZeroVLM (M), using both single-view and multi-view datasets. The results, shown in Fig. 6, reveal that ZeroVLM excels in single-view conditions with an average accuracy of 79.28%, but its performance drops to 58.42% in multi-view conditions. ZeroVLM (M) performs less well overall, with average accuracy of 56.95% for single-view and 56.23% for multi-view. Overall, ZeroVLM (L) outperforms ZeroVLM (M) in visual spatial reasoning tasks, particularly in single-view scenarios. While ZeroVLM (M) possesses unique advantages in handling multi-modalities, there is still room for improvement in specific visual spatial reasoning tasks [3]. The reason that multi-view models failed might be due to the fact that there are too many elements in the multi-view image dataset and the model cannot distinguish them correctly.

Table 3. Performance comparison of ZeroVLM (L) under different view combinations. L-V represents the left-view images, R-V represents the right-view images, Ra-V represents the random-view images, and M-V represents the multi-view images (excl. the original image). Bests are in **bold**, and second bests are underlined.

View Type	View	View Prompt	VSR (Random Split)	VSR (Zero Shot)	What'sUp (A)	What'sUp (B)
Single-View	Origin	✗	70.29	70.94	71.14	<u>80.76</u>
	L-V	✗	81.80	82.35	82.69	71.15
	R-V	✗	78.60	79.41	80.76	78.84
	Ra-V	✗	80.60	83.33	78.84	73.07
	L-V	✓	**89.20**	88.63	<u>88.62</u>	76.32
	R-V	✓	87.60	<u>89.41</u>	**90.38**	**84.21**
	Ra-V	✓	<u>88.40</u>	**90.09**	87.42	79.56
Multi-View	M-V	✗	55.60	60.78	59.61	57.69
	Origin + L-V	✓	64.60	50.98	63.46	65.23
	Origin + L-V + R-V	✓	67.40	61.76	69.23	68.38
	Origin + M-V	✓	72.20	59.80	65.38	63.21

Effect on Different View Prompts. In this experiment, we aim to explore the potential enhancement of visual spatial reasoning abilities in VLMs by employing different view prompts. We sought to investigate if leveraging contextual connections through textual cues could significantly improve the performance of VLMs in understanding and reasoning about visual spatial relationships. To achieve this, we applied various view prompts with ZeroVLM and assessed its visual spatial reasoning abilities across both single-view and multi-view datasets. These view prompts were designed to provide contextual cues that could aid the model in interpreting visual spatial information more effectively. The results of this comprehensive assessment are presented in Table 3. The experiment demonstrated that the use of different prompts can indeed enhance the visual spatial reasoning capabilities of VLMs. Overall, our study concludes that employing a view prompt can enhance the visual spatial reasoning abilities of VLMs.

Case Study. Our study aims to investigate the impact of 3D reconstruction on the visual spatial reasoning capabilities of VLM. We assess whether 3D reconstruction (Zero-1-to-3) enhances these capabilities from the original dataset to the single-view dataset and compare the performance of ZeroVLM (L) and ZeroVLM (M) using single-view images after 3D reconstruction. The comparative analysis focuses on the visual spatial reasoning capabilities of ZeroVLM on both datasets. Figure 7 illustrates the enhancement by ZeroVLM using the single-view dataset. Figure 8 presents the performance comparison between ZeroVLM (L) and ZeroVLM (M). Results show that ZeroVLM (L) has improved visual spatial reasoning with the single-view dataset after 3D reconstruction and outperforms ZeroVLM (M). This suggests that 3D reconstruction provides useful spatial information aiding visual reasoning.

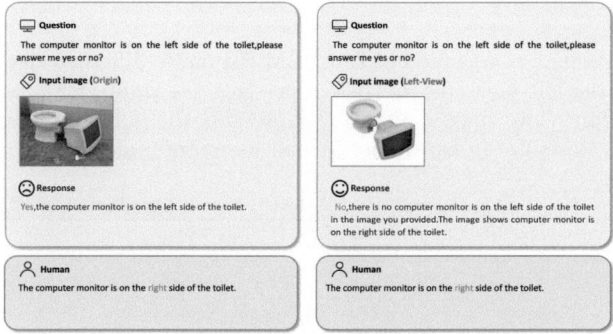

Fig. 7. Different results were obtained by ZeroVLM when evaluating datasets with and without 3D reconstruction. View prompts are omitted to save space.

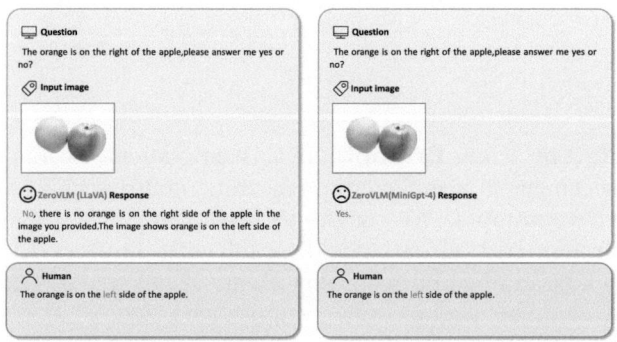

Fig. 8. Different results were obtained when inputting the 3D reconstructed datasets into ZeroVLM (L) and ZeroVLM (M). View prompts are omitted to save space.

5 Conclusion

This work studies the task of visual spatial reasoning and presents a simple and novel model, called ZeroVLM, for enhancing the visual spatial reasoning capability of VLMs through 3D reconstruction. In particular, ZeroVLM uses the Zero-1-to-3 model to generate different views over different angles of the input image, and uses VLMs to generate spatial reasoning answers with the stitched view image and a specially designed view prompt. We validate the effectiveness of our VLMs by comparative experiments from various views, including single-view and multiple-view images, and evaluated the performance of LLaVA and MiniGPT-4 under our ZeroVLM. The experimental results suggest that 3D reconstruction with a view prompt from a single perspective can effectively enhance the model's visual spatial reasoning ability. Future research could also develop models that dynamically adjust view prompts based on task requirements and integrate additional modal information, such as video and audio, to enhance multi-modal processing capability.

6 Limitations

Although ZeroVLM demonstrates significant performance improvements, we still identify the following limitations of our work: (1) Data dependency: ZeroVLM used specific visual spatial reasoning datasets in our experiments. Although these datasets cover a variety of scenarios, they may not fully represent all the complex spatial relationships in the real world; (2) Diversity of datasets: Although we used multiple datasets for testing, these datasets may not fully cover all possible application scenarios. Therefore, the model may need further training and adjustment to ensure its generality and robustness when processing different types of images and tasks; (3) The generalization ability of the model: Although the Zero-1-to-3 model performs well in zero-shot generalization, in some extreme cases, the model may still not accurately capture the spatial relationship. Therefore, considering other methods for the 3D reconstruction module is one of our future work directions.

7 Potential Risks

The development and deployment of VLMs for visual spatial reasoning present several potential risks. One significant risk is the dependency on specific datasets for training, which may not encompass the full diversity of spatial relationships encountered in real-world scenarios. This can lead to models that perform well in controlled environments but fail to generalise effectively. Additionally, the computational resources required for 3D reconstruction and multi-view generation are substantial, posing scalability and real-time application challenges. Another concern is the potential for bias in the datasets, which can result in models that unfairly represent or perform poorly on underrepresented spatial arrangements or object types. Furthermore, privacy and security issues arise when handling large amounts of visual data, necessitating strict adherence to data protection guidelines. Lastly, there are ethical considerations regarding the misuse of enhanced spatial reasoning capabilities for surveillance or other invasive applications, underscoring the need for transparency and accountability in the deployment of these technologies. Addressing these risks is essential to ensure the effective and responsible use of VLMs in visual spatial reasoning.

Appendix

This section contains additional results. Figure 9 illustrates the differences between LLaVA and ZeroVLM (L). In our study, we prepare the required questions in JSON file format and modify ZeroVLM (L) to recognise and accept JSON file inputs. We enable ZeroVLM (L) to identify the corresponding questions by matching the input image names with the image names in the JSON file. Figure 10 illustrates the single-view and multi-view datasets obtained after 3D reconstruction of the VSR dataset and the What'sUp dataset.

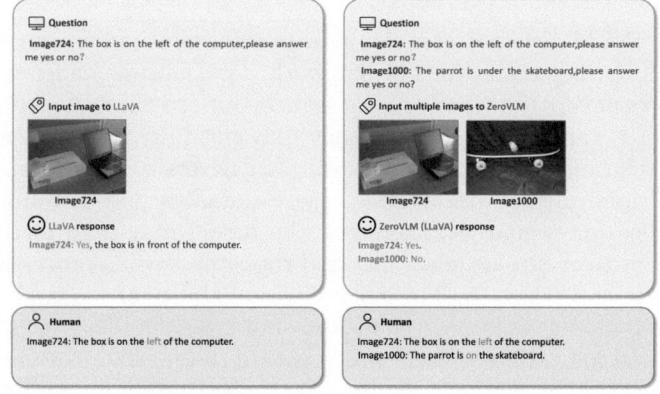

Fig. 9. The primary difference between LLaVA and ZeroVLM (L) lies in their input handling. LLaVA processes a single image as input, whereas ZeroVLM (L) is designed to handle multiple images. Due to the limited expressive capacity of individual images, we restrict the input for ZeroVLM (L) to two images.

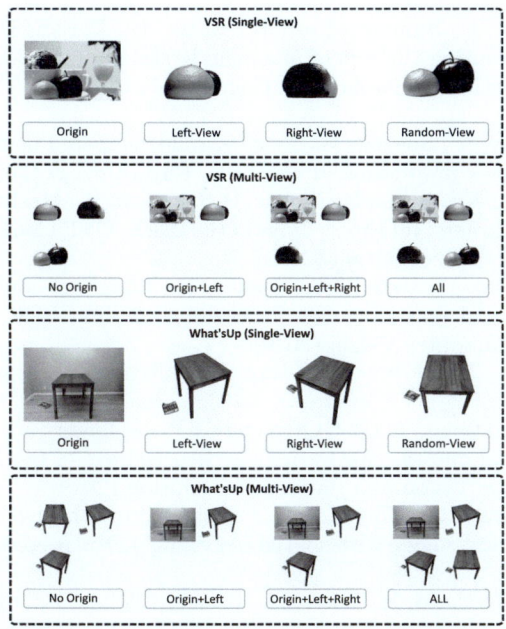

Fig. 10. The 3D reconstructed single-view and multi-view versions of each dataset are presented.

References

1. Achiam, J., et al.: GPT-4 technical report. arXiv preprint arXiv:2303.08774 (2023)
2. Bao, H., et al.: VLMO: unified vision-language pre-training with mixture-of-modality-experts. arXiv preprint arXiv:2111.02358 (2021)
3. Battaglia, P.W., et al.: Relational inductive biases, deep learning, and graph networks. arXiv (2018)
4. Cao, A.Q., De Charette, R.: Monoscene: monocular 3D semantic scene completion. In: Proceedings of the IEEE/CVF Conference on Computer Vision and Pattern Recognition (2022)
5. Chen, B., et al.: Spatialvlm: endowing vision-language models with spatial reasoning capabilities. In: Proceedings of the IEEE/CVF Conference on Computer Vision and Pattern Recognition (2024)
6. Chen, F., Chen, X., Xu, S., Xu, B.: Improving cross-modal understanding in visual dialog via contrastive learning. In: 2022 IEEE International Conference on Acoustics, Speech and Signal Processing (ICASSP), ICASSP 2022 (2022)
7. Chen, X., et al.: Pali: a jointly-scaled multilingual language-image model. arXiv preprint arXiv:2209.06794 (2022)
8. Chiang, W.L., et al.: Vicuna: an open-source chatbot impressing GPT-4 with 90%* chatgpt quality (2023)
9. Dai, B., Fidler, S., Lin, D.: A neural compositional paradigm for image captioning. In: Advances in Neural Information Processing Systems (2018)
10. Dosovitskiy, A., et al.: An image is worth 16 × 16 words: transformers for image recognition at scale. arXiv preprint arXiv:2010.11929 (2020)

11. Goyal, Y., Khot, T., Summers-Stay, D., Batra, D., Parikh, D.: Making the V in VQA matter: elevating the role of image understanding in visual question answering. In: 2017 IEEE Conference on Computer Vision and Pattern Recognition (CVPR) (2017)
12. Guchait, M., Roy, A., Sharma, S.: Probing mild-tempered neutralino dark matter through top-squark production at the LHC. Phys. Rev. D (2021)
13. He, K., Chen, X., Xie, S., Li, Y., Dollár, P., Girshick, R.: Masked autoencoders are scalable vision learners. In: Proceedings of the IEEE/CVF Conference on Computer Vision and Pattern Recognition (2022)
14. Hu, R., Rohrbach, A., Darrell, T., Saenko, K.: Language-conditioned graph networks for relational reasoning. In: Proceedings of the IEEE/CVF International Conference on Computer Vision (2019)
15. Huang, Y., et al.: Interformer: real-time interactive image segmentation. In: Proceedings of the IEEE/CVF International Conference on Computer Vision (2023)
16. Hudson, D.A., Manning, C.D.: GQA: a new dataset for real-world visual reasoning and compositional question answering. In: Proceedings of the IEEE/CVF Conference on Computer Vision and Pattern Recognition (2019)
17. Kamath, A., Hessel, J., Chang, K.W.: What's up with vision-language models? Investigating their struggle with spatial reasoning. arXiv preprint arXiv:2310.19785 (2023)
18. Khattak, M.U., Rasheed, H., Maaz, M., Khan, S., Khan, F.S.: Maple: multi-modal prompt learning. In: Proceedings of the IEEE/CVF Conference on Computer Vision and Pattern Recognition (CVPR) (2023)
19. Kiela, D., Bhooshan, S., Firooz, H., Perez, E., Testuggine, D.: Supervised multimodal bitransformers for classifying images and text. arXiv preprint arXiv:1909.02950 (2019)
20. Kosoy, E., et al.: Decoupling the components of geometric understanding in vision language models. arXiv preprint arXiv:2503.03840 (2025)
21. Li, F., et al.: Vision-language intelligence: tasks, representation learning, and large models. arXiv preprint arXiv:2203.01922 (2022)
22. Li, G., Duan, N., Fang, Y., Jiang, D., Zhou, M.: Unicoder-VL: a universal encoder for vision and language by cross-modal pre-training. arXiv (2019)
23. Li, L.H., Yatskar, M., Yin, D., Hsieh, C.J., Chang, K.W.: Visualbert: a simple and performant baseline for vision and language. arXiv preprint arXiv:1908.03557 (2019)
24. Li, X., et al.: Vision-language models in medical image analysis: from simple fusion to general large models. Inf. Fusion 102995 (2025)
25. Li, Y., et al.: Voxformer: sparse voxel transformer for camera-based 3d semantic scene completion. In: Proceedings of the IEEE/CVF Conference on Computer Vision and Pattern Recognition (2023)
26. Liu, F., Bugliarello, E., Ponti, E.M., Reddy, S., Collier, N., Elliott, D.: Visually grounded reasoning across languages and cultures. arXiv preprint arXiv:2109.13238 (2021)
27. Liu, F., et al.: Deplot: one-shot visual language reasoning by plot-to-table translation. arXiv preprint arXiv:2212.10505 (2022)
28. Liu, F., Emerson, G., Collier, N.: Visual spatial reasoning. Transactions of the Association for Computational Linguistics (2023)
29. Liu, H., Li, C., Li, Y., Lee, Y.J.: Improved baselines with visual instruction tuning. arXiv preprint arXiv:2310.03744 (2023)
30. Liu, H., Li, C., Wu, Q., Lee, Y.J.: Visual instruction tuning. In: Advances in Neural Information Processing Systems (2024)

31. Liu, R., Wu, R., Van Hoorick, B., Tokmakov, P., Zakharov, S., Vondrick, C.: Zero-1-to-3: zero-shot one image to 3D object. In: Proceedings of the IEEE/CVF International Conference on Computer Vision (2023)
32. Liu, Y., Wei, Y.S., Yan, H., Li, G.B., Lin, L.: Causal reasoning meets visual representation learning: a prospective study. Mach. Intell. Res. (2022)
33. Liu, Z., et al.: Internchat: solving vision-centric tasks by interacting with chatbots beyond language. arXiv preprint arXiv:2305.05662 (2023)
34. Long, J., Shelhamer, E., Darrell, T.: Fully convolutional networks for semantic segmentation. In: 2015 IEEE Conference on Computer Vision and Pattern Recognition (CVPR) (2015)
35. Menon, S., Vondrick, C.: Visual classification via description from large language models. arXiv preprint arXiv:2210.07183 (2022)
36. Podell, D., et al.: SDXL: improving latent diffusion models for high-resolution image synthesis. arXiv preprint arXiv:2307.01952 (2023)
37. Qi, D., Su, L., Song, J., Cui, E., Bharti, T., Sacheti, A.: Imagebert: cross-modal pre-training with large-scale weak-supervised image-text data. arXiv preprint arXiv:2001.07966 (2020)
38. Radford, A., et al.: Learning transferable visual models from natural language supervision. In: International Conference on Machine Learning (2021)
39. Rajabi, N., Kosecka, J.: Towards grounded visual spatial reasoning in multi-modal vision language models. arXiv preprint arXiv:2308.09778 (2023)
40. Rasheed, H., et al.: Glamm: pixel grounding large multimodal model. arXiv preprint arXiv:2311.03356 (2023)
41. Redmon, J., Divvala, S., Girshick, R., Farhadi, A.: You only look once: unified, real-time object detection. In: 2016 IEEE Conference on Computer Vision and Pattern Recognition (CVPR) (2016)
42. Su, W., et al.: VL-BERT: pre-training of generic visual-linguistic representations. arXiv preprint arXiv:1908.08530 (2019)
43. Tan, H., Bansal, M.: Lxmert: learning cross-modality encoder representations from transformers. arXiv preprint arXiv:1908.07490 (2019)
44. Touvron, H., et al.: Llama: open and efficient foundation language models. arXiv preprint arXiv:2302.13971 (2023)
45. Vaswani, A., et al.: Attention is all you need. In: Advances in Neural Information Processing Systems (2017)
46. Wang, J., Yan, M., Zhang, Y., Sang, J.: From association to generation: text-only captioning by unsupervised cross-modal mapping. arXiv preprint arXiv:2304.13273 (2023)
47. Wang, P., et al.: OFA: unifying architectures, tasks, and modalities through a simple sequence-to-sequence learning framework. In: International Conference on Machine Learning, pp. 23318–23340. PMLR (2022)
48. Xie, N., Lai, F., Doran, D., Kadav, A.: Visual entailment: a novel task for fine-grained image understanding. arXiv preprint arXiv:1901.06706 (2019)
49. Yang, C., et al.: Improving vision-and-language reasoning via spatial relations modeling. In: Proceedings of the IEEE/CVF Winter Conference on Applications of Computer Vision (2024)
50. Yang, J., et al.: Vision-language pre-training with triple contrastive learning. In: Proceedings of the IEEE/CVF Conference on Computer Vision and Pattern Recognition (2022)
51. Yang, L., et al.: Diffusion models: a comprehensive survey of methods and applications. ACM Comput. Surv. (2023)

52. Yu, L., Poirson, P., Yang, S., Berg, A.C., Berg, T.L.: Modeling context in referring expressions. In: Leibe, B., Matas, J., Sebe, N., Welling, M. (eds.) ECCV 2016. LNCS, vol. 9906, pp. 69–85. Springer, Cham (2016). https://doi.org/10.1007/978-3-319-46475-6_5
53. Zakari, R.Y., Owusu, J.W., Wang, H., Qin, K., Lawal, Z.K., Dong, Y.: VQA and visual reasoning: an overview of recent datasets, methods and challenges. arXiv preprint arXiv:2212.13296 (2022)
54. Zellers, R., Bisk, Y., Farhadi, A., Choi, Y.: From recognition to cognition: visual commonsense reasoning. In: Proceedings of the IEEE/CVF Conference on Computer Vision and Pattern Recognition (2019)
55. Zhang, J., Huang, J., Jin, S., Lu, S.: Vision-language models for vision tasks: a survey. IEEE Trans. Pattern Anal. Mach. Intell. **46**(8), 5625–5644 (2024). https://doi.org/10.1109/TPAMI.2024.3369699
56. Zhang, P., et al.: Vinvl: revisiting visual representations in vision-language models. In: Proceedings of the IEEE/CVF Conference on Computer Vision and Pattern Recognition (2021)
57. Zhang, X., Meng, Z., Lever, J., Ho, E.S.: Libra: leveraging temporal images for biomedical radiology analysis. arXiv preprint arXiv:2411.19378 (2024)
58. Zhao, W.X., et al.: A survey of large language models. arXiv preprint arXiv:2303.18223 (2023)
59. Zhou, B., Zhao, H., Puig, X., Fidler, S., Barriuso, A., Torralba, A.: Scene parsing through ade20k dataset. In: 2017 IEEE Conference on Computer Vision and Pattern Recognition (CVPR) (2017)
60. Zhu, D., Chen, J., Shen, X., Li, X., Elhoseiny, M.: MiniGPT-4: enhancing vision-language understanding with advanced large language models. arXiv preprint arXiv:2304.10592 (2023)

BladeLoRA: An Enhanced LoRA Method with Adaptive Rank Selection and Pruning for Efficient Fine-Tuning

Anqi Liu, Baoyuan Qi, and Xuedan Hu(✉)

Xiaomi Inc., Beijing, China
{liuanqi6,qibaoyuan,huxuedan}@xiaomi.com

Abstract. Large pre-trained language models (PLMs) are being updated continuously. To handle massive amounts of training data and adapt to various downstream tasks, model fine-tuning has become increasingly crucial. Among the existing parameter-efficient fine-tuning methods, Low-Rank Adaptation (LoRA) and its variants are quite popular because they do not incur additional inference costs. However, the current LoRA-based methods still have room for improvement in terms of their ability to adapt to specific downstream tasks. Considering the differences in the importance of different layers in large models, we optimize the selection of rank values in LoRA, making LoRA pay more attention to the information in the deeper layers of the model through linearly increasing rank values. In order to make the performance of the fine-tuned model reach or exceed that of full-parameter fine-tuning, so that the generated content better meets the requirements of downstream tasks, we adjust the matrix weights to align them with those of full-parameter fine-tuning. To mitigate the increased computational load and resource consumption caused by the increase in rank values and gradient alignment, we incorporate two pruning methods to handle large models of different scales. Therefore, we propose BladeLoRA, which consists of three parts. First, we design an increasing sequence of rank values. Then, we adjust the weights of specific layers to approximate the results of full-parameter fine-tuning. Finally, we apply different algorithmic pruning techniques to pre-trained large models of different scales. We conduct experiments on the T5 and Llama2 models, and the experimental results fully validate the effectiveness of BladeLoRA.

Keywords: Large Language Model · Parameter-Efficient Fine-Tuning · LoRA Variants

1 Introduction

Today, large language models are booming and possess enormous potential for downstream tasks. However, the massive parameter scale of large language models poses challenges for the adaptation of downstream tasks. Full-parameter fine-tuning [1] demands astronomical computing resources; for example, GPT-3 with 175 billion parameters would require a massive GPU cluster, incurring high costs [2].

To address this issue, numerous parameter-efficient fine-tuning methods have been developed, and several classic methods among them include: Adapter Tuning, Low-Rank Adaptation (LoRA) [3], Prefix Tuning [4], Prompt Tuning [5], and P-tuning [6]. Among them, Low-Rank Adaptation (LoRA) [3] significantly reduces the number of parameters that needs to be trained by incorporating a low-rank decomposition matrix into the Transformer architecture. As a result, it enables efficient parameter fine-tuning on a single GPU. Meanwhile, the LoRA matrix has extremely low memory usage, which facilitates task-specific fine-tuning and weight replacement during inference. This is highly beneficial for handling multiple downstream tasks. By injecting low-rank decomposition matrices, LoRA drastically cuts the number of trainable parameters [7,8]. In the Transformer architecture, with a rank of 8, trainable parameters dropped from 32,768 to 4,608 (an 86% reduction). It enables single-GPU fine-tuning, reducing resource needs and costs, and has a small memory footprint for multi-task handling.

LoRA and its variants have made certain progress in performance optimization, yet there is still room for improvement. On the one hand, although LoRA can significantly reduce the number of parameters, in some tasks with extremely high precision requirements, there may still be a certain gap compared with full-parameter fine-tuning. On the other hand, with the continuous increase of tasks and the continuous development of models, the demand for reducing resource consumption has become more and more urgent. When dealing with multiple downstream tasks simultaneously, how to further enhance the generation quality and improve computational efficiency remains an urgent problem to be solved [2,7].

We design BladeLoRA to enhance the quality of the content generated by the fine-tuned model without increasing computational load. Firstly, to improve the model's fine-tuning performance, BladeLoRA incorporates linear rank growth and gradient alignment. To approximate the effect of comprehensive fine-tuning, BladeLoRA adjusts the weights of key layers to accurately capture semantic and syntactic information related to the task, thereby enhancing the model's adaptability to specific tasks. Secondly, BladeLoRA employs different methods to prune pre-trained large models of various scales. This adaptive pruning strategy effectively eliminates redundant parameters introduced by incremental rank and gradient alignment, improving training efficiency and reducing memory consumption, enabling the model to operate optimally in resource-constrained environments.

The summary of our contributions is as follows:

- We introduce BladeLoRA, an improved and optimized Parameter-Efficient Fine-Tuning (PEFT) method. This method combines the advantages of LoRA and pruning methods, enabling a learning capacity that approaches or even exceeds that of full-parameter fine-tuning.
- We introduce the adaptive selection of pruning methods for different large language models, combined with the linear increase of rank values and gradient alignment, to enhance the effectiveness of fine-tuning training.
- We evaluate BladeLoRA in terms of general language understanding, text perplexity, and the accuracy of commonsense reasoning. BladeLoRA outperforms LoRA, and the evaluation results meet or even exceed those of full-parameter fine-tuning.

2 Related Work

2.1 Reparameterized Fine-Tuning

Parameter-efficient fine-tuning, like Reparameterized Fine-tuning, adjusts few parameters in pre-trained models for task adaptation. It reparameterizes model parameters, cutting resource use substantially [7,8]. This approach reduces computational, storage, and time costs. The LoRA, for example, slashes trainable parameters via low-rank decomposition matrices. In a natural language task with 65,536 trainable parameters [3], LoRA with rank 8 reduces trainable parameters to 11.71% of full-tuning, easing computing demands. Storage-wise, it only stores a few changed parameters; small LoRA matrices can be fine-tuned for different text classifiers and swapped during inference, sparing storage for multiple task-specific models [1,3]. Time-cost savings are also notable. Fewer parameters mean faster training. Traditional full-parameter tuning may take days or weeks, while parameter-efficient tuning can be done in hours or less, boosting model development efficiency.

2.2 Low-Rank Adaptation

LoRA (Low-Rank Adaptation) [3] is a technique used for fine-tuning large language models. Typically, in the fine-tuning of large language models (LLMs), it is expected to update the model using new domain training data and learn a matrix to update the model parameters into a specific form. However, due to the huge size of this matrix and its identical dimension to the original model parameters, fine-tuning the model parameters consumes a large amount of computational and memory resources.

LoRA transforms this parameter through matrix transformation, i.e., it changes it into the form of $\boldsymbol{W} = \boldsymbol{W}_0 + \boldsymbol{BA}$, where $\boldsymbol{W}_0$ is the pre-trained weight, and $\boldsymbol{W}_0$ does not have to be changed during the fine-tuning training. Only the matrices $\boldsymbol{B}$ and $\boldsymbol{A}$ must be calculated, thus notably reducing the number of weight parameters that ought to be maintained. For example, suppose a training task takes hundreds of GPU hours, but with LoRA, it can be reduced to tens of GPU hours or even less. In the context of storage, as only the parameters of low-rank matrices need storage, rather than the entire model's parameters, storage demands are significantly cut. Take a multi-billion-parameter model: full-parameter fine-tuning might need hundreds of gigabytes or more of storage, whereas LoRA might need only dozens of megabytes or less.

2.3 Variants of Low-Rank Adaptation

The success of LoRA has led to the emergence of numerous variant methods, which improve and expand LoRA in various aspects.

DoRA [9] decomposes the pre-trained weight into two components, magnitude and direction, for directional updates in LoRA to efficiently minimize the number of trainable parameters. However, DoRA suffers from the problem of high computational complexity. rsLoRA [10] improves the training stability and performance by modifying the scaling factor of the low-rank adapter to be divided by the square root of the rank. However, for some complex tasks or tasks that are notably different from the pre-training tasks, the expressive ability of rsLoRA is relatively limited. LoRA+ [11] assigns distinct learning rates to matrices, rendering parameter tuning intricate. AdaLoRA [12] adaptively allocates the parameter budget among the weight matrices based on the importance scores of these weight matrices. However, in comparison with the traditional LoRA, AdaLoRA demands more computation and debugging during the training process, which is likely to increase the complexity of the training. LoRA-GA [13] improves the initialization method of LoRA, making the convergence speed of training close to that of full-parameter fine-tuning . However, its optimization of the fine-tuning effect is limited. ReLoRA [14] based on the properties of matrix rank, makes use of the idea of LoRA's low-rank update. By restarting LoRA multiple times, it increases the total rank of the updates. However, it is necessary to achieve a full-rank warm-up in order to reach the baseline performance. LoRAPrune [15] cuts down the parameter number and computational cost through pruning, but it may cause information loss and degrade model performance. These LoRA variants each bring their own improvements, yet all are accompanied by novel issues.

In conclusion, the variants of LoRA improve LoRA in different aspects, but they also have some drawbacks. Based on LoRA, BladeLoRA aims to make the fine-tuning results closer to full-scale fine-tuning while taking into account the importance of different layers. BladeLoRA optimizes the rank selection of LoRA, aligns the matrix weights with full-scale fine-tuning, and employs different pruning methods to improve the training efficiency and reduce the memory consumption.

3 BladeLoRA

In the realm of large language models, fine-tuning techniques are of paramount importance for enhancing the model's performance in specific tasks. BladeLoRA, through meticulous fine-tuning of the model, aims to assist large language models in precisely and efficiently enhancing their capabilities in professional domains. Just as a sharp blade can swiftly and accurately cut into the target and hit the core, our method is also dedicated to enabling large language models to play a crucial and efficient role in professional applications. Based on this, we name the method BladeLoRA.

3.1 Overall Framework

BladeLoRA focuses on the fine-tuning effectiveness of model performance and integrates three key improvements on the basis of the LoRA framework: linear growth of rank, gradient optimization of the attention output layer, and targeted pruning based on parameter scale. The overall architecture of BladeLoRA is presented in Fig. 1.

For large-language models with a parameter scale of less than or equal to 2 billion, the overall process of BladeLoRA is as follows: First, during the fine-tuning phase, linearly increase the rank values of matrices A and B from the bottom layer to the top layer. Then, in the training process, adjust the gradients of the attention output layer to approximate full-parameter fine-tuning. Finally, apply weight sparsification pruning to the large model (Fig. 2).

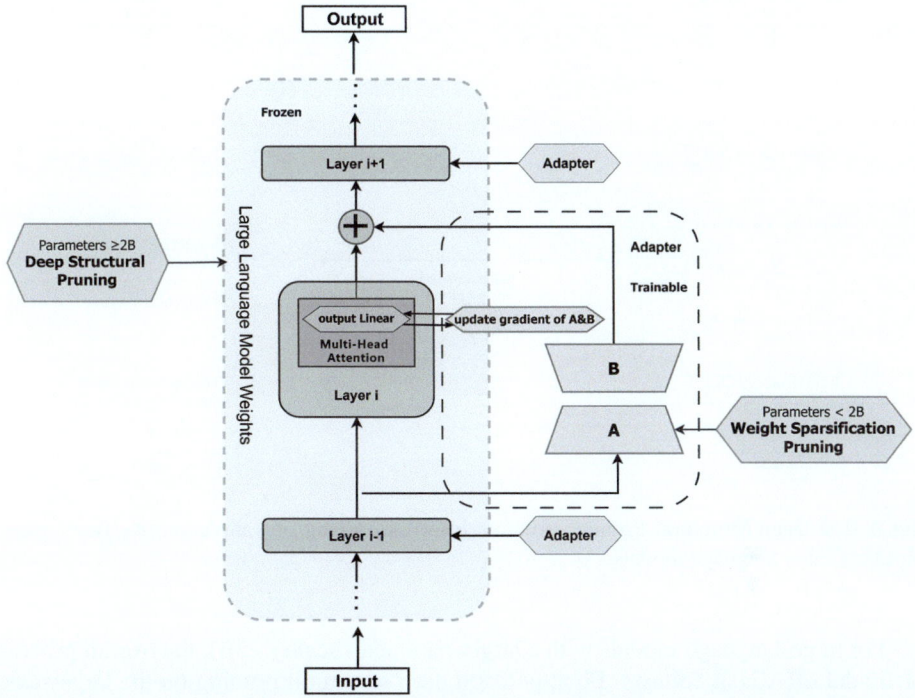

Fig. 1. The overall framework structure of BladeLoRA. BladeLoRA selects pruning methods specifically for large models of different scales. The ranks of the LoRA matrices A and B are set to increase linearly with the number of layers. Meanwhile, it calculates the equivalent gradients for the output layer of the attention mechanism.

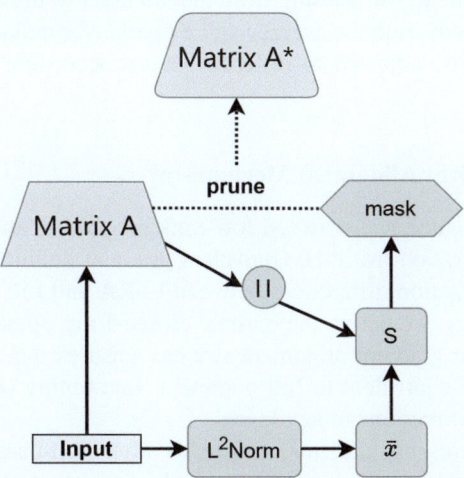

Fig. 2. The calculation process of the importance matrix S based on the weights of matrix A (Weight Sparsification Pruning).

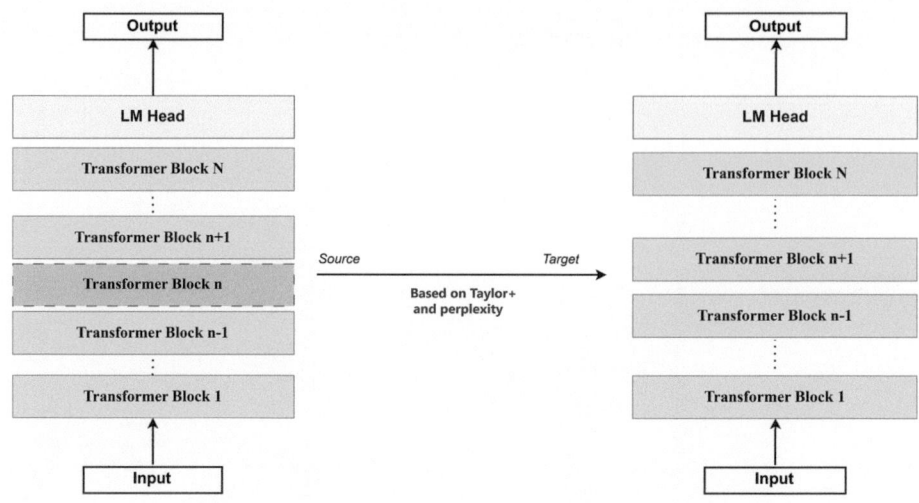

Fig. 3. The Deep Structural Pruning structure involves pruning operations on the Transformer blocks of large language models.

For large-language models with a larger parameter scale ($\geq$2B), the overall process of BladeLoRA is as follows: First, perform deep structural pruning on the large-scale language model (Fig. 3). Next, during the fine-tuning phase, linearly increase the rank values of matrices A and B from the bottom layer to the top layer. Finally, in the training process, process the gradients of the attention output layer to make them close to those of full-parameter fine-tuning.

For the rank r selection of matrices A and B, the range is set as $r \in [r_{min}, r_{max}]$, with the rank values linearly increasing from the 0th layer to the last layer. Let the rank of the i-th layer be r_i, ensuring the average value of all layer ranks meets: $\frac{1}{n}\sum_{i=0}^{n-1} r_i = r_{avg}$ where r_{avg} can be adjusted to different values according to specific tasks and models.

3.2 Dynamic Gradient Alignment Mechanism

To bridge the performance gap between low-rank adaptation and full-parameter fine-tuning, we draw inspiration from the equivalent gradient definition in LoRA-Pro [16] to quantify the optimization differences between LoRA and full fine-tuning. By minimizing this discrepancy, we derive the optimal closed-form update solution for LoRA. BladeLoRA's selective gradient alignment strategy ensures that parameter updates of the LoRA module are equivalent to full-parameter fine-tuning (FT) gradients by constraining the gradient directions of key layers.

Suppose W_{ft} represents the model weights after full-parameter fine-tuning. It is derived by performing gradient updates on all parameters, leveraging pre-trained weights. W_{ft} is associated with matrices A and B in the Low-Rank Adaptation (LoRA) module, and is expressed as $W_{ft} = W_0 + \alpha BA$, where W_0 is the pre-trained weight,

α is a scaling factor (commonly $\alpha = r$, with r being the rank of the low-rank matrix), and A and B are the low-rank matrices to be trained within the LoRA module.

∇W_{ft} denotes the gradient of the model weight W_{ft} during full-parameter fine-tuning. Let the objective function be J, which is a function of the model weight W_{ft}. By the definition of the gradient, $\nabla W_{ft} = \frac{\partial J}{\partial W_{ft}}$, signifying the partial derivative of the objective function J with respect to the model weight W_{ft}.

In BladeLoRA, the update of the LoRA module is optimized by establishing an equivalence between the gradient of the LoRA module ∇W_{lora} and the gradient of full-parameter fine-tuning ∇W_{ft}. The relevant formula is $\nabla W_{lora} = \alpha B^T \Delta A + \alpha \Delta B A$, which can also be written as:

$$\nabla W_{lora} = \frac{\partial(W_0 + \alpha BA)}{\partial A} \cdot \Delta A + \frac{\partial(W_0 + \alpha BA)}{\partial B} \cdot \Delta B \qquad (1)$$

The update amounts ΔA and ΔB are determined by minimizing the Frobenius norm of the gradient difference between the two, given by:

$$\mathcal{L} = \|\nabla W_{lora} - \nabla W_{ft}\|_F^2 \qquad (2)$$

To obtain the update amounts ΔA and ΔB, we take the variation of the matrix with respect to the variables and set the gradients to zero, solving the resulting system of simultaneous equations. The specific derivation is as follows: Assume the objective function J is a function of the model weights W_{ft}, and W_{ft} is related to matrices A and B. In BladeLoRA, the update of W_{ft} depends on A and B, with $W_{ft} = W_0 + \alpha BA$ (W_0 being the pre-trained weight).

By the chain rule of differentiation, to calculate the partial derivative of J with respect to A, denoted as $\frac{\partial J}{\partial A}$, we first find the partial derivative of W_{ft} with respect to A, $\frac{\partial W_{ft}}{\partial A} = \alpha B^T$. Then, $\frac{\partial J}{\partial A} = \frac{\partial J}{\partial W_{ft}} \cdot \frac{\partial W_{ft}}{\partial A} = \nabla W_{ft} \cdot \alpha B^T$, where $\nabla W_{ft} = \frac{\partial J}{\partial W_{ft}}$. Setting $\frac{\partial J}{\partial A} = 0$, we get $\nabla W_{ft} \cdot \alpha B^T = 0$, which can be rearranged to $\alpha B^T \nabla W_{ft} = 0$.

In practical calculations for updating ΔA, we transform the equation to $\alpha B^T \Delta A = B^T \nabla W_{ft}$. When $B^T B$ is invertible (a condition typically met in practical model training and matrix operations), we multiply both sides of the equation on the left by $(B^T B)^{-1}$, obtaining $(B^T B)^{-1} \alpha B^T \Delta A = (B^T B)^{-1} B^T \nabla W_{ft}$. Since α is a scaling factor (usually $\alpha = r$, with r being the rank of the low-rank matrix) for notational convenience and alignment with calculation habits, we divide both sides of the equation by α^2, ultimately getting:

$$\Delta A = \frac{1}{\alpha^2}(B^T B)^{-1}(B^T \nabla W_{ft} - \alpha \Delta B A) \qquad (3)$$

Similarly, to calculate the partial derivative of the objective function J with respect to B, denoted as $\frac{\partial J}{\partial B}$, we first find the partial derivative of W_{ft} with respect to B, $\frac{\partial W_{ft}}{\partial B} = \alpha A$. Then, by the chain rule, $\frac{\partial J}{\partial B} = \frac{\partial J}{\partial W_{ft}} \cdot \frac{\partial W_{ft}}{\partial B} = \nabla W_{ft} \cdot \alpha A$. Setting $\frac{\partial J}{\partial B} = 0$, we get $\nabla W_{ft} \cdot \alpha A = 0$.

Rearranging the terms, we have $\alpha \Delta B A = \nabla W_{ft} A^T$. When AA^T is invertible (as is often the case in practical operations), we multiply both sides of the equation on the right by $(AA^T)^{-1}$, obtaining $\alpha \Delta BA(AA^T)^{-1} = \nabla W_{ft}A^T(AA^T)^{-1}$. Dividing both sides of the equation by α^2, we obtain:

$$\Delta B = \frac{1}{\alpha^2}(\nabla W_{ft}A^T - \alpha B\Delta A)(AA^T)^{-1} \qquad (4)$$

Among them, α is the scaling factor (usually taken as $\alpha = r$), and $X \in \mathbb{R}^{r \times r}$ is a free matrix used to balance the degrees of freedom in the update direction. The final update magnitude is controlled by the learning rate η:

$$A \leftarrow A - \eta \Delta A, \quad B \leftarrow B - \eta \Delta B \qquad (5)$$

This mechanism directly aligns the gradient directions through a closed-form solution, eliminating the need for additional calculations of the gradients in full-parameter fine-tuning. Moreover, it ensures the invertibility of the matrix through regularization.

3.3 Targeted Pruning Strategy

We adopt differentiated pruning approaches for large language models (LLMs) with varying parameter scales: weight sparsification pruning [17] is applied when the parameter count is < 2 billion, while deep structural pruning [18] is employed for models with parameters ≥ 2 billion.

Weight Sparsification Pruning (Parameters < 2B). For large language models with parameter scales below 2 billion, applying deep structural pruning may significantly impact model performance. Therefore, we adopt dynamic weight sparsification pruning to refine parameter optimization. The method dynamically evaluates the weight criticality for fine-grained parameter pruning. First, input feature statistics are analyzed by calculating the sliding average of feature L2 norms:

$$\bar{X} = \gamma \cdot \bar{X} + (1 - \gamma) \cdot \sqrt{\sum_{m,n} X_{mn}^2} \qquad (6)$$

where $\gamma = 0.9$ is the smoothing coefficient and the statistical window is set to 200 training steps. An importance matrix is then constructed:

$$S_{pq} = |A_{pq}| \cdot \bar{X}_q \qquad (7)$$

Every $\tau = 120$ training steps, a binary mask is generated based on the importance matrix:

$$M_{pq} = \begin{cases} 1, & \text{if } S_{pq} \text{ is among the top k\% important values} \\ 0, & \text{otherwise} \end{cases} \qquad (8)$$

Parameter sparsification is finally achieved through element-wise matrix multiplication:

$$A_{pruned} = A \odot M \qquad (9)$$

After every i training steps, the above pruning procedure is applied to matrix A to continuously adjust its sparsity during training.

Deep Structural Pruning (Parameters $\geq$ 2B). This study employs the deep pruning method proposed by [18], which reduces computational costs while maintaining model performance through structural pruning. This aligns closely with our objective of enhancing model efficiency. The method performs coarse-grained pruning at the Transformer block level, evaluating module importance using the Taylor+ [19] metric and perplexity (PPL) [20] metric:

Taylor Expansion Metric:

$$I_T^n = \sum_{i,j,k} \left| \nabla_{W_{ijk}^n} L \cdot W_{ijk}^n \right| \tag{10}$$

This evaluates module importance by calculating the gradient contribution of weight parameters to the loss function, where W is the linear weight matrix and L is the training loss on calibration dataset D.

Perplexity Metric:

$$I_P^n = \exp\left(-\frac{1}{|\mathcal{D}|} \sum_{x \in \mathcal{D}} \log p_{\theta^{-n}}(x)\right) \tag{11}$$

Here, θ^{-n} denotes the model parameters with the n-th block removed, and $\mathcal{D}$ is the calibration dataset. This metric assesses block importance by measuring the language model's next-token prediction accuracy after block removal; smaller PPL changes indicate lower block contributions.

Fuse the rankings of the two metrics using $I_{avg} = \frac{1}{2}\left(\frac{I_T}{\max I_T} + \frac{I_P}{\max I_P}\right)$, and remove the blocks with low scores according to the target compression ratio. Due to the isomorphism of Transformer blocks, the pruning ratio can be precisely controlled through the linear relationship $N_{retained} = N_{original} \times (1 - s)$.

4 Experiment

To verify the performance of BladeLoRA in fine-tuning models of different magnitudes, we conduct experiments on two large models, T5-Base [21] and Llama-2-7B [22]. We apply BladeLoRA to the T5-Base model with 220 million parameters, and evaluate this method on several natural language understanding benchmarks included in the General Language Understanding Evaluation (GLUE) [23]. Additionally, we evaluate the perplexity of Wikitext on the Llama-2-7B model. We implement the method using PyTorch and Hugging Face Transformers. All experiments are conducted on an NVIDIA A800-SXM4-80GB GPU. In the future, we will attempt to conduct experimental research on large models (such as Llama3-405B) using multiple GPUs.

4.1 Experimental Setup

Full-Parameter Fine-Tuning [1]. In the fine-tuning stage, the model is initialized with the pre-trained parameters, and all model parameters go through gradient updates.

LoRA [3]. LoRA is a method for parameter-efficient fine-tuning. Its core idea is, without changing the original weights of the pre-trained model, to capture task-related information by inserting a small number of trainable low-rank matrices into specific layers of the model, thus achieving the fine-tuning of the model.

rsLoRA [10]. rsLoRA is a large model fine-tuning technique that improves upon the LoRA method. By modifying the scaling factor of the low-rank adapter to be divided by the square root of the rank.

AdaLoRA [12]. Parameterizes the incremental updates in the form of singular value decomposition for a given parameter.

DoRA [9]. DoRA is a technique that decomposes the weights of a pre-trained model into two parts: magnitude and direction. It directly fine-tunes the magnitude and efficiently fine-tunes the direction using LoRA.

LoRA-GA [13]. The method aligns the gradients of the low-rank matrix product with those of full-parameter fine-tuning by improving the initialization method, enabling LoRA to achieve a convergence speed comparable to that of full-parameter fine-tuning.

LoRA-Pro [16]. By introducing the concept of equivalent gradients, it narrows the performance gap between LoRA and full-parameter fine-tuning and optimizes the convergence process of LoRA.

Parameter Settings. In our research, we conduct experiments on different distributions while keeping the total number of parameters unchanged, and found that the method approximating full-parameter fine-tuning for the output layer would yield better results. Considering the time-consuming problem of fine-tuning training, we limit the rank value within the range of [4, 12].

4.2 Experiments on GLUE Benchmark

Table 1 shows our results in the evaluation of T5-base model [21] on GLUE [23] dataset tasks (CoLA, MRPC, QNLI, SST-2, MNLI). BladeLoRA has an impressive high accuracy rate of 87.07% in the CoLA task, far exceeding other models. This indicates that it has unique advantages in judging the linguistic acceptability of sentences. LoRA-GA ranks second with an accuracy rate of 80.63%, still showing a certain gap compared with BladeLoRA. This suggests that although LoRA-GA performs well in this task, it may not be as precise as BladeLoRA in feature extraction or model decision-making.

BladeLoRA once again demonstrates excellent performance in the MRPC task, with an accuracy rate reaching 91.96%. LoRA-Pro closely follows with an accuracy rate of 85.54%. These two models perform outstandingly in judging the semantic equivalence of sentence pairs, being able to deeply understand the semantic connotations of sentences and effectively identify the semantic similarities and differences between sentences. The accuracy rates of rsLoRA and DoRA in this task are 73.28% and 66.42% respectively, which are relatively low. This may be because they are not precise enough in processing semantic feature extraction and comparison, or the design of their model architectures is not targeted enough for the task of semantic equivalence judgment.

Table 1. Comparison of the Experimental Results of Fine-tuning the T5-Base Model on GLUE. **Bold** indicates the highest score.

Methods	Accuracy Rate (%)				
	CoLA	MRPC	QNLI	SST-2	MNLI
Full-tuning	81.98	87.50	93.15	93.92	86.33
LoRA	74.49	65.93	92.97	93.69	85.26
rsLoRA	77.95	73.28	92.88	93.81	85.91
AdaLoRA	67.59	65.68	92.62	92.43	85.76
DoRA	74.21	66.42	92.98	93.58	86.19
LoRA-GA	80.63	83.82	93.21	94.15	85.69
LoRA-Pro	81.11	85.54	92.84	**94.27**	**86.64**
BladeLoRA	**87.07**	**91.96**	**94.8**	93.69	86.44

In the QNLI task, the accuracy of BladeLoRA reaches 94.8%, which is higher than other methods. This indicates that in natural language inference tasks, BladeLoRA surpasses these methods in terms of the ability to understand the logical relationships between sentences and make reasonable inferences. LoRA-Pro attains the highest accuracy rate of 94.27% in the SST-2 task, and LoRA-GA closely follows with 94.15%. This indicates that these two models perform excellently in the sentiment classification task and can accurately capture the sentiment tendencies in the text. BladeLoRA has an accuracy rate of 93.69% in this task. Although slightly lower than the results of LoRA-Pro and LoRA-GA, it still remains at a relatively high level. BladeLoRA also demonstrates a strong capability in emotion classification. Although the pruning operation in the method may affect some of the results, it can still better understand and classify the emotion information in the text.

In the MNLI task, BladeLoRA attains an accuracy of 86.44%, slightly higher than the full-parameter fine-tuning result of 86.33%. In contrast, traditional LoRA only reaches 85.26%, rsLoRA achieves 85.91%, and LoRA-Pro attains 86.64%. The outstanding performance of BladeLoRA on MNLI demonstrates that it not only achieves high accuracy on single tasks but also exhibits robust cross-genre generalization capabilities, which holds significant value for practical applications involving diverse text processing.

BladeLoRA showcases cross-task robustness in the GLUE benchmark tests. It notably outperforms all baseline methods in the language acceptability judgment task CoLA (87.07%), the semantic equivalence judgment task MRPC (91.96%) and the natural language inference task QNLI (94.8%). Moreover, it achieves competitive results in the sentiment classification task SST-2 (93.69%). Notably, in the MNLI multi-genre reasoning task (86.44%), BladeLoRA outperforms full-parameter fine-tuning (86.33%). The consistency of its performance across tasks validates the effectiveness of the model design. By using a dynamic rank adjustment strategy $r \in [4, 12]$ and gradient alignment technology, BladeLoRA can effectively capture the language features of different tasks, such as syntactic structures, semantic relationships, and emotional inclinations. Its training framework demonstrates generalization capabilities for complex NLP tasks.

4.3 Experiment on Fine-Tuning Llama2-7B

This section aims to conduct a detailed analysis of the experimental results of the Llama2-7B [22] model under different fine-tuning methods (LoRA and BladeLoRA). Table 2 presents data on language model tasks (measured by perplexity on the Wikitext2 [24] and PTB [25] datasets) and commonsense reasoning tasks (including accuracies on the BoolQ [26], PIQA [27], HellaSwag [28], WinoGrande [29], ARC-e [30], ARC-c [30], and OBQA [31] datasets) to evaluate the impact of different fine-tuning methods on the model performance.

Table 2. Comparison of the Experimental Results of Fine-tuning the Llama2-7B Model. **Bold** indicates the highest score.

Methods	PPL		Accuracy of Commonsense Reasoning (%)						
	Wikitext2	PTB	BoolQ	PIQA	HellaSwag	WinoGrande	ARC-e	ARC-c	OBQA
LoRA	17.91	65.39	58.5	74.97	66.06	56.67	66.59	35.07	38.6
BladeLoRA	**15.36**	**58.71**	**78.96**	**75.32**	**75.32**	**66.77**	**76.14**	**45.82**	**48.23**

The experimental results of BladeLoRA on the Llama2-7B model indicate that this method has made substantial headway in performance improvement in both language modeling and commonsense reasoning tasks. In language modeling, the perplexity (PPL) of BladeLoRA on the Wikitext2 and PTB datasets is 15.36 and 58.71 respectively, representing a 14.2% and 10.2% reduction compared to LoRA (17.91/65.39), which verifies the effectiveness of the dynamic rank adjustment strategy in capturing long-range dependencies and complex language patterns.

In commonsense reasoning tasks, BladeLoRA has achieved significantly improved accuracy ($p < 0.01$) in tasks such as BoolQ (78.96% vs. 58.5%), HellaSwag (75.32% vs. 66.06%), and OBQA (48.23% vs. 38.6%), validating the enhancing effect of the gradient alignment technology on semantic understanding. The hierarchical pruning strategy has preserved the integrity of key reasoning modules in tasks like PIQA (75.32% vs. 74.97%) and WinoGrande (66.77% vs. 56.67%). However, for the ARC-c task (45.82% vs. 35.07%), it should be noted that the small sample size may affect the statistical significance of the leading result.

In terms of resource efficiency, the VRAM occupation of BladeLoRA has increased by 1.65% (from 20.61 GB to 20.95 GB), and the training time is 3 h and 47 min, which is longer compared to LoRA's 1 h and 49 min. The slightly higher VRAM occupation of BladeLoRA than LoRA may be due to the more complex parameter adjustment strategy adopted during the fine-tuning process, resulting in a greater need for VRAM to store model parameters and intermediate calculation results during operation. The significantly longer running time of BladeLoRA than LoRA is because BladeLoRA performs more refined parameter adjustments or adopts more complex calculation processes during training. Although this may bring certain performance improvements, it also increases the consumption of computing resources and the cost of running time.

Overall, through the synergistic effect of dynamic rank adjustment, gradient alignment, and hierarchical pruning, BladeLoRA has achieved a balance between performance and efficiency in multi-task scenarios. It has significant advantages, especially in reasoning tasks that require deep semantic understanding, providing a feasible optimization solution for large language model deployment.

5 Discussion

The performance differences of different models across various tasks are remarkable, and the selection of a model should be grounded in the specific requirements of the task. For the task of judging linguistic acceptability (CoLA), BladeLoRA is a more preferable option. In terms of semantic equivalence judgment (MRPC), both BladeLoRA and LoRA-Pro perform outstandingly. In the natural language inference (QNLI) task, the gap among different methods is relatively small, but BladeLoRA performs relatively well. In the sentiment classification (SST-2) task, LoRA-Pro and LoRA-GA exhibit excellent performance.

In language model tasks, BladeLoRA is slightly superior to LoRA in terms of perplexity, indicating that it has a certain improvement in language modeling ability. Although the gap is small, the relatively lower perplexity of BladeLoRA may be attributed to its parameter adjustment strategy during the fine-tuning process, enabling it to better capture the statistical patterns and semantic information in language data.

In the commonsense reasoning task, BladeLoRA demonstrates higher accuracy on most datasets, indicating relatively stronger overall commonsense reasoning capabilities. Overall, BladeLoRA achieves higher accuracy than LoRA on most commonsense reasoning datasets, which implies that BladeLoRA helps the model better learn and apply commonsense knowledge for accurate reasoning and judgment. On the PIQA dataset, BladeLoRA also performs slightly better than LoRA. When dealing with physical commonsense problems, the BladeLoRA method may be more suitable for the characteristics of this dataset.

In future research, it is feasible to continue exploring the adaptive adjustment of rank values according to the training progress to further enhance the fine-tuning effect of BladeLoRA. In the future, we hope to conduct in-depth research on the applicability of BladeLoRA in vision-language models (such as LLaVA). Regarding the improvement of memory and inference efficiency, we also aim to develop a joint optimization scheme that combines BladeLoRA with model quantization techniques to further boost its performance.

6 Conclusion

BladeLoRA employs a strategy of linearly increasing the rank and performs gradient alignment for specified layers to approximate the effect of full-parameter fine-tuning. Meanwhile, BladeLoRA adopts different pruning schemes for large language models of different scales. BladeLoRA enhances the fine-tuning effect and improves task adaptability to some extent. Moreover, BladeLoRA utilizes different pruning methods according to the magnitude differences of pre-trained large models. It can reduce redundant parameters while guaranteeing performance, significantly boost training efficiency, decrease memory consumption, and ensure that the model can operate efficiently even in resource-constrained environments.

References

1. Lv, K., Yang, Y., Liu, T., Guo, Q., Qiu, X.: Full parameter fine-tuning for large language models with limited resources. In: Ku, L.W., Martins, A., Srikumar, V. (eds.) Proceedings of the 62nd Annual Meeting of the Association for Computational Linguistics (Volume 1: Long Papers), Bangkok, Thailand, pp. 8187–8198 (2024). https://doi.org/10.18653/v1/2024.acl-long.445. https://aclanthology.org/2024.acl-long.445/
2. Chen, J., et al.: When large language models meet personalization: perspectives of challenges and opportunities. World Wide Web **27**(4), 42 (2024)
3. Hu, E.J., et al.: LoRA: low-rank adaptation of large language models. In: International Conference on Learning Representations (2022). https://openreview.net/forum?id=nZeVKeeFYf9
4. Li, X.L., Liang, P.: Prefix-tuning: optimizing continuous prompts for generation. In: Zong, C., Xia, F., Li, W., Navigli, R. (eds.) Proceedings of the 59th Annual Meeting of the Association for Computational Linguistics and the 11th International Joint Conference on Natural Language Processing, pp. 4582–4597 (2021). https://doi.org/10.18653/V1/2021.ACL-LONG.353
5. Lester, B., Al-Rfou, R., Constant, N.: The power of scale for parameter-efficient prompt tuning. In: Proceedings of the 2021 Conference on Empirical Methods in Natural Language Processing, pp. 3045–3059 (2021). https://doi.org/10.18653/v1/2021.emnlp-main.243. https://aclanthology.org/2021.emnlp-main.243
6. Gavrilov, D., Balagansky, N.: Ahead-of-time p-tuning. Computing Research Repository abs/2305.10835 (2023). https://doi.org/10.48550/ARXIV.2305.10835. https://doi.org/10.48550/arXiv.2305.10835
7. Han, Z., Gao, C., Liu, J., Zhang, J., Zhang, S.Q.: Parameter-efficient fine-tuning for large models: a comprehensive survey. Trans. Mach. Learn. Res. (2024). https://openreview.net/forum?id=lIsCS8b6zj
8. Xu, L., Xie, H., Qin, S.Z.J., Tao, X., Wang, F.L.: Parameter-efficient fine-tuning methods for pretrained language models: a critical review and assessment. arXiv preprint arXiv:2312.12148 (2023). https://doi.org/10.48550/arXiv.2312.12148
9. Liu, S.Y., et al.: Dora: weight-decomposed low-rank adaptation. In: Forty-First International Conference on Machine Learning (2024)
10. Kalajdzievski, D.: A rank stabilization scaling factor for fine-tuning with lora. arXiv preprint arXiv:2312.03732 (2023). https://doi.org/10.48550/arXiv.2312.03732
11. Hayou, S., Ghosh, N., Yu, B.: Lora+: efficient low rank adaptation of large models. In: Forty-First International Conference on Machine Learning, ICML 2024, Vienna, Austria, 21–27 July 2024. OpenReview.net (2024). https://openreview.net/forum?id=NEv8YqBROO
12. Zhang, Q., et al.: Adalora: adaptive budget allocation for parameter-efficient fine-tuning. arXiv preprint arXiv:2303.10512 (2023). https://doi.org/10.48550/arXiv.2303.10512
13. Wang, S., Yu, L., Li, J.: LoRA-GA: low-rank adaptation with gradient approximation. In: Advances in Neural Information Processing Systems, vol. 37, pp. 54905–54931 ((2024))
14. Lialin, V., Shivagunde, N., Muckatira, S., Rumshisky, A.: Relora: high-rank training through low-rank updates. In: The Twelfth International Conference on Learning Representations, ICLR 2024, Vienna, Austria, 7–11 May 2024. OpenReview.net (2023). https://openreview.net/forum?id=DLJznSp6X3

15. Dery, L., Kolawole, S., Kagy, J.F., Smith, V., Neubig, G., Talwalkar, A.: Everybody prune now: Structured pruning of LLMs with only forward passes. Computing Research Repository abs/2402.05406 (2024). https://doi.org/10.48550/ARXIV.2402.05406
16. Wang, Z., Liang, J., He, R., Wang, Z., Tan, T.: Lora-pro: are low-rank adapters properly optimized? arXiv preprint arXiv:2407.18242 (2024)
17. Benedek, N., Wolf, L.: Prilora: pruned and rank-increasing low-rank adaptation. arXiv preprint arXiv:2401.11316 (2024)
18. Kim, B.K., et al.: Shortened llama: depth pruning for large language models with comparison of retraining methods. arXiv preprint arXiv:2402.02834 (2024)
19. Molchanov, P., Mallya, A., Tyree, S., Frosio, I., Kautz, J.: Importance estimation for neural network pruning. In: Proceedings of the IEEE/CVF Conference on Computer Vision and Pattern Recognition, pp. 11264–11272 (2019)
20. Kulkarni, S., et al.: PPL bench: evaluation framework for probabilistic programming languages. arXiv abs/2010.08886 (2020). https://api.semanticscholar.org/CorpusID:224705971
21. Raffel, C., et al.: Exploring the limits of transfer learning with a unified text-to-text transformer. J. Mach. Learn. Res. **21**(140), 1–67 (2020)
22. Touvron, H., et al.: Llama 2: open foundation and fine-tuned chat models. arXiv preprint arXiv:2307.09288 (2023)
23. Wang, A., Singh, A., Michael, J., Hill, F., Levy, O., Bowman, S.R.: Glue: a multi-task benchmark and analysis platform for natural language understanding. arXiv preprint arXiv:1804.07461 (2018)
24. Merity, S., Xiong, C., Bradbury, J., Socher, R.: Pointer sentinel mixture models. In: International Conference on Learning Representations (2017)
25. Marcus, M.P., Santorini, B., Marcinkiewicz, M.A.: Building a large annotated corpus of English: the Penn treebank. Comput. Linguist. **19**(2), 313–330 (1993). https://aclanthology.org/J93-2004/
26. Clark, C., Lee, K., Chang, M.W., Kwiatkowski, T., Collins, M., Toutanova, K.: Boolq: exploring the surprising difficulty of natural yes/no questions. In: Proceedings of the 2019 Conference of the North American Chapter of the Association for Computational Linguistics: Human Language Technologies (2019)
27. Bisk, Y., Zellers, R., Le Bras, R., Gao, J., Choi, Y.: Piqa: reasoning about physical commonsense in natural language. In: Proceedings of the AAAI Conference on Artificial Intelligence (2020)
28. Zellers, R., Holtzman, A., Bisk, Y., Farhadi, A., Choi, Y.: Hellaswag: can a machine really finish your sentence? In: Proceedings of the 57th Annual Meeting of the Association for Computational Linguistics (2019)
29. Sakaguchi, K., Le Bras, R., Bhagavatula, C., Choi, Y.: Winogrande: an adversarial winograd schema challenge at scale. Commun. ACM **64**(9), 99–106 (2019). https://doi.org/10.1145/3474381
30. Clark, P., et al.: Think you have solved direct-answer question answering? Try arc-da, the direct-answer AI2 reasoning challenge. Computing Research Repository abs/2102.03315 (2021). https://arxiv.org/abs/2102.03315
31. Mihaylov, T., Clark, P., Khot, T., Sabharwal, A.: Can a suit of armor conduct electricity? A new dataset for open book question answering. In: Proceedings of the 2018 Conference on Empirical Methods in Natural Language Processing (2018)

Evaluating Knowledge Graph Sources for Non-personalized Financial Asset Recommendation: 10K Reports vs. Wikidata

Lubingzhi Guo[✉], Javier Sanz-Cruzado, and Richard McCreadie

University of Glasgow, Glasgow G12 8QQ, UK
l.guo.1@research.gla.ac.uk,
{javier.sanz-cruzadopuig,richard.mccreadie}@glasgow.ac.uk

Abstract. Financial asset recommender (FAR) systems suggest investment assets to customers based on past market information. Many of these models choose those securities which they estimate to be more profitable for customers. Financial knowledge graphs (KGs) – data structures containing information about assets and their relations to other involved entities (companies, people) – have been one of the data sources exploited to drive asset selection. Although the construction of knowledge graphs from different sources (news, reports) has previously been investigated, there has been limited analysis of the effect these construction strategies have for FAR. In this work, we compare two different knowledge graphs representing U.S. stocks under a unified FAR framework: a knowledge graph crawled from a general knowledge base, Wikidata, and a knowledge graph built by extracting entities and relations from 10K financial reports using the GoLLIE open information extraction model. We show that integrating these KGs in FAR can lead up to 10.7% improvements in monthly ROI. However, the nature of these graphs makes algorithms prone to bias the recommendations towards different asset types. Therefore, we further propose and evaluate an adaptive graph selection strategy, which dynamically chooses the suitable graph prediction model—trained on either the 10K Graph or the Wikidata Graph—for each asset. The findings indicate that stock-level and sector-level selection strategies respond differently to the length of the recency window, reflecting, respectively, a preference for short-term responsiveness and long-term stability.

Keywords: Knowledge Graph Construction · Stock Recommendation · Information Extraction

1 Introduction

Financial asset recommender systems are tools to assist investors in making informed investment decisions [24,40,44,45]. These technologies aim to produce a ranking of financial securities (e.g. stocks) on which a customer might invest. As one of the main targets of these methods is to help customers increase their wealth, the majority of the methods proposed in this field rely on historical pricing information of assets to predict stock price movement [29,55]. This core signal is then often augmented through the integration of evidence from external information sources such as textual data from news and social media [9, 10, 18].

A *financial knowledge graph* (KG) is a data structure that can be used to store such external information [10, 11, 50, 57]. In such a graph, nodes represent entities (companies, people), while edges represent relations between them (e.g. between-company or board member relationships). Multiple methods have been proposed for the creation of financial KGs, including crawling general knowledge bases like Wikidata [14] or extracting facts and events from financial reports [20, 33] or news [10, 13].

Different KG creation techniques have advantages and disadvantages. On the one hand, graphs extracted from financial documents (such as news or financial reports) include timely information about companies and related entities, which is specific to the financial domain. However, they are generated by applying information extraction techniques over (typically) unstructured text documents [4], and as such are prone to hallucinating incorrect facts [32]. On the other hand, graphs produced from general knowledge bases like Wikidata or DBPedia have their factoids assessed by human annotators to ensure their correctness [48], but often incorporate connections that are irrelevant for the financial domain and are updated infrequently. While both approaches have been tested in isolation previously, no prior works have quantitatively compared these two different strategies. This is an important gap, as intuitively the graphs produced by these two strategies are likely to benefit different types of assets being recommended, introducing a structured bias. For instance, general knowledge bases result in larger graphs with imbalanced coverage toward well-known/long standing companies. Meanwhile, news-based graphs are smaller and more focused on companies that are newsworthy.

Hence, in this work, we tackle the above gap by analysing the impact that these two knowledge graph construction strategies have when predicting the future profitability of U.S. stocks. First, we produce a financial knowledge graph containing information about companies from Wikidata. Second, we build a knowledge graph by applying automated information extraction techniques over 10K reports using large language models (LLMs) [39]. As required by the U.S. Securities and Exchange Commission, these annual reports disclose detailed financial performance and announcements about publicly traded companies to stock investors and unsurprisingly trigger immediate market responses [15]. We then compare the utility of these knowledge graphs under a unified profitability prediction framework integrating knowledge graph embeddings [49] as features for the task. Afterwards, we analyze which types of assets are better promoted by each knowledge graph on the stock recommendation task and, finally, we propose and test ensemble strategies that adaptively select the best knowledge graph for scoring different stocks.

Specifically, the primary contributions of this work are fourfold:

- We construct a financial KG from 10K reports using fine-tuned LLMs for open information extraction.
- We crawl a financial KG from Wikidata as a general knowledge base.
- We compare the effect these knowledge graphs have on profitability prediction over the U.S. stock market, demonstrating that integrating these KGs can lead up to 10.7% higher in monthly ROI. We also demonstrate that different KG construction strategies bias their results towards separate sets of assets.

– We compare two different adaptive graph selection methods that combines two distinct knowledge graphs for stock recommendation, showing that well-designed selection criteria can consistently enhance monthly ROI.

2 Related Work

To integrate external evidence into an asset recommendation system using a knowledge graph as an intermediate representation, we need two technologies: 1) a graph generator, that takes information about financial topics and extracts associated entities as well as their relations that form the graph; and 2) an entity embedder, which given an asset produces a vector embedding that encodes information related to the asset from the graph. We introduce past works regarding each below:

2.1 Knowledge Graph Generation

The first step in knowledge graph generation is to select the type of content that you want to extract information from. If producing a new knowledge graph from scratch, the most popular data source to use is financial news articles, as intuitively significant events that affect an asset will have associated news content, but conversely much irrelevant information will also be captured [13]. Instead, a clean data source such as financial filings can be used, which is more targeted and in-depth, but are published infrequently [20,33]. Alternatively, rather than building a completely new graph, some works have bootstrapped from an existing knowledge-base, such as DBPedia, where a large general knowledge graph needs to be filtered down to a useful subset for the financial domain [48]. To contain the scope for this initial work, we compare approaches to model what a company (that can be invested in) *is and does*. As such, we use U.S. 10K financial reports as a company provided overview of their operations and compare it to company information from WikiData.

Once we have selected our data sources, we next need to extract the entities and relationships that will form each graph. Depending on the type of data being used, the approach here will differ. If using an existing knowledge graph, then a set of filtering rules needs to be defined, as well as potentially entity disambiguation performed. However, for text-based data sources, Information Extraction (IE) techniques need to be applied to the raw text. This is usually comprised of two components: 1) entity identification (and linking), which identifies financial entities (companies, people, places) in the text; and 2) relationship extraction, which generates likely relationship tags between pairs of entities [33][1]. For instance:

$$\text{Entity1 }_{\text{'Nik Jhangiani'}}, \text{Relationship }_{\text{'CFO'}}, \text{Entity2 }_{\text{'Diageo'}} \qquad (1)$$

Of note is that for relationship extraction, approaches can be either closed domain (a set of target relationship types are defined beforehand) or open domain (any relationship tag

---

[1] Relationships may also have extracted properties/qualifiers, such as an indicated date for when the relationship was formed.

can be generated) [19]. While most works focus on closed-domain extraction, the emergence of effective large language models has opened the door to less error-prone open-domain extraction than was previously possible, with models such as GoLLIE [39]. In this work, we use GoLLIE over 10K filings to perform open-domain extraction, where the model is guided to look for either business, transaction or personnel-related relationships.

2.2 Entity Embedding

Once we have a financial knowledge graph, given a financial asset representing a company that we want to recommend, we need to produce an embedding representing what the knowledge graph has about that company. To do this, knowledge graph embedding (KGE) models are used, which produce a low-dimensional vector representation given a starting graph node or edge to represent [49]. There are three families of KGE models:

Translation-Based. Translation-based techniques represent entities as points and relationships as transformations (translations or rotations) in vector spaces. The idea is that, if we apply the relation to the head entity vector, the resulting vector will be close to the tail entity. An early representation of this group of algorithms is TransE [6], which considers relations as translations between head and tail entities in a common embedding space. As this simple model struggles with one-to-many, many-to-one, symmetric or transitive relations [37], subsequent models like TransH [37] and TransR [22] introduce additional spatial dimensions to handle a variety of relations. TransH handles complex relationships via hyperplane projections, whereas TransR separates entity and relation spaces. Beyond translations, RotatE [42] represents relations as rotations in a complex vector space.

Factorization-Based. Factorization methods on the other hand implement a scoring function based on semantic similarity to estimate the plausibility of a given triplet, typically by mining the latent semantics between entities and relations [37]. These models include RESCAL [31] which leverages three-way tensor factorization techniques and represents relations as full-rank matrices, outperformed but is computationally demanding. Several methods have made progress in refining the tensor factorization procedure in comparison to RESCAL, resulting in increased computational efficiency while preserving the ability to handle asymmetric relations. DistMult [54] simplifies the procedure by representing each relation as a diagonal matrix, thus shrinking the parameter space. TuckER [5] uses Tucker decomposition and combining relations in low-rank matrices. HolE [30] reduces the number of parameters by employing circular correlation operation.

Neural Network-Based. Neural networks are considered a promising solution in many domains since their large number of parameters enable them to learn complicated patterns and also encode weights and biases observed [37]. Therefore, several KGE methods have taken these algorithms as a basis. ConvE [12] introduces the utilization of 2-dimensional convolutions over embeddings for link prediction. Other models investigate the generalisation power of graph neural networks (GNNs) for the task. An early example of these methods is the RGCN model [41], which adapts graph convolutional networks for their use on link prediction and entity classification on knowledge graphs. Subsequently, building upon graph attention networks [47], KGAT [51] effectively applies the attention mechanism for higher-order relation modelling.

In our later experiments, we compare asset embeddings produced by a range of algorithms across these three types for both 10K filings and Wikidata-based knowledge graphs.

2.3 Financial Asset Recommendation

Finally, having produced a knowledge graph embedding for a company/asset, we can then use that embedding to augment a downstream task. In this work, we target Financial Asset Recommendation as that task, where given a day, we want to rank assets on that day such that the future return-on-investment of the top ranked assets is maximised [2,3,14]. For this, we rely on non-personalized regression models like the ones used by [35,40]

Similarly to our work, several models have integrated pricing and knowledge graph information for stock predictions [14,56]. These models either exploit similarities between assets [23,50,56] or integrate KGs as features [10,11,57]. We explore the second way. However, previous feature-based approaches need specific KG structures or data sources to build those KGs. Differently, we propose a simple framework which integrates knowledge graph embeddings as features. This allows the use of any financial KG as input to our models – something that we can use to compare the effect that different knowledge graph structures have on the recommendations.

3 Knowledge Graph Construction

In this work, we construct two financial knowledge graphs from two different sources to compare the performance for financial asset recommendation/stock recommendation.

3.1 Knowledge Graph Definition

We first provide a formal definition of a knowledge graph. Following the property graph model defined by [16], a knowledge graph $\mathcal{G}$ is defined by 5 components $\mathcal{G} = \langle \mathcal{E}, \mathcal{L}, \mathcal{V}, \mathcal{R}, \mathcal{P} \rangle$. $\mathcal{E}$ is the set of entities in the graph. Entities represent objects, companies, people or abstract concepts. For instance, the board gaming company Hasbro and the Dungeons & Dragons (D&D) tabletop game represent entities in a knowledge graph. $\mathcal{L}$ represents the relation labels (types) in the knowledge graph. An example of relation label is 'CEO'. $\mathcal{V}$ is the set of literal values which can be used to represent properties of entities and relations, such as a date or a number. The set $\mathcal{R} \subset \mathcal{E} \times \mathcal{L} \times \mathcal{E}$ contains triplets $r = (e_h, l, e_t)$ representing directed links between entities in the knowledge graph, where $e_h \in \mathcal{E}$ is the origin or head entity, $e_t \in \mathcal{E}$ is the destination or tail entity, and $l \in \mathcal{L}$ represents the type of the relation. An example of a relation would be $r = $ (Hasbro, CEO, Chris Cocks) – indicating that Chris Cocks is the CEO of Hasbro. Finally, $\mathcal{P} \subset (\mathcal{E} \cup \mathcal{R}) \times \mathcal{L} \times \mathcal{V}$ is the set of properties of entities and relations. For

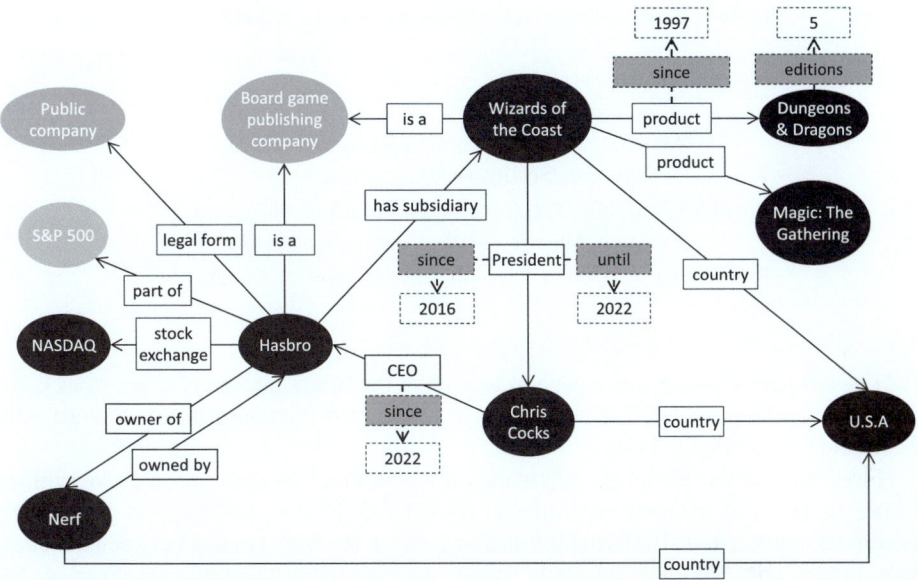

Fig. 1. Example of a knowledge graph. (Color figure online)

instance, (D&D, editions, 5) is a property of the D&D entity indicating that 5 editions of this game have been released, while the tuple $(r, \text{since}, 2022)$ referred to the previously mentioned relation indicates that Chris Cocks has been the CEO of Hasbro since 2022.

We show a graphical representation of an example knowledge graph centered on the entity Hasbro in Fig. 1 – which shows all the aforementioned examples. In the figure, entities are shown as ellipses. Entity colour represents the type of entity: companies/organizations in blue, people in green, products in brown, financial indexes in yellow, locations in black and entities representing more abstract concepts in grey. Relations between entities are indicated by continuous arrows, with white boxes showing the relation type. Dashed arrows represent the properties of an entity/relationship, with the property label represented by a light blue box with dashed lines, and the property value as a white box with dashed lines.

3.2 Wikidata Graph

Firstly, we extract a financial knowledge graph from a general knowledge base, Wikidata [48]. Wikidata includes information about entities in the financial domain that we can integrate into a graph. However, as Wikidata contains a broad range of information beyond the financial domain, we need to filter and retrieve the relevant data for our knowledge graph, following the procedure we detail next.

Seed Entity Matching. As a first step, we need to identify some seed entities in Wikidata. For this, we take the stocks trading in NASDAQ, NYSE and AMEX at December

Table 1. Entity, relation and property types in the Wikidata graph.

Element	Valid types
Entity	Organization, Person, Location, Market, Product, Material, Activity, Award, Legal form, Form of government, Gender, Health problem
Relation	Ownership, Employment, Part of, Creation, Award, Location, Material, Skills, Condition, Sequence
Property	Time, Position, Location, Item or service, Amount

2021 as our seed entities, since we aim to predict the future pricing of these stocks. We employ a semi-automated three-step process to match those companies with entities in the Wikidata knowledge base:

First, we use the SPARQL Wikidata Query Service[2] to filter and retrieve entities related to the stock exchanges of interest (NASDAQ, NYSE, AMEX) and gather their identifiers, names, and aliases in multiple languages. If a direct match between the company tickers and Wikidata entries is found, we link them automatically. Second, for assets without direct matches, we use DBpedia Spotlight [25] for entity recognition and linking to entries in DBPedia (another public knowledge base), which are then cross-referenced to Wikidata identifiers. We verify the results manually to ensure accuracy. Finally, for any unmatched entities, we conduct a manual search in Wikidata. If a company does not match any entity, it is excluded from our dataset, assuming no association with Wikidata exists. We started with a total of 5,823 assets from NASDAQ, NYSE and AMEX. Via entity matching we mapped 3,370 of these (57.9%) to Wikidata pages.

Entity and Relation Extraction. Starting with mapped Wikidata entries, we extract metadata, relations, and properties for each entry, including any available temporal information for the relations. Our crawling method follows a breadth-first search algorithm, beginning with seed entities and expanding outward in a first-found, first-served manner. To avoid crawling information outside the financial domain, we cap the search depth from the seed entities. Furthermore, we have specified a list of valid financial relations and entity types to guide our crawler. The broad types of those entities and relations are summarized in Table 1.

3.3 10K Reports Graph

Second, we create a graph from financial texts using automated relation extraction. In this work, we construct our automated knowledge graph using some of the most comprehensive and official financial reports: the 10K annual filings. We next provide details of our information extraction procedure.

---

[2] https://query.wikidata.org/.

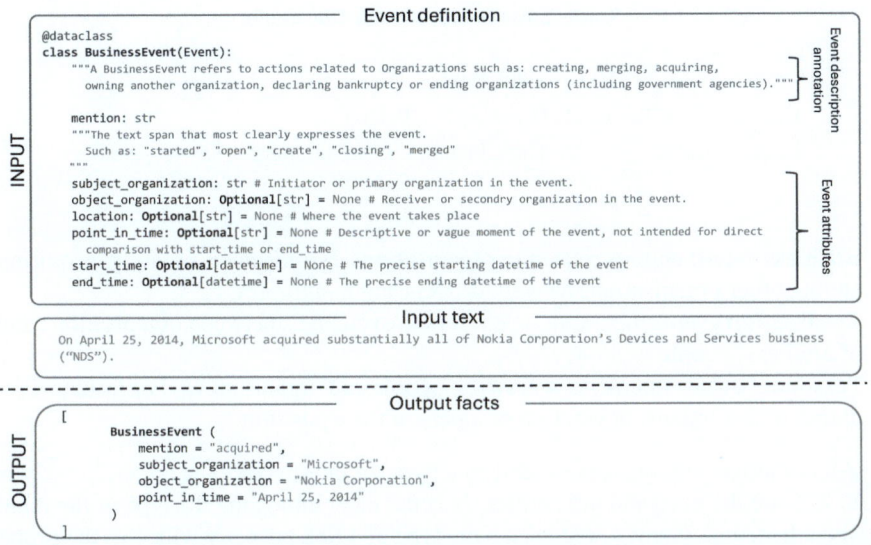

Fig. 2. An example of extracted hyper-relational facts.

Pre-processing. Considering that financial reports are lengthy and exceed the context window of the LLM we use, we initially perform sentence segmentation on each report, converting it into a list of sentences using Stanford NLP [34]. This enables us to generate hyper-relational facts. Furthermore, as in most reports, terms such as 'we', 'the company' and 'the corporate' refer to the reported company, as such we resolve/replace these with their corresponding company names.

Entity and Relation Extraction. Our information extraction pipeline is based on GoL-LIE [39]. GoLLIE is a recent LLM-based model for zero-shot information extraction (IE). This model has been successfully applied to multiple IE tasks across multiple domains, so we use it in our work to extract financial entities and relations from the 10K filings. This model is based on Code-LLaMA [38] and represents both input and output using Python classes. It receives two inputs: first, a text from which to extract information, a second, a list of Python class definitions describing the information to extract. For each label, there is a Python class detailing its structure (where class attributes represent specific information pieces to extract). Extraction guidelines are embedded as comments in the Python class to assist the model. The output of the model is a list of instances of the pre-defined Python classes, each containing a pair of entities, a relation and any relevant properties.

In our information extraction procedure, we perform event argument extraction to produce hyper-relational facts using event templates provided for GoLLIE[3]. We define three types of events to extract:

---

[3] https://github.com/hitz-zentroa/GoLLIE/blob/main/notebooks/EventExtraction.ipynb.

Table 2. Entity types in the 10K graph.

Entity	Valid Type
Head Entity & Tail Entity	Organization, Person
Property Label	Time, Position, Location, Item or service, Amount

- **Business event:** actions related to organisations. For instance, creating, acquiring or ending other organisations as well as declaring bankruptcy.
- **Transaction event:** this event type refers to exchanges between organisations, either of artefacts, people or money.
- **Personnel event:** interactions between people and organisations. For instance, foundation of a company, or election of a person for a position.

All of these events are represented by a hyper-relational fact (e_h, l_r, e_t, l_p, v), where $e_h, e_t \in \mathcal{E}$ are the head and tail entities, l_r is the label indicating the type of the relation between them and, if any, l_p represents the type of a link property with v as the property value. For each event type, we define the types of the entities, and allow the model to extract the relation types. We broadly classify the link properties into five groups: 'time', 'position', 'location', 'item or service' and 'amount'.

Figure 2 shows an example of the input and output of the model. In the predefined 'BussinessEvent' data class, we first provide a text describing the types of events we want to extract as a comment. In order to capture the business facts related to organizations, we define the head entity as 'subject organization', and tail entity as 'object organization', adding location and time as properties. As it is common that the extracted facts may not always include all the components we thus define Optional typings to handle diverse matching patterns. This example demonstrates an extracted 'BusinessEvent' instance from the input text, with 'Microsoft' as the head entity and 'Nokia Corporation' as the tail entity. The relationship between them is described by the term 'acquired', with 'April 25, 2014' serving as the only time-related property.

Relation Clustering. The identified relational phrases are continuous text spans directly extracted from the sentence, which tend to be noisy. Therefore, additional steps are needed to match different relation types. Inspired by Hu et al. [17], we use clustering to group similar relational facts in an unsupervised manner.

We first perform lemmatization on the extracted relations to reduce variations in their word representation. To perform the clustering, we represent the relation mentions as vectors using the Sentence-BERT pretrained language model [36]. This enables us to establish distances between relation phrases, which we can use to perform the clustering. Then, we use agglomerative clustering [26] to group the vectors and combine similar relations – thus shrinking the number of different relations in our knowledge graph. We use this simple and hierarchical algorithm as it allows us to establish a distance threshold for grouping instead of a number of clusters – something that aligns well with our open information extraction task. In our configuration, we consider that two vectors with distance (within-cluster variance) smaller than 1 belong to the same cluster. Finally, to further refine our dataset with higher qualified relations, we exclude relations that occurred with a frequency below the 75th percentile threshold for the entire collection (6 times in our data).

Entity Linking. Similar to extracted relations, the entities extracted from texts are text spans that need to be unified and linked to real-world entities. Given the difficulty in accurately mapping individual names, we only focus on organisations. We apply two methods. First, we use a zero-shot entity linking method based on BERT known as BLINK [53]: this approach matches spans of text to entities in Wikipedia. Second, we use the company name normalisation functionality of the John Snow Labs NLP library[4] This feature maps extracted company names to the name registered with the SEC in the Edgar Database, which is useful when handling 10K filings and aims to enhance the accuracy of linking organisational entities.

Both methods provide, as outputs, an entity name and a confidence score. To ensure reliability of the collected entities, for each method, we only keep those text-entity pairs with confidence scores above the median score obtained for all the analysed text spans. We keep the matching if the confidence score for one of the two methods is above the median for the entity linker. In case we have positive matchings for a company in both methods, we keep the one provided by BLINK.

4 Profitability Prediction with Knowledge Graph Embeddings

After constructing our financial knowledge graphs, we aim to use them to improve price prediction accuracy, where future predicted prices are used to recommend financial assets. We therefore define a simple aggregation framework that enables us to combine knowledge graph information with temporal pricing information, depicted in Fig. 3.

For a point in time t, given a set of financial assets, we first feed the gathered knowledge graph into a knowledge graph embedding (KGE) model. These models produce embeddings summarizing the information we have about the entities representing the assets in the knowledge graph. Separately, the historical price data is processed to create the technical indicator sequence for each stock. Both technical indicators and knowledge graph embeddings are then concatenated and given as input to a profitability prediction method that estimates the future profitability of the assets and then ranks them in descending order according to that estimation.

This is a classical feature aggregation approach that has previously been shown to be effective in a wide range of scenarios and so we won't discuss it further. Rather, in the remainder of this section we describe how the two types of features (technical indicators and entity embeddings) are generated in more detail and provide a general definition of the profitability prediction regression algorithms.

4.1 Asset Vector Generation

As a first step to perform profitability prediction, we need a representation of the different financial assets that we want to predict for. There are two types of information

---
[4] https://github.com/JohnSnowLabs/johnsnowlabs.

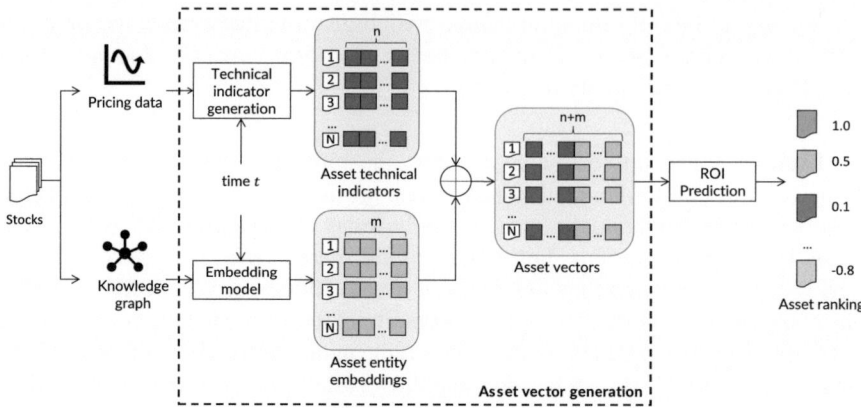

Fig. 3. Profitability Prediction Architecture.

that we consider in this work to represent assets: 1) asset past technical data (i.e. information derived from the price of an asset over time); and 2) information regarding the company associated to the asset (based on our knowledge graph). Notably, these asset features will vary over time, as market pricing is updated frequently and information about the company gets updated periodically.

Given a particular time, t, we represent a stock $s \in \mathcal{S}$ as a numerical vector of dimension D, which we denote as $s(t) \in \mathbb{R}^D$. In our framework, $s(t)$ is defined as

$$s(t) = s_{TI}(t) \oplus s_{KG}(t) \qquad (2)$$

where $s_{TI}(t) \in \mathbb{R}^n$ is a vector containing technical indicators for the asset s at time t, with n representing the number of indicators and $s_{KG}(t) \in \mathbb{R}^d$ is a d-dimensional embedding of the entity representing the asset in the knowledge graph at time t. We provide more information about these vectors next.

Technical Indicators. Technical indicators (also known as key performance indicators, KPIs) are heuristics that encode some aspect of the past pricing information of a financial asset. These heuristics have been shown to provide useful signals when predicting the future profitability of financial assets [28], and are widely used when training price prediction models [27,28,40]. Technical indicators do not commonly analyse the whole time series before a given time t. Instead, they usually summarize a fixed period of time, given by a window Δt. Examples of technical indicators include the average price of a stock during a period of time, the return on investment of the stock in the last month, or the volatility of the asset price (standard deviation of the stock price between two points in time).

We can mathematically define a financial technical indicator as a function $f : \mathcal{S} \times \mathbb{R}^+ \times \mathbb{R}^+ \to \mathbb{R}$. This function receives as an argument (a) the price time series of an asset $s \in \mathcal{S}$, (b) the time t and (c) the time window Δt. The technical indicator studies then the time series $s[t - \Delta t, t]$ (i.e. the pricing information of the asset between $t - \Delta t$

and t) and provides a numerical value. In our framework, we define a technical indicator vector as:
$$s_{TI}(t) = \{f_i\left(s, t, (\Delta t)_i\right)\}_{i=1}^{n} \qquad (3)$$
where $\{f_i\}_{i=1}^{n}$ represents the technical indicators to use and $(\Delta t)_i$ represents the time window chosen for the technical indicator f_i. We allow the use of different time windows as the value and meaning of an indicator might differ according to Δt. For instance, the technical indicator [return on investment (ROI)] for the prior 1 week may tell us something different than [return on investment (ROI)] for the prior year. The set of technical indicators used are summarized later in Table 4.

Asset Entity Embeddings. Knowledge graph embedding (KGE) models aim to encode the information in the knowledge graph into a low dimensional space, with each entity in the graph represented by an embedding vector, while preserving the important properties of the graph [8]. Entity embeddings are computed considering not only the information about each entity, but also that entity's relationship with other entities in the graph (thereby encoding information about related assets and relations within the embedding). In this work, we experiment with a range of methods for generating knowledge graph embeddings for our financial assets that we use downstream as features for profitability prediction.

An important consideration here is that entities and relations might appear and disappear over time, and, if we are predicting the price of stocks at a given point in time t, we should not have any information in the knowledge graph that appeared after time t (i.e. we need to avoid including information from the future). For instance, if we predict the profitability of NASDAQ stocks in 2003, we should not have any information about Meta or Twitter (which were founded, respectively, in 2004 and 2006). Using the properties of the entities and relations, we can remove future information from the graph. We define the knowledge graph containing only information before time t as $\mathcal{G}(t)$.

Formally, we want to produce a representation of an asset s as a vector $s_{KG}(t)$ containing the embedding of the entity related to that asset in the knowledge graph. We can formulate a KGE model as a function $g : \mathcal{G} \rightarrow \mathcal{E} \times \mathbb{R}^d$ where $\mathcal{G}$ is a knowledge graph, $\mathcal{E}$ is the set of entities and d is the dimension of the embedding space. If we denote the entity associated to asset s in the knowledge graph $\mathcal{G}(t)$ as e_s, we can define $s_{KG}(t) \in \mathbb{R}^d$ as the vector embedding of e_s in the knowledge graph $\mathcal{G}(t)$:

$$s_{KG}(t) = g\left(\mathcal{G}(t)\right)[e_s] \qquad (4)$$

In order to generate those embeddings, KGE models establish an scoring function $g_s : \mathcal{E} \times \mathcal{L} \times \mathcal{E} \rightarrow \mathbb{R}$ for every possible triplet (e_h, l, e_t), denoting the plausibility of every relation. The learning process of these models preserves the structure of the graph by maximizing that scoring function for the existing relationships $\mathcal{R}$.

There are many knowledge graph embeddings models that have previously been proposed, as discussed previously in Sect. 2.2. However, to-date these models have not been compared on the profitability prediction task. Hence, we select a representative set of both popular and state-of-the-art models from the literature and experiment with them our later experiments. While exhaustively describing each embedding model is out-of-the-scope of this work, we provide a brief formulation of each KGE model we use below to highlight the differences between them, where $|\mathcal{E}|$ denotes the number of entities, $|\mathcal{R}|$ denotes the number of relations, d denotes the dimension of the embeddings and, to simplify the notation, e_h and e_t represent here, respectively, the embeddings of the head and tail entities:

Translation-Based Embeddings

- **TransE** [6]: this method represents relations as translations between entities in the same embedding space. The tail entity vector e_t should be near to the head entity vector e_h plus the relation vector l, i.e., $e_h + l \approx e_t$. Hence, we use as scoring function g_s to optimize the negative L1-norm distance between $e_h + l$ and e_t:

$$g_s(e_h, l, e_t) = -\|e_h + l - e_t\|_1$$

- **TransH** [52]: TransH extends TransE by representing relations as vectors in a $d-1$-dimensional hyperplane with normal vector w_l. This method projects the entity vectors e_h and e_t, respectively, onto the hyperplane as:

$$e_h^\perp = e_h - w_l^T e_h w_l$$
$$e_t^\perp = e_t - w_l^T e_t w_l$$

Hence, the relation vector l is thus regarded as the connection between $e_h^\perp$ and $e_t^\perp$ in the hyperplane, and the scoring function g_s to optimize is then defined as:

$$g_s(e_h, l, e_t) = -\|e_h^\perp + l - e_t^\perp\|_2^2$$

- **TransR** [22]: TransR breaks the restrictive assumption of TransE and TransH that entities and relations live in the same semantic space. Instead, it represents them in distinct vector spaces by projecting entities ($e_h, e_t \in \mathbb{R}^d$) to relation space using a projection matrix $M_l \in \mathbb{R}^{k \times d}$.

$$e_h^l = e_h M_l$$
$$e_t^l = e_t M_l$$

With $l \in \mathbb{R}^k$, the scoring function g_s to optimize is defined as:

$$g_s(e_h, l, e_t) = -\|e_h^l + l - e_t^l\|_1^2$$

- **RotatE** [43]: RotatE represent each relation as an element-wise rotation from the head entity to the tail entity. This method expects that

$$e_t \sim e_h \circ l, \quad \text{where } \|l_i\| = 1 \, \forall i \in \{1, ..., d\}$$

where $\circ$ represents the Hadamard product and relations are represented as vectors $l \in \mathbb{C}^d$ in the complex d-dimensional sphere of radius equal to 1. The scoring function g_s for each relation is then defined as:

$$g_s(e_h, l, e_t) = -\|e_h \circ l - e_t\|$$

Factorization-Based Embeddings

- **RESCAL** [31]: RESCAL employs tensor factorization to model latent entity representations and their interactions. Entities are represented as vectors, while every relation l is represented as an asymmetric matrix $L \in \mathbb{R}^{d \times d}$. The scoring function is defined as:
$$g_s(e_h, l, e_t) = e_h^T \cdot L \cdot e_t$$
- **HolE** [30]: HolE combines the advantages of RESCAL and TransE and improves efficiency by using the circular correlation operator $*: \mathbb{R}_d \times \mathbb{R}_d \to \mathbb{R}_d$, which can be seen as a compression of the tensor product that does not increase the dimensionality of the representation. The scoring function is then defined as:
$$g_s(e_h, l, e_t) = \sigma(l^T(e_h * e_t))$$
where l is a vector in $\mathbb{R}^d$ representing the relation.
- **TuckER** [5]: Based on Tucker decomposition [46], TuckER decomposes the binary tensor representation of the knowledge graph into two factor matrices ($E \in \mathbb{R}^{|\mathcal{E}| \times d}$, $L \in \mathbb{R}^{|\mathcal{L}| \times d_l}$) and a core tensor $W \in \mathbb{R}^{d \times d_l \times d}$. E represents the head/tail entity embedding matrix, L represents the relation embedding matrix, and W indicates the level of interaction between the different factors and contributes to the parameter-sharing ability. Its scoring function is defined as:
$$g_s(e_h, l, e_t) = W \times_1 e_h \times_2 l \times_3 e_t$$
where e_h, l, e_t are the rows of corresponding factor matrices, and $\times_i$ denotes the mode-i tensor product.

Neural Network-Based Embeddings

- **ConvE** [12]: ConvE takes advantage of convolutional neural networks (CNNs) for computing the embeddings. This method models the complex interactions between subject entities and relations by using convolutional and fully-connected layers. It first applies a two-dimensional convolution layer with filters ω on reshaped and concatenated head entity and relation embeddings, $\bar{e}_h$ and $\bar{l}$ denote a 2D reshaping of e_h and l, respectively. The resulting feature map tensor is then vectorized and projected into d-dimensional entity space using a linear transformation by W and matched with the e_t via an inner product. The scoring function is defined as:
$$g_s(e_h, l, e_t) = f(vec(f([\bar{e}_h; \bar{l}] * \omega))W)e_t$$
- **RGCN** [41]: RGCN is an extension of a graph convolutional network (GCN) [21] that applies relation-specific transformations by replacing the weighting scheme in which all edges have the same value with a weight that varies depending on the relation type. It consists of the RGCN encoder, which computes entity representations, and the DistMult [54] factorization scoring function. Scores for each triple are defined as:
$$g_s(e_h, l, e_t) = e_h^W \cdot L \cdot e_t^W$$
where W is the final level of the encoder, and $L \in \mathbb{R}^{d \times d}$ is a diagonal relation matrix.

4.2 Profitability Prediction

Once we have the vector representation for the assets at time t, we train a regression model to estimate the future profitability of the assets. Formally, the regression model acts as a function $h : \mathbb{R}^D \to \mathbb{R}$, which receives the feature vector of an asset s at time t and estimates the return of investment of the asset at time $t + \Delta t$. (where Δt is the time window we want to predict for). Notably, any regression model can be used here: from simple methods like linear regression or random forest to more complex approaches like long short-term memory networks (LSTMs) or gated recurrent units (GRUs). Finally, as most downstream use-cases for price prediction involve finding the most profitable assets, we rank all assets by their predicted profitability (in descending order).

As we are in a temporal scenario where we can only train using data prior to the time we are to produce predictions for, given a prediction time t, we train a model using asset feature vectors for different time points preceding t (with the end of the training period referred to as t_{train}). For example, given a training vector for an asset s computed for the training time point $t - 1y$ (1 year before the prediction time), its regression target is the return on investment (ROI) between $t - 1y$ and $t - 1y + \Delta t$, i.e. the percentage change in closing price over the Δt period starting at $t - 1y$. Note that training time points t_{train} must be less than or equal to $t - \Delta t$ to avoid requiring information from the future when evaluating. Return on investment is calculated as follows:

$$\text{ROI}(s, t, \Delta t) = \frac{\text{Close}(s, t + \Delta t) - \text{Close}(s, t)}{\text{Close}(s, t)} \quad (5)$$

where $\text{Close}(s, t)$ represents the closing price of $s \in \mathcal{S}$ at time t. As the loss function for our regression algorithms, we use the squared error:

$$\mathcal{L} = \sum_{t=t_0}^{t_{train} - \Delta t} \sum_{s \in \mathcal{S}} \left(\text{ROI}\left(s, t, \Delta t\right) - h\left(s(t)\right) \right)^2 \quad (6)$$

where t_0 is the initial time.

5 Experimental Setup

To assess the effectiveness of the two constructed knowledge graphs in predicting stock market profitability, we carry out experiments using U.S. stock market data. Here, we detail the dataset and the experimental setup used for our analysis.

5.1 Dataset

To conduct our experiments, we collected a dataset from three major U.S. stock exchanges: NASDAQ, NYSE, and AMEX.

Pricing Data: We collect daily pricing data from Yahoo! Finance[5] including open, close, high, low, and volume prices for 5,823 assets from January 2018 to September 2022.

---
[5] http://finance.yahoo.com.

Wikidata Graph: Using the approach described in Sect. 3.1, we collected 3,370 assets entities from Wikidata, resulting in more than 100k entities and 450k relations crawled for our knowledge graph. Table 3 summarises the total properties of the crawled Wiki graph.

Table 3. Graph Properties

Property	Wikidata	10K
Number of entities	102,739	8,380
Number of relation types	114	450
Number of links	457,758	36,973

10K Graph: We successfully retrieved 2,264 assets with 10K reports[6] based on the linked assets in the Wikidata graph, resulting in 5,399 filings from 2017–2022. We incorporated an additional year of data prior to 2018 to ensure a rich dataset for constructing the initial knowledge graph. Table 3 summarizes the global 10K graph properties.

Dataset Split: For each time point, technical indicators and knowledge graph versions from prior dates are used as input to predict price changes over a six-month horizon (Δt). For our experiments, time points on or before the 31st of December 2019 are used for training and the six months following the 30st of June 2020 are used for testing, maintaining a six-month gap between those sets to avoid data leakage. Within the dataset, time points are spaced 1 week apart, selecting the Monday of each week as t. In total, the training set includes 73 time points, while the test set contains 25.

Dataset Post-processing: To ensure data consistency and reduce discrepancies, we take the intersection of assets listed in the pricing data, Wikidata entities and 10K reports. This results in 2,042 assets for our training set and 2,096 assets for our testing set. We also exclude 421 upper outliers from our test set when profits exceed 1.5 times the interquartile range above the third quartile, which indicate unusually high profits. These outliers include penny stocks, companies coming back from bankruptcy, and phenomena like the 2021 meme stock trading (e.g., GameStop). Including these assets leads to unstable evaluations, as their presence among the top-ranked assets can significantly skew metrics like ROI@10.

5.2 Metrics

In order to evaluate our predictions, we consider two different metrics: 1) a ranking-oriented metric, monthly return on investment (ROI), and 2) a global error metric, root mean squared error (RMSE). We summarise each below:

---

[6] https://sec-api.io/.

Table 4. Summary of financial technical indicators

Indicator (financial days)	Time period Δt
Average price	28, 63, 126
Return on investment	28, 63, 126
Volatility	28, 63, 126
Momentum	14, 21, 28
Moving average convergence divergence	26
Rate of change	14, 21, 28
Relative strength index	14
Detrended close oscillator	22
Force index	1
Minimum	14, 21, 28
Maximum	14, 21, 28
Chaikin oscillator	10
Average true range	14
Average directional index	14
Vortex indicator	14

- **Monthly return on investment (ROI@k):** we analyse the average monthly return on investment over the top k ranked assets. In our experiments, we take $k = 10$ and compute the ROI over the 6 months following the date of the recommendations.
- **Root mean-squared error (RMSE):** To understand the model accuracy, we compute the square root of the average squared difference between predicted and real ROI.

5.3 Model Configuration

Technical Indicators: In our experiments, we use 16 different KPIs derived from the pricing time series as technical indicators, summarized in Table 4. In order to generalise the comparison of two knowledge graphs, and reduce the influence of KPIs on the comparison result, we have chosen two groups of technical indicators:

- **BasicKPIs**: average price, return on investment, and volatility.
- **AdvKPIs**: all KPIs in Table 4.

Knowledge Graph Embeddings: We select a set of both popular and state-of-art KGE models for the experiment, specifically, 9 KGE models are tested:

- **Translation-based embeddings**: TransE [6], TransH [52], TransR [22] and RotatE [43]
- **Factorization-based embeddings**: RESCAL [31], HolE [30] and TuckER [5]

Table 5. Performance of random forest regression methods with assets embeddings derived from two knowledge graphs, when predicting six months into the future. The best value for each algorithm and metric is highlighted in bold. † denotes significant improvements (Wilcoxon test $p < 0.05$) with respect to the only KPIs baseline. * indicates significant improvements compared to the corresponding graph model for the other graph.

Group	Algorithm	BasicKPIs				AdvKPIs			
		ROI@10		RMSE		ROI@10		RMSE	
		10K Graph	Wikidata	10K Graph	Wikidata	10K Graph	Wikidata	10K Graph	Wikidata
Baseline (Only KPIs)		0.010		0.4574		0.0466		0.4299	
Translation-based models	KPIs + TransE	**0.0454***	0.0368	0.4439†	0.4415†	0.0474*	0.0393	0.4277†	0.4289
	KPIs + TransH	0.0409	0.0419	0.4408†	0.4383†	0.0467	0.0434	0.4257†	0.4275
	KPIs + TransR	0.0435	0.0422	0.4442†	0.4385†*	0.0442	0.0454	0.4276†	0.4259†
	KPIs + RotatE	0.0427*	0.0385	0.4423†	0.4371†	0.0472*	0.0403	0.4254†	0.4256†
Factorization-based models	KPIs + RESCAL	0.0418	0.0418	0.4474†	0.4439†*	0.0451	0.0447	0.4329	0.4243†*
	KPIs + HolE	0.0418	0.0407	0.4448†	0.4353†*	0.0441	0.0442	0.4285	0.4239†*
	KPIs + TuckER	0.0400	0.0409	0.4442†	0.4334†*	0.0412	0.0445*	0.4298	0.4226†*
Neural network models	KPIs + ConvE	0.0407	0.0450*	0.4433†	0.4304†*	0.0435	0.0451	0.4269†	0.4207†*
	KPIs + RGCN	0.0423	0.0447	0.4479†	**0.4192†***	0.0423	**0.0502***	0.4322	**0.4126†***
Market		0.0345		-		0.0345		-	
S&P 500		0.0266		-		0.0266		-	

- **Neural network-based embeddings**: ConvE [12] and RGCN [41]

We use the PyKeen library [1] to generate 50-dimensional embeddings for entities (companies) associated with each asset. We repeat embeddings generation 5 different times to analyse the variability across the runs. However, we use just one random seed for the RGCN model due to its high computational cost.

Regression Model. We opt to use a Random Forest regression algorithm with 100 trees as our prediction model.

6 Results

In this section we compare the impact of incorporating two distinct knowledge graphs sourced from Wikidata and 10K reports on the prediction of asset profitability. In particular, we investigate the following research questions:

- **RQ1**: How does the use of the Wikidata and 10K graphs affect the effectiveness of profitability prediction?
- **RQ2**: How different are the profitable assets recommended for each knowledge graph?

6.1 RQ1: Graph Performance Comparison

We begin by examining the core question posed in this work: how do knowledge graphs derived from financial reports vs. a knowledge base affect financial asset recommendation (FAR) effectiveness? In particular, we would like to know whether one knowledge graph provides more useful information than the other, and whether the approach used to embed the graph for each company impacts performance.

To answer this question, we compare FAR approaches with and without knowledge graph embeddings. In particular, we start with a price-prediction-based baseline referred as *Baseline (Only KPIs)*, which uses past pricing data to predict the future price of an asset. For a day, all assets are ranked by their predicted return-on-investment (ROI) after 6 months. To evaluate performance, we report both error between the prediction and actual ROI (RMSE, lower is better) and the actual (monthly) ROI of the top 10 recommendations (ROI@10, higher is better). We have two baseline variants, denoted BasicKPIs and AdvKPIs, where the latter includes more technical indicators. As we can see from Table 5, the baseline models achieve an ROI@10 of 4.1% (BasicKPIs) to 4.66% (AdvKPIs), which is higher than both the market average (Market) and S&P 500 (a common index benchmark) for the same period (also reported at the bottom of Table 5).

Having established our baseline, we now contrast this baseline to the same model when augmented with the embeddings derived from our two knowledge graphs. In Table 5, for each metric, we include two columns (10K Graph and WikiData) reporting performance when the baseline is augmented by each knowledge graph. As there are a range of possible graph embedding techniques (see Sect. 4.1), we include one row for each embedding technique tested, denoted *KPIs + <KGE>* (where <KGE> is a knowledge graph embedding approach, e.g. TransE). The best metric values are highlighted in bold, and statistically significant increases (pairwise Wilcoxon test at $p < 0.05$) in comparison to the Baseline (Only KPIs) model is denoted †. We also highlight significance differences between the application of the same model on the two knowledge graphs as ∗.

The first observation is that integrating KGE for profitability prediction generally results in RMSE reductions with respect to the baselines (33/36 times). In 30 cases, this reduction is significant, thus showcasing the capability of knowledge graph information to generate more accurate predictions. When comparing both graphs, the Wikidata KG obtains lower errors in 15 out of 18 cases (with 11 of them showing a significant difference) – therefore showing that this graph provides more accurate results than the 10K graph.

We observe a different pattern when we study the return on investment over the top-10 ranked results however: even when most methods using KGE reduce the prediction error, this fact does not necessarily result in more profitable recommendation rankings. This is particularly notable for the methods using the larger set of indicators, where only four models beat the baseline (TransE, TransH and RotatE for the 10k graph and RGCN for the Wikidata graph). However, for both baselines, it is possible to find at least one model for each graph improving its profitability. In the case of the BasicKPIs baseline, the best models are TransE for the 10K graph (4.54% ROI@10) and ConvE for the Wikidata graph (4.47% ROI@10). For AdvKPIs, TransE is again the best for the 10K graph (4.74% ROI@10), whereas RGCN is the best for Wikidata (5.02% ROI@10). This illustrates that both knowledge graphs are capable of providing a useful profitability signal for the task.

When we compare the effectiveness of the graphs in terms of ROI@10, we also see that there is a different relationship between the complexity of the embedding approach and ROI gain across the two graphs. Specifically, the 10k graph yields higher ROI for the translation-based algorithms (particularly the simpler TransE and RotatE models) that perform poorly when applied on Wikidata. Meanwhile, for the most complex of tested algorithms (TuckER, and both neural network approaches, ConvE and RGCN), the Wikidata graph provides a stronger profitability signal. According to Table 3, the Wikidata graph contains approximately ten times the number of entities and links as the 10K graph, indicating a greater complexity and graph size. Although the simple knowledge graph embedding models are capable of providing useful summaries of the 10k graph information, we hypothesize that the more complex knowledge graph embedding models (specially those based on neural networks) need a much larger number of links to learn how to extract stronger profitability signals from knowledge graphs – hence why RGCN performs well on Wikidata but not the 10K filings.

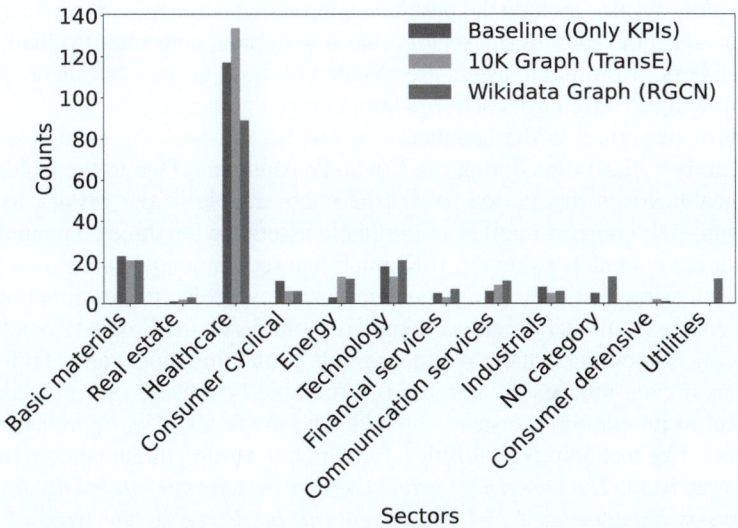

Fig. 4. Distribution of profitable assets in the top-10 recommendation rankings across sectors.

To answer RQ1: *Both knowledge graphs are capable of enhancing the accuracy of the predictions – with Wikidata achieving better results. If we look at returns, however, it highly depends on the embedding method used. The simpler translation-based methods favour the use of the smaller 10K graph, whereas the most complex neural-based methods require more information to work, which they can obtain from the Wikidata graph.*

6.2 RQ2: Profitable Asset Sector Analysis

Besides raw algorithm performance, we hypothesize that different knowledge graph construction methodologies lead to the promotion of specific types of assets in the recommendations. For instance, general knowledge graphs might promote well-known companies as they have more information about them. As studying these differences is important to understand the inner workings of these methods, we provide a preliminary analysis where we study the distribution of recommended profitable assets across sectors.

To perform this analysis, we identify assets with positive ROI in the top-10 of the asset rankings and count how many times each sector is represented. We compare two top performing models using the basic indicators: TransE for the 10K graph, and RGCN for the Wikidata graph. Although ConvE provides slightly better performance when using the basic KPIs for the Wikidata graph, we choose RGCN as it is the best overall method for this KG. Both BasicKPIs + TransE (10k) and BasicKPIs + RGCN (WikiData) provide similar ROI@10 values (4.54% vs. 4.47%), but we hypothesise that source of that profitability might be different.

Figure 4 displays the results of our experiment, where the x axis shows the different sectors and the y axis shows the number of profitable assets for each algorithm and sector. In the plot, we also include the baseline using only technical indicators as features, for comparison. For many of the sectors (basic materials, consumer cyclical, energy), similar numbers of profitable assets are selected by both graphs, but there are sectors which highlight the differences between both knowledge bases.

The most important is the healthcare sector. In our data, the studied test period (June-December 2020) runs during the Covid-19 pandemic. Due to the pandemic, the value of healthcare in this period rose. This is observable in our results, as it is the sector counting the biggest number of profitable assets for the three compared models. However, it is the models using the 10K graph that recommends more assets from this sector. Considering that 10K filings contain company projection information, in this case, they enable the model to capture company outlooks on the Covid-19 pandemic and exploit them – something that the Wikidata graph, containing more general information, does not, as it even reduces the number of profitable healthcare recommended assets with respect to the baseline. Instead, the Wikidata graph takes its improvements from other sectors, like technology or utilities, for which the graph might contain more data.

To answer RQ2: *The knowledge graph construction strategy markedly impacts the types of assets recommended and this appears to be driven by the types of relationships and properties captured within each graph, although further investigation will be needed to conclusively show this.*

7 Adaptive Graph Selection

The differences on sector-level performance across knowledge graphs observed in Sect. 6.2 suggest that each knowledge graph may be better suited to predict the profitability of specific types of stocks. Motivated by this observation, we investigate whether adaptively selecting the suitable graph for each stock can improve profitability. To analyze this, we propose an ensemble method that switches between knowledge graph-based models depending on the stock.

7.1 Algorithm Description

We propose a switching ensemble model [7] for profitability prediction, that adaptively selects a previously trained ROI prediction algorithm for each stock. We show the architecture of the ensemble in Fig. 5. The ensemble chooses among the possible models following their performance on the training set. We consider two possible strategies for choosing the model for each individual stock:

- **Stock-level strategy:** Given a stock, we choose the profitability prediction algorithm that minimizes RMSE during the training period.
- **Sector-level strategy:** All stocks within a sector are assigned to the same profitability prediction model – the model minimizing the average RMSE of the sector stocks during the training period.

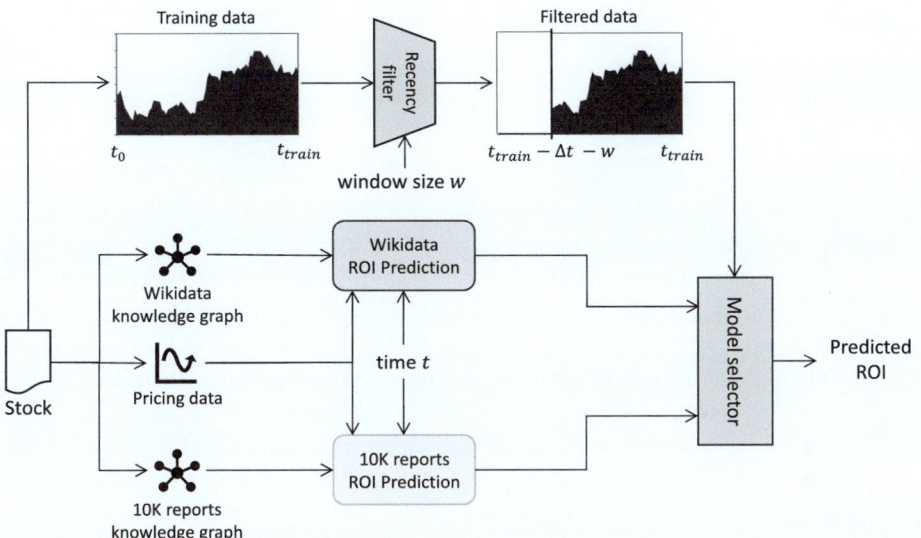

Fig. 5. Architecture of the adaptive ensemble.

While using the complete training data for the model selector is a possibility, in the financial sector, the time of the input information matters. We hypothesize that, by choosing the most recent training points, the performance of our ensemble model should increase. To deal with this, we apply a recency filter to our training data. This filter receives as input a window size w (measured in weeks). If we define t_{train} as the end of the training period, this recency filter keeps the training time points in the $(t_{train} - \Delta t - w, t_{train})$ period.[7]

---

[7] As the last time point of the training period is at $t_{train} - \Delta t$, we take the starting point of the windowed period as $t_{train} - \Delta t - w$ to take all the examples within a period of length w.

7.2 Experiments

We compare our adaptive method under the same experimental setup defined in Sect. 5. To build our ensemble, we use the best-performing KPIs + <KGE> model for each knowledge graph as the baseline: TransE for the 10K graph and RGCN for the Wikidata graph. We also include these two models as baselines in our experiment.

For our ensembles, we experiment with multiple window sizes, ranging from 1 to 78 weeks (corresponding to 73 data points, as some holidays were excluded). This window selection allows us to assess how the length of historical windows for graph selection affects recommendation effectiveness.

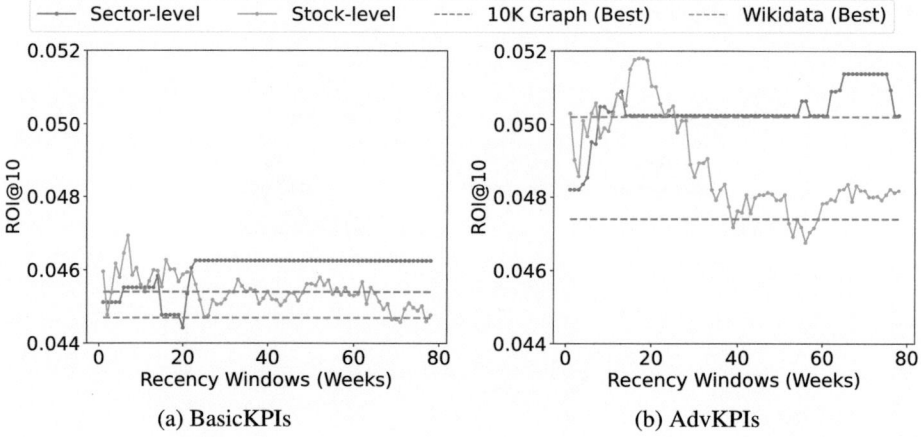

Fig. 6. Comparison of ROI@10 Across Different Graph Selection Strategies.

7.3 Results

In this section, we examine the influence of adaptive graph selection strategy on asset recommendation performance. Specifically, we focus on the following research questions:

- **RQ3:** How does the adaptive combination of two knowledge graphs impact the effectiveness of investment profitability?
- **RQ4:** How does the choice of recency window length affect the proportion of each graph selected?

RQ3: Dynamic Selection Performance. We begin by addressing the key question in the section: whether dynamically choosing the predicted best graph for each stock or sector can enhance profitability in asset recommendation. Thus, we compare the performance of both stock-level and sector-level strategies across all possible recency windows to examine the overall performance against the performance of the best KPIs + <KGE> models (that use a single knowledge graph as input). Figure 6 illustrates the ROI@10 performance of the tested methods for different KPIs – BasicKPIs on Fig. 6(a), on the left, and AdvKPIs on Fig. 6(b), on the right. Here, the x-axis represents the length of the recency window in weeks (as we go towards the right part of each graph, we are using more – and older – examples to choose the best model for each stock). Figure 6 shows, in orange, the adaptive stock-level model and, in blue, the adaptive sector-level model. We include, as reference the best model for the 10K graph (KPIs + TransE) and the Wikidata graph (KPIs + RGCN), respectively, as green and purple dashed lines.

We observe distinct patterns achieved by the two adaptive strategies. The stock-level approach exhibits volatile performance and outperforms the single-graph baseline over shorter recency windows—up to 20 weeks for BasicKPIs and 15–25 weeks for AdvKPIs. The highest improvement reaches 3.39% (0.04694 vs. 0.0454) for BasicK-PIs and 3.19% (0.05180 vs. 0.0502) for AdvKPIs, compared to the best-performing single-graph method. In contrast, the sector-level method demonstrates more stable performance over longer recency windows and consistently outperforms or performs comparably to the best-performing baseline when the window size exceeds 20 weeks, with the highest improvement of 1.89% (0.04626 vs. 0.0454) and 2.35% (0.05138 vs. 0.0502) for BasicKPIs and AdvKPIs, respectively. This suggests that shorter recency windows are more suitable for fine-grained selection, whereas longer windows are better suited for coarse-grained sector-level strategies that benefit from broader temporal aggregation.

To answer RQ3: *An adaptive graph selection method that predicts and assigns a graph to each asset can lead to improved recommendation ROI. However, our findings suggest that the recency window has a significant impact on the performance of different adaptive selection strategies: shorter windows benefit stock-level strategy by emphasizing recent fluctuations, while longer windows support sector-level methods through stable temporal smoothing.*

RQ4: Effect of Recency Window Length. As the recency window sizes plays an important role in the way of dynamically combine different graphs, we hypothesize that different varying window lengths promote the use of different graphs. In particular, we investigate how the length of the recency window influences the graph selection across both the top-10 recommended stocks and the entire stock set. Fig. 7 and Fig. 8 show the variation in the percentage of 10K Graph usage across different recency windows (x-axis) for BasicKPIs and AdvKPIs, respectively. For each KPI set, results are presented for both stock-level and sector-level strategies, with proportions shown separately for the top-10 recommended stocks (Figs. 7 (a) and 8(a)) and for the full stock set (Figs. 7(b) and 8(b)).

We first compare the graph selection with the profitability of our adaptive approaches. A first observation from Figs. 7 and 8 is that, as the recency window increases, we observe a trend toward more balanced and stable use of the graph across the entire stock set, in both stock and sector-level configurations. This is particularly noteworthy in the sector level strategy, which barely modifies the stock allocation to each method on recency windows bigger than 20 weeks – explaining the stability of the

ROI performance for this method in Fig. 6. Indeed, the improvement in performance under long recency windows in Fig. 6(b) can be explained by the increase of usage of the 10K graph when we use those long recency windows. The performance of the stock-level strategy, however, it is not so easily explainable by changes in graph usage: while the usage of different graphs tends to estabilize as we consider longer time periods, the performance does not. This implies that, although the proportion of stocks selected for each graph is the same, the stocks are not – making the stock selection strategy very sensitive to changes in the recency window.

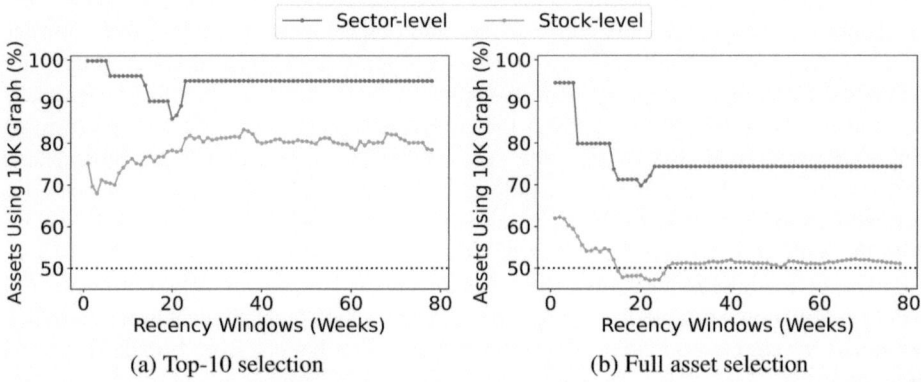

Fig. 7. A comparison of the proportion of 10K graphs selected (a) in the top 10 recommended stocks and (b) across all stocks under the BasicKpis setting.

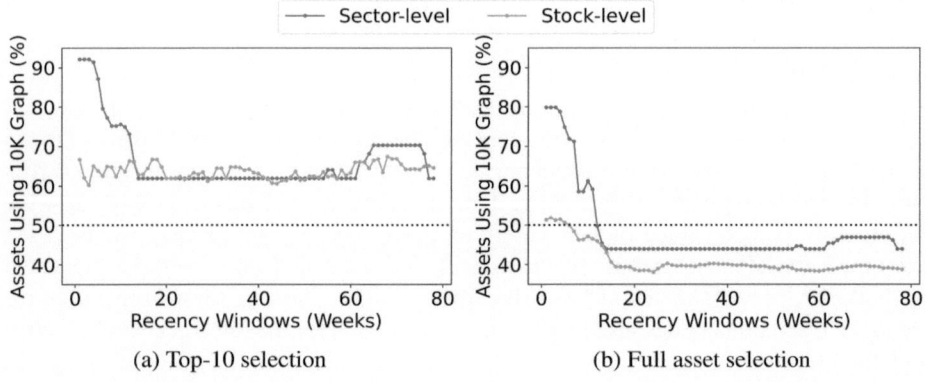

Fig. 8. A comparison of the proportion of 10K graphs selected (a) in the top 10 recommended stocks and (b) across all stocks under the AdvKpis setting.

Interestingly, there are changes in the stock selection trend when we look at the top-10 selection (Figs. 7 and 8(a)) and the complete set of stocks (Figs. 7 and 8 (b)). When we look at the full set of stocks, there is a different dominant graph for BasicKPIs and AdvKPIs – specially when we use longer recency windows. The BasicKPIs model tends to favor the 10K graph – which is used to predict the profitability of slightly more than 50% of the stocks predicted by the stock-level model, and between 70–95% of the stocks predicted by the sector-level model. On the other hand, the AdvKPIs model tends to favor the Wikidata graph – limiting the usage of the 10K graph to 40–50% of the stocks. Considering the overall ROI@10 performance reported in Sect. 6.1, where the best BasicKPIs model uses the 10K graph, and the best AdvKPIs model uses the Wikidata graph, this is what we expected for both the top-10 and the complete selection. However, for both BasicKPIs and AdvKPIs, in the top-10 assets, the selection is dominated by the 10K graph (predicting between 60–99% of the stocks in the top-10, depending on the recency window).

Following Fig. 4, this mismatch between the top-10 and the complete set of stocks might be explained by the preference of the 10K graph to promote healthcare stocks. These stocks were highly important during the Covid-19 pandemic period on which the test period runs – and their selection on the top 10 explains the preference of the 10K graph over the Wikidata graph for the top-10 stocks. However, both sector and stock-based adaptive models can benefit from a mixture of the two graphs – as it allows a greater diversification of assets in the recommendation and greater performance.

To answer RQ4: *The length of recency window has differing effects on graph usage patterns and asset selection for investment – with longer recency windows leading to more stable graph usage selections. While overall graph selection appears relatively balanced across the full stock set, the top-10 recommended assets consistently favor the 10K Graph across most settings.*

8 Conclusion and Future Work

In this work, we have explored the impact that two KG construction strategies have when predicting the future returns of U.S. stocks. For this, we collected a Wikidata subgraph and a built a graph by automatically extracting factoids from annual 10K filings. We have compared these methods under a unified FAR model that estimates the profitability of stocks. This method integrates price technical indicators with asset KG vectors extracted from the graphs by 9 different knowledge graph embedding models.

Our findings show that both graph types can improve the profitability of recommendations with respect to only using price information by up-to 10.7%. However, different graphs favour different embedding strategies: graphs extracted from financial reports tend to be smaller, and therefore benefit from translation-based models like TransE [6] or RotatE [43], whereas the bigger Wikidata graph favours complex neural network models like RGCN [41].

We have also analysed the distribution of the profitable assets recommended by the models across sectors, showing that different knowledge graph construction strategies might present biases towards certain types of assets. In our experiments, the 10K graph has been able to leverage the information regarding global events (in particular, the Covid-19 pandemic) available in the reports to promote profitable healthcare stocks, while the more static Wikidata graph has identified profitable assets in sectors like utilities. Based on this observation, we further investigated the effectiveness of adaptive graph selection strategies at stock and sector levels. Our findings indicate that dynamically selecting graphs based on past performance can enhance profitability, supporting that different knowledge graphs indeed offer complementary strengths for different asset types. However, different strategies exhibit varying preferences for recency window sizes, reflecting their sensitivity to temporal granularity. Moreover, while longer windows generally result in more balanced graph usage, the top-10 assets consistently favor the 10K Graph, largely due to its alignment with high-performing healthcare sectors during the Covid-19 pandemic.

As future work, we aim to compare these knowledge graphs with others that include other types of financial information, such as news or press releases. We also aim to further investigate more fine-grained adaptive methods that integrate additional properties of different knowledge graphs for improved stock recommendation. Finally, as in this work we have only used random forests, we aim to test other FAR algorithms, including those directly targeting asset ranking [2].

References

1. Ali, M., et al.: PyKEEN 1.0: a python library for training and evaluating knowledge graph embeddings. J. Mach. Learn. Res. **22**(82), 1–6 (2021)
2. Alsulmi, M.: From ranking search results to managing investment portfolios: exploring rank-based approaches for portfolio stock selection. Electronics **11**(23), 4019 (2022). https://doi.org/10.3390/electronics11234019
3. Alzaman, C.: Deep learning in stock portfolio selection and predictions. Expert Syst. Appl. **237**, 121404 (2024). https://doi.org/10.1016/j.eswa.2023.121404
4. Bach, N., Badaskar, S.: A review of relation extraction. Lit. Rev. Lang. Stat. **II**(2), 1–15 (2007)
5. Balazevic, I., Allen, C., Hospedales, T.: TuckER: tensor factorization for knowledge graph completion. In: 2019 Conference on Empirical Methods in Natural Language Processing and the 9th International Joint Conference on Natural Language Processing (EMNLP-IJCNLP 2019), Hong Kong, China, pp. 5185–5194. Association for Computational Linguistics (2019). https://doi.org/10.18653/v1/D19-1522
6. Bordes, A., Usunier, N., Garcia-Durán, A., Weston, J., Yakhnenko, O.: Translating embeddings for modeling multi-relational data. In: 27th Conference on Neural Information Processing Systems (NeurIPS 2013), Stateline, Nevada, USA. Curran Associates, Inc. (2013)
7. Burke, R.: Hybrid web recommender systems. In: Brusilovsky, P., Kobsa, A., Nejdl, W. (eds.) The Adaptive Web. LNCS, vol. 4321, pp. 377–408. Springer, Heidelberg (2007). https://doi.org/10.1007/978-3-540-72079-9_12
8. Cai, H., Zheng, V.W., Chang, K.C.C.: A comprehensive survey of graph embedding: problems, techniques, and applications. IEEE Trans. Knowl. Data Eng. **30**(9), 1616–1637 (2018). https://doi.org/10.1109/TKDE.2018.2807452
9. Chen, Q.: Stock movement prediction with financial news using contextualized embedding from BERT. CoRR abs/2107.08721 (2021)
10. Cheng, D., Yang, F., Wang, X., Zhang, Y., Zhang, L.: Knowledge graph-based event embedding framework for financial quantitative investments. In: 43rd International ACM SIGIR Conference on Research and Development in Information Retrieval (SIGIR 2020), Online, China, pp. 2221–2230. ACM (2020). https://doi.org/10.1145/3397271.3401427

11. Deng, S., Zhang, N., Zhang, W., Chen, J., Pan, J.Z., Chen, H.: Knowledge-driven stock trend prediction and explanation via temporal convolutional network. In: The Web Conference 2019 (WWW 2019 Companion), San Francisco, CA, USA, pp. 678–685. ACM (2019). https://doi.org/10.1145/3308560.3317701
12. Dettmers, T., Minervini, P., Stenetorp, P., Riedel, S.: Convolutional 2D knowledge graph embeddings. In: 32nd of the AAAI Conference on Artificial Intelligence (AAAI 2018), New Orleans, LA, USA, pp. 1811–1818. AAAI Press (2018). https://doi.org/10.1609/aaai.v32i1.11573
13. Elhammadi, S., et al.: A high precision pipeline for financial knowledge graph construction. In: 28th International Conference on Computational Linguistics (COLING 2020), pp. 967–977. International Committee on Computational Linguistics, Online, Barcelona, Spain (2020). https://doi.org/10.18653/v1/2020.coling-main.84
14. Feng, F., He, X., Wang, X., Luo, C., Liu, Y., Chua, T.S.: Temporal relational ranking for stock prediction. ACM Trans. Inf. Syst. **37**(2), 1–30 (2019). https://doi.org/10.1145/3309547
15. Griffin, P.A.: Got information? Investor response to form 10-K and form 10-Q EDGAR filings. Rev. Acc. Stud. **8**, 433–460 (2003)
16. Hogan, A., et al.: Knowledge graphs. ACM Comput. Surv. **54**(4), 71:1–71:37 (2021). https://doi.org/10.1145/3447772
17. Hu, X., Wen, L., Xu, Y., Zhang, C., Yu, P.: SelfORE: self-supervised relational feature learning for open relation extraction. In: Webber, B., Cohn, T., He, Y., Liu, Y. (eds.) 2020 Conference on Empirical Methods in Natural Language Processing (EMNLP 2020), pp. 3673–3682. Association for Computational Linguistics, Online (2020). https://doi.org/10.18653/v1/2020.emnlp-main.299. https://aclanthology.org/2020.emnlp-main.299
18. Hu, Z., Liu, W., Bian, J., Liu, X., Liu, T.Y.: Listening to chaotic whispers: a deep learning framework for news-oriented stock trend prediction. In: 11th ACM International Conference on Web Search and Data Mining (WSDM 2018), Los Angeles, CA, USA, pp. 261–269. ACM (2018). https://doi.org/10.1145/3159652.3159690
19. Kaur, S., et al.: REFinD: relation extraction financial dataset. In: the 46th International ACM SIGIR Conference on Research and Development in Information Retrieval (SIGIR 2023), Taipei, Taiwan, pp. 3054–3063. ACM (2023)
20. Kertkeidkachorn, N., Nararatwong, R., Xu, Z., Ichise, R.: FinKG: a core financial knowledge graph for financial analysis. In: 17th IEEE International Conference on Semantic Computing (ICSC 2023), Laguna Hills, CA, USA, pp. 90–93. IEEE (2023). https://doi.org/10.1109/ICSC56153.2023.00020
21. Kipf, T.N., Welling, M.: Semi-supervised classification with graph convolutional networks. In: 10th International Conference on Learning Representations (ICLR 2017), Toulon, France. OpenReview (2017)
22. Lin, Y., Liu, Z., Sun, M., Liu, Y., Zhu, X.: Learning entity and relation embeddings for knowledge graph completion. In: 29th AAAI Conference on Artificial Intelligence (AAAI 2015), Austin, TX, USA, pp. 2181–2187. AAAI Press (2015). https://doi.org/10.1609/aaai.v29i1.9491
23. Long, J., Chen, Z., He, W., Wu, T., Ren, J.: An integrated framework of deep learning and knowledge graph for prediction of stock price trend: an application in Chinese stock exchange market. Appl. Soft Comput. **91**, 106205 (2020). https://doi.org/10.1016/j.asoc.2020.106205
24. McCreadie, R., et al.: Next-generation personalized investment recommendations. In: Soldatos, J., Kyriazis, D. (eds.) Big Data and Artificial Intelligence in Digital Finance: Increasing Personalization and Trust in Digital Finance using Big Data and AI, pp. 171–198. Springer, Cham (2022). https://doi.org/10.1007/978-3-030-94590-9_10

25. Mendes, P.N., Jakob, M., García-Silva, A., Bizer, C.: DBpedia spotlight: shedding light on the web of documents. In: 7th International Conference on Semantic Systems (I-Semantics 2011), Graz, Austria, pp. 1–8. ACM (2011). https://doi.org/10.1145/2063518.2063519
26. Murtagh, F., Legendre, P.: Ward's hierarchical agglomerative clustering method: which algorithms implement ward's criterion? J. Classif. **31**, 274–295 (2014)
27. Naik, N., Mohan, B.R.: Stock price movements classification using machine and deep learning techniques-the case study of indian stock market. In: Macintyre, J., Iliadis, L., Maglogiannis, I., Jayne, C. (eds.) EANN 2019. CCIS, vol. 1000, pp. 445–452. Springer, Cham (2019). https://doi.org/10.1007/978-3-030-20257-6_38
28. Neely, C.J., Rapach, D.E., Tu, J., Zhou, G.: Forecasting the equity risk premium: the role of technical indicators. Manage. Sci. **60**(7), 1772–1791 (2014). https://doi.org/10.1287/mnsc.2013.1838
29. Nelson, D.M.Q., Pereira, A.C.M., Oliveira, R.A.: Stock market's price movement prediction with LSTM neural networks. In: 2017 International Joint Conference on Neural Networks (IJCNN 2017), Anchorage, AK, USA, pp. 1419–1426. IEEE (2017). https://doi.org/10.1109/IJCNN.2017.7966019
30. Nickel, M., Rosasco, L., Poggio, T.: Holographic embeddings of knowledge graphs. In: 30th AAAI Conference on Artificial Intelligence (AAAI 2016), Phoenix, AZ, USA, pp. 1955–1961. AAAI Press (2016). https://doi.org/10.1609/aaai.v30i1.10314
31. Nickel, M., Tresp, V., Kriegel, H.P.: A three-way model for collective learning on multi-relational data. In: 28th International Conference on Machine Learning (ICML 2011), Bellevue, WA, USA. pp. 809–816. Omnipress (2011)
32. Pejić Bach, M., Krstić, Ž, Seljan, S., Turulja, L.: Text mining for big data analysis in financial sector: a literature review. Sustainability **11**(5), 1277 (2019). https://doi.org/10.3390/su11051277
33. Pujara, J.: Extracting knowledge graphs from financial filings: extended abstract. In: 3rd International Workshop on Data Science for Macro–Modeling with Financial and Economic Datasets (DSMM 2017), colocated with the 2017 International Conference on Management of Data (SIGMOD/PODS 2017), Chicago, IL, USA, pp. 5:1–5:2. ACM (2017). https://doi.org/10.1145/3077240.3077246
34. Qi, P., Zhang, Y., Zhang, Y., Bolton, J., Manning, C.D.: Stanza: a python natural language processing toolkit for many human languages. In: 58th Annual Meeting of the Association for Computational Linguistic: System Demonstrations (ACL 2020), pp. 101–108. Association for Computational Linguistics, Online (2020). https://doi.org/10.18653/v1/2020.acl-demos.14
35. Rather, A.M., Agarwal, A., Sastry, V.N.: Recurrent neural network and a hybrid model for prediction of stock returns. Expert Syst. Appl. **42**(6), 3234–3241 (2015). https://doi.org/10.1016/j.eswa.2014.12.003
36. Reimers, N., Gurevych, I.: Sentence-bert: sentence embeddings using siamese bert-networks. In: 2019 Conference on Empirical Methods in Natural Language Processing and the 9th International Joint Conference on Natural Language Processing (EMNLP-IJCNLP 2019), Hong Kong, China, pp. 3982–3992. Association for Computational Linguistics (2019). https://doi.org/10.18653/v1/D19-1410
37. Rossi, A., Barbosa, D., Firmani, D., Matinata, A., Merialdo, P.: Knowledge graph embedding for link prediction: a comparative analysis. ACM Trans. Knowl. Discov. Data **15**(2), 14:1–14:49 (2021). https://doi.org/10.1145/3424672
38. Roziere, B., et al.: Code llama: open foundation models for code. arXiv preprint arXiv:2308.12950 (2023)

39. Sainz, O., García-Ferrero, I., Agerri, R., de Lacalle, O.L., Rigau, G., Agirre, E.: GoLLIE: annotation guidelines improve zero-shot information-extraction. In: The 12th International Conference on Learning Representations (ICLR 2024), Vienna, Austria. OpenReview (2024). https://openreview.net/forum?id=Y3wpuxd7u9
40. Sanz-Cruzado, J., McCreadie, R., Droukas, N., Macdonald, C., Ounis, I.: On transaction-based metrics as a proxy for profitability of financial asset recommendations. In: 3rd International Workshop on Personalization & Recommender Systems in Financial Services (FinRec 2022), colocated with the 16th ACM Conference on Recommender Systems (Rec-Sys 2022), Seattle, WA, USA, pp. 1–9 (2022)
41. Schlichtkrull, M., Kipf, T.N., Bloem, P., Berg, R., Titov, I., Welling, M.: Modeling relational data with graph convolutional networks. In: Gangemi, A., et al. (eds.) ESWC 2018. LNCS, vol. 10843, pp. 593–607. Springer, Cham (2018). https://doi.org/10.1007/978-3-319-93417-4_38
42. Sun, Y., Fang, M., Wang, X.: A novel stock recommendation system using Guba sentiment analysis. Pers. Ubiquit. Comput. **22**(3), 575–587 (2018). https://doi.org/10.1007/s00779-018-1121-x
43. Sun, Z., Deng, Z.H., Nie, J.Y., Tang, J.: RotatE: knowledge graph embedding by relational rotation in complex space. In: 7th International Conference on Learning Representations (ICLR 2019), New Orleans, LA, USA. OpenReview (2019)
44. Takayanagi, T., Chen, C.C., Izumi, K.: Personalized dynamic recommender system for investors. In: Proceedings of the 46th International ACM SIGIR Conference on Research and Development in Information Retrieval, SIGIR 2023, pp. 2246–2250. Association for Computing Machinery, New York (2023). https://doi.org/10.1145/3539618.3592035
45. Takayanagi, T., Izumi, K., Kato, A., Tsunedomi, N., Abe, Y.: Personalized stock recommendation with investors' attention and contextual information. In: Proceedings of the 46th International ACM SIGIR Conference on Research and Development in Information Retrieval, SIGIR 2023, pp. 3339–3343. Association for Computing Machinery, New York (2023). https://doi.org/10.1145/3539618.3591850
46. Tucker, L.R.: The extension of factor analysis to three-dimensional matrices. In: Contributions to Mathematical Psychology, pp. 109–127. Holt, Rinehart and Winston (1964)
47. Veličković, P., Cucurull, G., Casanova, A., Romero, A., Liò, P., Bengio, Y.: Graph attention networks. In: 6th International Conference on Learning Representations (ICLR 2018), Vancouver, BC, Canada. OpenReview (2018)
48. Vrandečić, D., Krötzsch, M.: Wikidata: a free collaborative knowledgebase. Commun. ACM **57**(10), 78–85 (2014). https://doi.org/10.1145/2629489
49. Wang, M., Qiu, L., Wang, X.: A survey on knowledge graph embeddings for link prediction. Symmetry **13**(3), 485:1–485:29 (2021). https://doi.org/10.3390/sym13030485
50. Wang, T., Guo, J., Shan, Y., Zhang, Y., Peng, B., Wu, Z.: A knowledge graph-GCN-community detection integrated model for large-scale stock price prediction. Appl. Soft Comput. **145**, 110595 (2023). https://doi.org/10.1016/J.ASOC.2023.110595
51. Wang, X., He, X., Cao, Y., Liu, M., Chua, T.S.: KGAT: knowledge graph attention network for recommendation. In: 25th ACM SIGKDD International Conference on Knowledge Discovery & Data Mining (KDD 2019), Anchorage, AK, USA, pp. 950–958. ACM (2019). https://doi.org/10.1145/3292500.3330989
52. Wang, Z., Zhang, J., Feng, J., Chen, Z.: Knowledge graph embedding by translating on hyperplanes. In: 28th AAAI Conference on Artificial Intelligence (AAAI 2014), Québec City, Québec, Canada, pp. 1112–1119. AAAI Press (2014). https://doi.org/10.1609/aaai.v28i1.8870

53. Wu, L., Petroni, F., Josifoski, M., Riedel, S., Zettlemoyer, L.: Zero-shot entity linking with dense entity retrieval. In: 2020 Conference on Empirical Methods in Natural Language Processing (EMNLP 2020), pp. 6397–6407. Association for Computational Linguistics, Online (2020)
54. Yang, B., Yih, W.T., He, X., Gao, J., Deng, L.: Embedding entities and relations for learning and inference in knowledge bases. In: Proceedings of the 3rd International Conference on Learning Representations (ICLR 2015), San Diego, CA, USA (2015)
55. Zhang, L., Aggarwal, C., Qi, G.J.: Stock price prediction via discovering multi-frequency trading patterns. In: 23rd ACM SIGKDD International Conference on Knowledge Discovery and Data Mining (KDD 2017), Halifax, Nova Scotia, Canada, pp. 2141–2149. ACM (2017). https://doi.org/10.1145/3097983.3098117
56. Zhang, Y., Yang, K., Du, W., Xu, W.: Predicting stock price movement direction with enterprise knowledge graph. In: 22nd Pacific Asia Conference on Information Systems (PACIS 2018), Yokohama, Japan, p. 237 (2018)
57. Zhao, Y., et al.: Stock movement prediction based on bi-typed hybrid-relational market knowledge graph via dual attention networks. IEEE Trans. Knowl. Data Eng. **35**(8), 8559–8571 (2023). https://doi.org/10.1109/TKDE.2022.3220520

Author Index

C
Chen, Yifang 87

F
Feng, Hui 71
Frisoni, Giacomo 36

G
Goyo, Manuel Alejandro 36
Guo, Lubingzhi 120

H
Hu, Xuedan 105

K
Kanoulas, Evangelos 19

L
Liu, Anqi 105

M
McCreadie, Richard 120
Meng, Zaiqiao 87

Merola, Carlo 3
Moro, Gianluca 36

N
Nanavati, Jay 71
Nguyen, Thong 19

Q
Qi, Baoyuan 105
Qiao, Jingfen 19

R
Reynares, Emiliano 71

S
Sanz-Cruzado, Javier 120
Sartori, Claudio 36
Singh, Jaspinder 3

Y
Yates, Andrew 19
Yin, Yuntzu 71

Z
Zhou, Hao 87

MIX
Papier aus verantwortungsvollen Quellen
Paper from responsible sources
FSC® C105338

If you have any concerns about our products,
you can contact us on
ProductSafety@springernature.com

In case Publisher is established outside the EU,
the EU authorized representative is:
**Springer Nature Customer Service Center GmbH
Europaplatz 3, 69115 Heidelberg, Germany**

Printed by Libri Plureos GmbH
in Hamburg, Germany